BURNHAM THORPE, THE BIRTHPLACE OF
ADMIRAL LORD NELSON

'There has always been a salt tang in the air blowing in at
the oddly assorted windows of the old Parsonage House
and on early mornings of silver frost, gulls stood on the
lawns. On wild nights a distant roar was eternally audible,
on wide summer days a ceaseless murmur. Of course such
a district had produced naval heroes.'

The Nelson Almanac

A BOOK OF DAYS
RECORDING NELSON'S LIFE
AND THE EVENTS THAT
SHAPED HIS ERA

Published in association with the WARWICK LEADLAY GALLERY

Edited by DAVID HARRIS

Picture editor ANTHONY CROSS

Naval
Institute
Press

In memory of my wife Julia (1936-1990) who, shortly
before her untimely death, persuaded me to accompany her
to Singapore where our friendship with Michael J Sweet
(1931-1994) began. Founder of The Antiques of the Orient
Gallery, *bon viveur* and author of *The Book of Days of Sir
Stamford Raffles* (1993), Mike it was who first encouraged
me to produce this companion volume. It is to both of them,
therefore, that I dedicate *The Nelson Almanac*.

Warwick Leadlay

First published in Great Britain in 1998 by
Conway Maritime Press,
an imprint of Brasseys (UK) Ltd,
33 John Street, London WC1N 2AT.

Published and distributed in the United States of America and
Canada by the Naval Institute Press, 118 Maryland Avenue,
Annapolis, MD 21402-5035.

Library of Congress Catalog Number 98-66111

ISBN 1-55750-647-7

This edition is authorized for sale only in the United States, its
territories and possessions, and Canada.

Half title: *quotation taken from* Nelson *by Carola Oman,
Hodder & Stoughton, 1947.*

Frontispiece: *'Victory of Trafalgar in the Van', one of a
suite of four aquatint engravings by Robert Dodd after his
own design, published on 1 March 1806, showing the
French Admiral Dumanoir and the ships of his division
making their escape to windward.*

The illustrations on pages 1, 14 (bottom), 51, 94, 97, 108, 112, 132,
138 (top), 152, 155, and 186 are from the archives of
Conway Maritime Press. All other illustrations reproduced
by permission of the Warwick Leadlay Gallery, unless otherwise
stated in the captions.

Project editor Alison Moss.
Designed by Peter Champion.
Printed and bound in China.

CONTENTS

INTRODUCTION 6
By David Harris

THE GREAT BUSINESS OF
BEING A SEA OFFICER 7
By Tony Ryan

JANUARY 12

THE FORTUNE OF THE DAY . . . 22
By Derek Allen

FEBRUARY 28

TRIA JUNCTA IN UNO 36
By Carol Evans

MARCH 42

DOWNRIGHT FIGHTING 50
By Hans Christian Bjerg

APRIL 54

THE STATION FOR HONOUR . . . 64
By Jimmy Pack

MAY 70

TINKERS, POETS, WHORES AND
SCOUNDRELS 78
By Tom Pocock

JUNE 82

NEVER FEAR THE EVENT 92
By John Boxall

JULY 98

HONOR EST A NILO 108
By Stephen Howarth

AUGUST 116

THE PROPERTY OF THE
KING OF NAPLES 124
By Fiona Fraser Thomson

SEPTEMBER 130

ENGLAND'S EXPECTATION . . . 138
By David Harris

OCTOBER 146

THE POSTMAN IN THE
PICKLE 154
By Anthony Cross

NOVEMBER 164

I HAVE ONE MORE SIGNAL
TO HOIST 172
By Robin Neillands

DECEMBER 180

SELECTED BIBLIOGRAPHY . . . 188

INDEX 189

INTRODUCTION

Almanacs were best-sellers in the eighteenth and nineteenth centuries. In Britain, total sales of all the various types of almanac surpassed any other publication, including the Bible, with more than half a million copies sold each year. Because they lay so close to the heart of popular literature, they were very often the primary means by which a sense of history passed to the people. These publications listed the so-called 'red letter' days, that is, the high days and holidays that punctuated the religious and secular year in an era that was still largely unregulated by clockwork time. Filling the spaces in between was (an admittedly) selective version of world history – biblical events, references to kings and queens, and so on. The idea of an almanac also extended to particular subject areas, such as *The Nautical Almanac* (see 6 January on page 13).

Spanning the years of Admiral Lord Nelson's celebrated lifetime, this almanac is a glorious jumble of facts and events brought together as a primer for the aspiring student of Nelson's era. Serious effort has gone into its creation: the articles are original, the research is thorough, some of the artwork hitherto unpublished and the treatment is unique.

Essentially, the book has three basic elements. It is biographical, with lively and provocative articles written by some of the most respected modern-day Nelson experts and writers. It is a book of his letters, with Nelson himself giving us first hand information of his experiences. And it is also an historical document encompassing revolution, invasion and war, discovery, invention and cultural achievement.

These elements have been woven together to produce a kaleidoscopic tapestry of the period. Structured as a diary, each month is prefaced with a relevant article scrutinising an aspect of Nelson's life or naval career by one of the contributory authors. Days of the week follow, each with a date for Nelson together with a date in history between 1758 and 1805. Certain events are given greater coverage in short articles and captioned illustrations, which appear on the opposite page to the diary entry.

An excellent way to learn about Nelson is to read his letters. In order to reveal more of the man than the main articles can provide, I have, with irreverent liberty, chosen a few words or lines from his papers for all the Nelson dates. Where there are no recorded letters, log or journal entries for a particular day, I have taken extracts from letters to him. These simple extracts illuminate the agility of his mind, his grasp of maritime and world events, his attention to the finest detail, his passions, his fears and his frustrations.

A few brief notes on the subject of time may be prudent here. Obviously, it is only in the broad daylight of history that we can discern a sensible pattern in the otherwise haphazard arrangement of past events, but there are the more practical difficuties to be encountered. For instance, time varies from place to place. An Englishman and a Frenchman will record the same event a few minutes, per degree, apart in, say, Greenwich and Paris. More seriously, the Admiralty changed date at noon. Authors were often without accurate information to hand, and sometimes took days over a letter that was then further delayed by the passage of the mail boat which was prey to all sorts of mischief en route. In addition, Nelson habitually wrote in similar terms to several addressees, often days, weeks or even months apart. Time then, did not so much fly, as loiter and stumble from place to place.

I might also add this last proviso: any anthology by definition, let alone necessity, excludes far more than it can possibly include. The parameters of Nelson's life and death, however, provide a good deal of scope. The further the reader delves into the book, the more he or she will find. Individual dates throughout the book will piece together the jigsaw of a particular episode in history, such as the American War of Independence, the French Revolution, and the rise of Napoleon. Furthermore it is possible to see how the different threads of history interweave and in some cases affect the outcome of related events.

David Harris

THE GREAT BUSINESS OF BEING A SEA OFFICER

NELSON'S CURRICULUM VITAE

Tony Ryan

H oratio Nelson, a small and reputedly delicate boy in his thirteenth year, entered the Royal Navy by going on board HMS *Raisonnable* (64), commanded by his maternal uncle Captain Maurice Suckling RN, in March 1771. Suckling's career, and hence his influence, was flourishing. In 1775 he was appointed Comptroller of the Navy, an office which he held until his death in 1778, and in 1776 was elected as the Member of Parliament for Portsmouth. Nelson passed the examination for lieutenant in 1777, was promoted commander in 1778 and posted captain in 1779. He thus made an advantageous beginning in a profession, the career mechanism of which was lubricated with dynasticism.

Since advancement from post-captain to flag rank was dependent upon seniority in the list of captains, it followed that Nelson could look forward to receiving his flag and with it the possibility of high command at a comparatively early age. A place in the élite of the naval profession however did not automatically follow. This was a prize reserved for a minority of sea officers, each with his own unique compound of personal and professional talents which transcended the gap between competence and distinction. Nelson planted his feet on the lower rungs of this particular ladder during service towards the end of the American war, in the Caribbean under Lord Hood, who noted his zeal and imagination.

In certain circumstances he was an awkward subordinate. In March 1784 he was made commander of *Boreas* (28) and given a peacetime posting to the Leeward Islands station where he was soon to be described by a correspondent of the widowed Frances Nisbet of Nevis as 'the captain of the *Boreas* of whom so much has been said' and as one of 'these odd sort of people'. Much indeed had been said; most of it critical. Despite the opposition of planter society, the exasperation of Sir Thomas Shirley, governor of the Leeward Islands and the unease of his command-

Nelson's uncle, Captain Maurice Suckling RN, was instrumental in introducing the young Horatio to life at sea.

Nelson's signature, written in 1777 when he was a lieutenant on board the Lowestoffe.

ing officer, Rear-Admiral Sir Richard Hughes, Nelson dedicated himself, in company with his friends the brothers Collingwood, to the exclusion from the British West Indies of merchantmen belonging to the United States of America on the ground that this admission was contrary to the provisions of the British Navigation Acts. In private correspondence he dismissed Hughes and all about him as 'great ninnies'; in correspondence with Hughes he declared his intent never to be subservient 'to the will of any Governor, nor co-operate with him in doing illegal acts. Presidents of Council I feel myself superior to'.

The twenty-five year old captain went further than this. Rejecting the pragmatic wisdom of his elders, he insisted that, even if the law were found to be incompatible with the interests of rich and influential people, it must be rigorously enforced. Although vindicated by the Admiralty, Nelson was ostracised by sections of polite society and lived under the threat of possible legal action with regard to the detention of United States merchantmen. He was sustained by consciousness of his own rectitude and by an exalted concept of the service to which he belonged. On 4 May 1786, during the courtship of his 'dearest Fanny', he reminded her that 'duty is the great business of a sea officer. All private considerations must give way to it, however painful it is'.

At the end of this tour of duty in 1787 Nelson experienced, as any officers do in peacetime, a spell of unemployment, mostly spent at Burnham Thorpe, on half pay. He was rescued from this irksome inactivity by the outbreak of war with Revolutionary France. On 30 January 1793 he was appointed to the command of *Agamemnon*, a 64-gun line-of-battle ship lying in ordinary at Chatham. The *Agamemnon* was assigned to duty in the Mediterranean under Lord Hood whose responsibilities were the containment of the Toulon fleet, the defence of British trade and the harassment of that of the enemy, and the consolida-

tion of alliances with Austria, the Kingdom of Naples and Sicily, Sardinia and Spain. It promised to be a tedious campaign with little prospect of either glory, for which Nelson craved, or of prize money which, despite occasional protestations to the contrary, he did not despise.

It was nevertheless principally within the Mediterranean that over the next five years Nelson achieved his ambitions to excel and to win fame. Fame was as strong a driving force as duty in motivating him; lack of recognition, real or imagined, wounded him. He complained bitterly about Hood's presentation of the operations leading to the occupation of Corsica in 1784.

'One hundred and ten days I have been actually engaged, at sea and on shore, against the enemy, I do not know that anyone has done more. I have had the comfort to be always applauded by my commander-in-chief, but never to be rewarded; and what is more mortifying, for services in which I have been wounded [the loss of sight in the right eye], others have been praised, who, at the time, were actually in bed, far from the scene of the action. They have not done me justice. But, never mind, I'll have a "Gazette" of my own.'

On 14 February 1797, after an unbroken period of almost incessant and frequently frustrating activity, this prophecy came near to fulfilment.

The occasion was the Battle of Cape St Vincent, where Nelson's manoeuvre in hauling *Captain* (74) out of the line to pursue and to board two heavy ships of the Spanish van clinched victory. It was a risky manoeuvre, for, had it misfired, he might well have found himself, to use one of his favourite expressions, in a confounded scrape. He was to emerge thick with honour; he was made a Freeman of the City of Norwich and created a Knight of the Bath. He had won public recognition as a national hero.

On 20 February 1797 Nelson received his flag in a routine promotion. In the months that followed he seems to have courted danger obsessively on service with the inshore squadron blockading Cadiz and as leader of an expedition to Tenerife in July. Launched with the approval of Sir John Jervis, by then the Earl of St Vincent, the expedition was a throwback to the Elizabethan strategy of treasure hunting at the expense of Spain, a supposedly weak and demoralised enemy. It was a public and personal disaster. Nelson, who showed throughout his career a penchant for land operations without ever excelling in the conduct thereof, was struck down at the head of a landing party at Santa Cruz. Three days later, on 27 July, he described himself as having become 'a burthen to my friends and useless to my country'. By 16 August his despondency was such that in a new and unfamiliar script he informed St Vincent that a 'left handed Admiral will never be considered as useful, therefore the sooner I get to a very humble cottage the better'.

Nelson's anxiety lest he be unemployed was groundless. After convalescence at Bath and London, which turned out to be the last time he lived with Lady Nelson, he hoisted his flag on board *Vanguard* (74), commanded by Captain Edward Berry, and sailed from Portsmouth on 10 April 1798 to rejoin St Vincent off Cadiz. Both St Vincent and Earl Spencer, First Lord of the Admiralty, were unanimous in their choice of the one-armed Nelson over other candidates, including officers senior to him, to deal with the Mediterranean crisis.

The arrival of the *Vanguard* within sight of St Vincent's flag marked the dawn of the 'Age of Nelson'. The year 1798 was his *annus miribilis*. It began modestly enough with his entry into the Mediterranean on a mission of reconnaissance at the head of a small detached squadron. It reached its climax, after reinforcements had increased its strength to thirteen 74-gun ships, with the almost total destruction of the French Toulon fleet in Aboukir Bay on 1 August. The names of Nelson and the Nile rang across Europe as the significance of the victory became clear. Not only had he cleared the Mediterranean of French sea power, he had wrecked Napoleon Bonaparte's Egyptian expedition by isolating in Egypt the army of 35,000 men. The news created in Europe a sense of confidence favourable to the reconstruction of the anti-French coalition; it inspired a musical monument

Lemuel Abbott's portrait of Nelson, the sleeve of his right arm empty and wearing in his cocked hat the chelengk, presented to him for services rendered at Aboukir Bay by the Sultan of Turkey.

– the nicknaming as the 'Nelson Mass' of Joseph Haydn's Mass in D minor of 1798.

The destruction wrought at Aboukir – eleven out of thirteen French sail of the line taken or destroyed – was deliberate. It chimed in with Nelson's concept of a sea battle as an exercise in annihilation. In this respect Nelson parted company with the eighteenth century. There is his well-known comment upon the satisfaction expressed by Vice-Admiral Sir William Hotham with the outcome of 'our little brush' with the Toulon fleet in March 1795 when *Ça-Ira* and *Censeur* were taken. 'We have done very well,' said Sir William; but according to Nelson, 'had we taken 10 sail and allowed the 11th to escape if possible to have been got at, I could never call it well done'.

The same spirit animated a letter from off Cadiz, dated 6 October 1805. Anticipating an early battle with the combined fleet, Nelson wrote of his anxiety for the arrival of reinforcements for 'it is, as Mr Pitt knows, annihilation that the Country wants, and not merely a splendid Victory of twenty-three to thirty-six honourable to the parties concerned, but absolutely useless in the extended scale to bring Bonaparte to his marrow bones; numbers can only annihilate'. The distinction drawn by Nelson between victory and annihilation had its roots in an ambition to go further than any man had done before, in an instinct that in the age which had dawned in 1789, victory as understood in the past was inadequate, and in a total confidence in the capacity of the British navy to overwhelm the enemy.

This confidence could be misunderstood. In the *Autobiography of a Seaman*, first published in 1859, Lord Cochrane recalled the impressions made upon him by Nelson at Palermo in 1799, describing him as 'an embodiment of dashing courage which would not take much trouble to circumvent an enemy, but being confronted with one would regard victory so much a matter of course as hardly to deem the chance of defeat worth consideration'. This recollection fails to register the efforts of intellect and imagination which went into the making of the Nelsonic victories at Aboukir Bay, in the hazardous slogging match with the Danish batteries at Copenhagen on 2 April 1801, and at Trafalgar. There is, to give but one example, the testimony of Edward Berry of the *Vanguard* of Nelson's consultations with his captains during the long, and at times apparently futile, search for the Toulon armament in 1798. 'There was no possible position', wrote Berry, 'in which they could be found that he did not take into his calculations, and for the most advantageous attack of which he had not digested and arranged the best possible disposition of the force which he commanded'.

The Band of Brothers. Nelson explains his plan of attack to his officers before Trafalgar. Nelson's strength as a naval leader lay in his ability to involve his captains in the meticulous planning that preceded a battle.

It was not Nelson's philosophy, however, that plans once made should, or could, be rigidly adhered to in all circumstances. 'I send you my plan of attack, as far as a man dare venture to guess at the very uncertain position the enemy may be found in. But my dear friend [Collingwood], it is to place you perfectly at ease respecting my intentions, and to give full scope to your judgement for carrying them into effect'.

A sense of the unpredictability of sea warfare was an essential aspect of the 'Nelson Touch' and was enshrined in the famous Trafalgar Memorandum of 9 October 1805 which contained a general design for the destruction of the enemy. It ends with the maxim that 'in case signals can neither be seen or perfectly understood no Captain can do very wrong if he places his Ship alongside that of the Enemy'. Only by taking this maxim out of context can it be made to chime in with Cochrane's assessment of Nelsonian tactics.

Nelson's popular reputation is associated almost entirely with the battles of Cape St Vincent, Aboukir Bay, Copenhagen and Trafalgar. But victory in battle was not always available as a final solution to a strategic problem. In May 1803 Nelson was appointed, on the renewal of war with France, to the command in the Mediterranean. Despite fighting without an ally, Britain had achieved ascendancy and influence throughout the area, thus providing for the security of Gibraltar, Sardinia, Naples and Sicily, Malta, 'a most important outwork of India', and Egypt. Nelson's first object therefore was to keep the Toulon fleet in check and if it came out 'to have force enough to annihilate them'. He could, however, no more command that a battle be fought than he could command the winds and the waves in the tempestuous Gulf of Lyons. If the Toulon fleet were to come out, it would do so at a moment chosen by itself. It could not be dislodged.

It was one of Nelson's boasts that Toulon was never blockaded and that 'every opportunity has been offered the enemy to put to sea, for it is there that we hope to realise hopes and expectations of our country'. Nelson's system was to keep Toulon under observation by an advanced force of frigates. His line of battle appeared occasionally, but generally kept itself at a distance beyond sight from the hills which surround the French base. He also made a practice of cruising in an area bounded by Spain, the Balearics, Corsica and Sardinia, partly to gather intelligence, partly to relieve the officers, himself included, and the men from the tedium of static blockade and partly to obtain supplies of fresh food and drink.

Under Nelson's regime the ships employed in the long watch were remarkably healthy. 'I really believe', he noted, 'that my shattered carcase [sic] is in the worst plight of the whole fleet'. In the sailing ship era no system of blockade could be watertight; and

Nelson's open system was not even intended to be so. This put a premium upon accurate anticipation of French intentions should they send the fleet to sea. The problem during 1803-5 was that the French had several entirely credible options as far as concerned the employment of the Toulon fleet. They included Ireland, Great Britain, the West Indies, Sardinia, Naples and Sicily, Malta, the Morea and Egypt. While not excluding a break out into the Atlantic, Nelson, influenced by 1798, was determined not to leave the Mediterranean until he could rule out operations there. The strength of this conviction was such that he lost vital time in pursuing Villeneuve and the Toulon fleet after the escape from Toulon on 30 March 1805. He eventually pursued the French to the West Indies and back to Europe without sighting them. Between 13 August 1803 and 18 August 1805, when *Victory* arrived at Spithead, the fleet had, according to his physician, Leonard Gillespie, enjoyed a state of health 'unexampled perhaps in any fleet or squadron heretofore employed on a foreign station'. Though thwarted of his prey, Nelson had achieved a notable victory over disease at sea.

After the triumph at Aboukir, Nelson lived as though all the world was his stage. The curtain rose on the theatrical reception at Naples in September 1798 of 'Nostro Liberatore' and on the celebrations which followed. It fell on the ceremonial funeral in St Paul's Cathedral on 9 January 1806. Between these dates his reception ranged from tumultuous applause to embarrassed dismay. His entanglement during 1798-1800 with the Neapolitan court, which was inevitably associated with his demonstrative infatuation with Emma Hamilton, did neither his professional nor his personal reputation any good. He was recalled on the pretext that his health, of which he was wont to complain, would benefit from a sojourn in England. Yet despite reserve in high places, he had become for the populace at large the one man who could save his country. This instinct was shared by Nelson himself. It was part of his magnetic appeal and of his inspirational genius. He did not seek to die at Trafalgar, but death in the cockpit of *Victory* ensured him an immortal place in the national memory.

Anthony N Ryan, MA FR Hist S, retired as Reader in History at the University of Liverpool in September 1991. A Julian Corbett Prizeman, he was Honorary General Editor of the Navy Records Society from 1973 to 1993. Editor of *The Saumarez Papers: The Baltic 1808-1812* and co-author with David B Quinn of *England's Sea Empire, 1550-1642,* he has contributed to several publications, British and foreign, including *The New Cambridge Modern History.* He has published in learned journals on subjects ranging from the Armada campaign of 1588 to the Royal Navy and the Continental System. He is a vice-president of the Navy Records Society, a member of the British Committee of the International Commission for Maritime History and a member also of the Editorial Board of the Society for Nautical Research.

Nelson leaves home to go to Sea
for the first time. 1771.

'What has poor Horace done, who is so weak, that he above all the rest should be sent to rough it out at sea? But let him come; and the first time we go into action, a cannon ball may knock off his head, and provide for him at once.'

Maurice Suckling

JOSIAH WEDGWOOD (1730-1795)

Josiah Wedgwood was born into a family of potters in the village of Burslem, Staffordshire, on 12 July 1730. He possessed a scientific intellect which he applied to his trade, concentrating on the effects of *glazing* ceramics. Having initially been in partnership with Thomas Whieldon, he went on to set up his own works in 1759 and began improving creamware. His success was assured when he furnished Queen Charlotte's household with pieces inevitably named Queens ware. It was to become the backbone of his enterprise.

In 1766 he built a new factory from which he pioneered the revival of neo-classicism. His early ornamental ware was known as 'black basalt' and then 'Jasper'. He then copied the Portland Vase which had been loaned to him by the Third Duke of Portland. It was a remarkably beautiful amphora believed to have been made early in the reign of the Emperor Augusta. Sir William Hamilton found it in Italy, sold it to the Dowager Duchess of Portland and it was finally acquired by the British Museum on the death of the Third Duke. Its style; white relief decoration on a blue ground, was immediately popular and hundreds of thousands of copies were sold.

Wedgwood also applied himself to improvements within the wider pottery trade; he invented the pyrometer, a means of measuring very high temperatures at the kilns, and introduced a steam engine in his factory in 1782 – the first industrial use of steam power. In 1783 he was elected fellow of the Royal Society.

1771 Nelson is rated on the books of Raisonnable aged 12 years 3 months. He had earlier written to his brother: 'Do, William, write to my father, and tell him that I should like to go to sea with Uncle Morrice'. Just 30 years later he is promoted to Vice-Admiral of the Blue.

1801 Union of Great Britain and Northern resulting in the union flag and present form of ensign. The act received Royal Assent on 1 August of the same year.

1805 To Commissioner Otway in Malta promising a frigate to convey him to Gibraltar on his being relieved. In the same letter he writes: 'Minorca, I should hope would be immediately taken; for I shall never send another ship to Malta. They are so far off, and act so very different to my wishes'.

1779 Fire breaks out in the tailor's shop below the Chapel of the Royal Naval College, Greenwich, gutting the Chapel. It is restored in the Rococco style.

1805 To the Mediterranean fleet after complaints by army and navy transports and victuallers: 'You are hereby required and directed, on no account or consideration whatever to impress, either Mates, Seamen or Boys, unless they shall be found drunk and rioting on shore, in which case I presume it may be proper to impress them for His Majesty's Ships of War'.

1795 Josiah Wedgwood, master potter and creator of a huge business empire, dies aged 64.

1798 Criticising Captain Williamson, Agincourt, at his court martial, accused of not doing his duty: 'I would have every man believe, I shall only take my chance of being shot by the enemy, but if I do not take that chance, I am certain of being shot by my friends'.

1805 The Spanish Admiral Gravina promises Decres of the French navy 30 Spanish ships for the war effort against England.

1800 Troubridge to Nelson on the deplorable conditions in Malta: 'I have this day saved 30,000 people from dying but with this day my ability ceases...if the Neapolitan Government will not supply corn, I pray your Lordship to recall us'.

1762 Tsarina Elizabeth Petrovna dies at the age of 52 and is succeeded by her nephew Peter III, maternal grandson of Peter the Great.

1802 To Sutton, nine years to the day after being recalled to duty by the Admiralty, on his hopes to be discharged: 'I cannot get my discharge. I asked yesterday: my answer was..."no person of any rank is to be discharged"'.

1767 'The Nautical Almanac', an annual publication giving celestial and terrestrial information to navigators, initiated by Dr Nevil Maskelyne, is published. It remained largely unaltered until its review in 1834.

1793 Nelson had been on the beach for five years before the Admiralty offered him a ship. To Fanny: 'Post nubila phoebus: after clouds comes sunshine. The Admiralty so smile upon me, that really I am as much surprised as when they frowned. Lord Chatham yesterday made many apologies for not having given me a Ship before this time, and said, that if I chose a 64 to begin with, I should be appointed to one as soon as she was ready'.

1781 The first air crossing of the English Channel by a hot air balloon is completed by Jean Pierre Blanchard and Dr John Jeffries. The flight from England to France takes two hours.

1st

2nd

3rd

4th

5th

6th

7th

The Funeral of Admiral Lord Nelson, 8-9 January 1806

Nelson's body was first preserved in a cask of brandy. At Gibraltar the brandy was changed to spirits of wine, and the cask was lashed to the mainmast and guarded night and day by a marine. *Victory* arrived at Spithead on 4 December, and at the Nore preparations began for the journey up the Thames to Greenwich, where his body lay in state. On 8 January, the coffin was carried by river barge to the Admiralty.

On the 9th, the funeral procession made its way to St Paul's. The car, was modelled at each end in imitation of the hull of *Victory*. Its head towards the horses was ornamented with a figure of Fame. The stern was carved and painted in the naval style, with the word 'Victory', in yellow raised letters on the lanthorn over the poop.

Nelson's funeral car which bore the coffin through the crowds that lined the streets from Whitehall to St Paul's.

Victory, under way from Portsmouth to the Downs, bearing the corpse of the late Admiral Lord Nelson (actually a reproduction of an earlier image of HMS Victory by Robert Dodd.)

'The coffin placed on the quarter deck with its head towards the stern, with the English Jack pendant over the poop lowered half staff. There was an awning over the whole, consisting of an elegant canopy supported by four pillars, in the form of palm trees...and partly covered in black velvet. The corners and sides were decorated with black ostrich feathers, and festooned with black velvet, richly fringed, immediately above which, in the front, was inscribed the word "Nile", at one end, on one side the following motto: "Hoste devicto, requievit", behind was the word "Trafalgar"; and on the other side the motto "Palmam qui meruit ferat". The carriage was drawn by six led horses, in elegant furniture.'

The Times, Friday, 10 January 1806.

On 8 January 1806 the body of Lord Nelson was carried in procession up the Thames from Greenwich Hospital, where it had lain in state in the Painted Hall. The miserable weather matched the solemnity of the occasion.

❧ **1799** ❧ To Earl Howe after the Battle of the Nile, referring to the captains under his command, who Nelson considered the greatest sea-officers the world had ever produced: 'I had the happiness to command a band of brothers; therefore, night was to my advantage. Each knew his duty, and I was sure each would feel for a French ship'.

❧ *1825* ❧ *Elias Whitney (b.1765), inventor of the cotton gin, dies. His invention enabled the United States to become Britain's main supplier of cotton. The first mill in the USA was opened by Samual Slater on 21 December 1790.*

❧ **1799** ❧ To Rear-Admiral His Excellency the Marquis de Niza of the Two Sicilies: 'You have some Turkish slaves on board. I beg, as a friend, as an English Admiral – as a favour to me, as a favour to my country – that you will give me the slaves. In doing this, you will oblige your faithful friend'.

❧ *1799* ❧ *Pitt the Younger introduces graduated duties on income, beginning with £60 per annum, to raise money to continue the Napoleonic Wars.*

❧ **1804** ❧ To Sir Evan Nepean at the Admiralty saying the French are still in Toulon, but suggesting they are about to sail for the Madelena Isles: 'You will please to acquaint the Lords Commissioners of the Admiralty, that the Enemy's Squadron at Toulon is still in port, and that Captain Donnelley's account, who reconnoitred them on the 6th Instant, they are apparently ready for sea'.

❧ *1806* ❧ *Cape Town capitulates to forces under Major-General Sir David Bird and Commodore Sir Home Riggs Popham, Diadem. Battle Honours are awarded.*

❧ *1804* ❧ To St Vincent on the subject of promotion: 'It was absolutely necessary merit should be rewarded on the moment; and that the officers of the fleet should look up to the Commander-in-Chief for their reward; for that otherwise the good or bad opinion of the C-in-C would be of no consequence'.

❧ *1794* ❧ *Lamourette, Bishop of Lyons since April 1791, is tried and guillotined. He had been taken prisoner by Republican troops on 29 September 1793, during the siege of Lyons.*

❧ *1785* ❧ On illegal trade: 'Whilst I have the honour to command an English man-of-war, I never shall allow myself to be subservient to the will of the Governor, nor co-operate with him in doing illegal acts. Presidents of Council I feel superior to. They shall make proper application to me, for whatever they may want to come by water'.

❧ *1792* ❧ *The Admiralty, by Order in Council, is directed to institute an inquiry into the working of each department against corruption.*

❧ *1801* ❧ The final separation from Lady Nelson: 'I call God to witness there is nothing in you or your conduct that I wish otherwise'.

❧ *1797* ❧ *Captain Sir Edward Pellew, Indefatigable, defeats Droits de l'Homme off Ushant. The French ship runs aground with terrible loss of life. Amazon, in support, also goes aground.*

❧ *1810* ❧ Emma's mother, Mrs Cadogan, dies. Mrs Bolton wrote: 'Dear blessed saint, was she not a mother to us all. Let us remember Mrs Cadogan. The silent sharer of her daughter's fortune and misfortune'.

❧ *1799* ❧ *Vizier Aly assassinates Mr Cherry, Captain Conway and others at Benares, India.*

8th

9th

10th

11th

12th

13th

14th

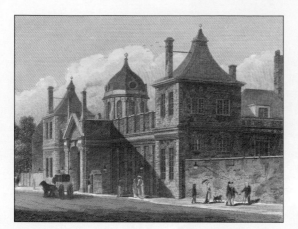

The British Museum in Great Russell Street c.1784. (See 15 January.)

Nelson's coat of arms (see 18 January) bearing his chosen motto: 'Palmam qui meruit ferat' (Let he who has deserved it, bear the palm), an obvious allusion to his finest hour at Aboukir Bay.

Australia was claimed as a British colony in 1770 when Captain Cook landed on the southeast coast. He named the area New South Wales due to its striking resemblance to the coast of the Bristol Channel. Botany Bay, a natural harbour, became the first recipient of British convicts after the loss of the American colonies.

The First Fleet, as the first convoy carrying convicts was known, comprising HMS *Sirius*, HMS *Supply*, three storeships and six transports, under the command of Captain Arthur Phillip, sailed from England on 13 May 1787. Philip went ahead of the fleet to Botany Bay where he arrived on 18 January 1788. Considering it unsuitable, he moved to Port Jackson where he raised the British flag on 27 January. He renamed Port Jackson as Sydney, after Viscount Sydney, the Under Secretary of State for Home Affairs who had succeeded Earl Temple during Pitt's first administration. Phillip became the first governor of Australia and remained there until ill health forced him to resign in 1792, and he returned to England. He was promoted to vice-admiral in 1810.

Louis XVI goes to the guillotine (see 21 January) – an illustration including a description of the 'beheading machine' that was to become one of the emblems of the Revolution – from a contemporary broadsheet.

MASSACRE OF THE FRENCH KING!

VIEW OF La Guillotine; OR THE

MODERN Beheading Machine, AT PARIS.

By which the unfortunate LOUIS XVI. (late King of France) suffered on the Scaffold, January 21st, 1793.

1815 Emma dies and is buried in Calais. Her grave is lost but an obelisk was finally erected in 1994 in a nearby park in her memory. Nelson wrote of her: 'My own dear wife, in my eyes and in the face of heaven'.

1759 *The British Museum opens at Montague House, Bloomsbury, London. Its first collection comprised books, curiosities and objects of natural history collected by Sir Hans Sloane. In 1803 the museum acquired the Elgin Marbles.*

15th

1804 To his squadron on the flag system of communications: 'The Lords Commissioners of the Admiralty having resolved that a change of the Numeral Flags described in page 14, of the Day Signal-Book, shall immediately take place, I have it in command from their Lordships to send you a painted copy of the flags as now altered, and to desire that you will paste the same on the 14th page of the Day Signal-Book in your possession'.

1792 *Three hundred and sixty one votes – exactly a majority – are cast for the death of King Louis XVI, against 360 for imprisonment, banishment or death with respite.*

16th

1801 To St Vincent on hoisting his flag in St Joseph: 'The St Joseph, as far as relates to Captain Hardy, is ready for sea, but the Dock-yard have not done with her. My cabin is not yet finished, of course – nor even painted; but that I do not care about: I shall live in Captain Hardy's. My wish is to get her into Torbay, and in seven days alongside the Ville de Paris. She will be perfection'.

1773 *Captain Cook's Resolution becomes the first ship to cross the Antarctic Circle.*

17th

1799 To his brother, The Reverend Nelson on his coat of arms: 'I thank you for your congratulations on what the generosity of our Country has done for me. I have very much your idea about the Arms, and if you will arrange it at the Heralds' Office, I shall feel very much obliged'.

1788 *Captain Arthur Phillip, Sirius, arrives in Botany Bay, in advance of the First Fleet carrying convicts.*

18th

1799 To Lord Minto: 'The state of this country [Sicily] is this – hate the French, love the English, discontented with their present Government, as Neapolitan councillors take the lead, to the entire exclusion of the Sicilians'.

1770 *A group of New Yorkers called the 'Sons of Liberty' engage British troops in a pitched battle in New York, in retaliation against the Quartering Act.*

19th

1805 Nelson, having passed through the Biche Channel expecting to find the French, records: 'At twenty-five minutes past nine, made the general signal "Prepare for Battle". At twenty-five minutes past eleven "Form the Established Order of Sailing in two Columns", and the signal "Keep in close Order".' Later he records: 'We are taken by a heavy gale at S.S.W. which has arrested our progress'.

1783 *The preliminaries of the Peace of Paris are signed at Versailles.*

20th

1805 Unknown to Nelson, (but later acknowledged in a letter to Briggs), some French ships are reported off Sardinia but they are not the battlefleet: 'The Seahorse saw a French Frigate off Pula, but it was so thick that he could not see three miles distant. I cannot, for want of Frigates send off this letter'.

1793 *Louis XVI of France, who was tried by the French Convention on 16 January, found guilty and sentenced to death, is executed in the Place de la Révolution, Paris.*

21st

ROBERT BURNS (1759-1796)

Robert Burns was the most revered of Scottish poets. His early lifestyle – that of a commoner – is reflected in his simple but earthy vernacular style. His subjects covered those things he most practised; independence of spirit, convivial drinking and love.

Although born into a farming family on 25 January 1759, his forte was with the pen not the plough. (He was later called the 'ploughman poet' by Edinburgh scholars.) Burn's first anthology of poems was published in Kilmarnock and became known as the *Kilmarnock Edition*. It earned him popular acclaim, first in Edinburgh and later throughout the whole of Scotland where he became a national hero. Burns resented this mantle and returned to farming, but ill health brought him an early death on 21 July 1796.

Burns has never waned in popularity. For over a century he influenced nearly all Scottish poets and while new styles continue to develope he will always be remembered for penning 'Auld Lang Syne'.

JOHN ADAMS (1735-1826)

A staunch upholder of the rights of the colonies, John Adams, in June 1776, seconded in the Continental Congress the resolution: 'these colonies are, and of right, ought to be, free and independent states.' He later became president, succeeding Washington in 1796.

President John Adams. (See 27 January.)

A chart of the Falkland Islands, 1771, published then because the islands were in the news as a point of conflict. (See 22 January.)

1805 Nelson, struggling against west by southwesterly gales towards Sardinia, believes Villeneuve is bound for Cagliari: 'I sincerely pray for a favourable wind; for we cannot be more than twenty leagues from them, and if Cagliari be their object, and the Sardes will but defend their capital, we shall be in time to save them: pray God it may be so.'

1771 The Falkland Islands are ceded to Britain by Spain. France founded the first settlement in 1764, a British colony was established in 1765, but Spain, despite objection from the British, sold 'las Malvinas' to the French in 1766.

1800 To Davison on the matter of sharing freight and prize money; both were to become subjects of law suits against St Vincent: 'Notwithstanding Dr Laurence's opinion, I do not believe I have any right to exclude the junior Flag Officers of the Fleet, and if I have, I desire that no such claims may be made'. The case was heard on 14 November 1803.

1806 William Pitt the Younger, dies after holding office for 18 years. It was said that Austerlitz killed him.

1801 The Corporation of Plymouth grant Lord Nelson the Freedom of their Borough in a silver box. He replied to the recorder: 'Whatever merit may have been attributed to [me] in the action of the Nile, it was only for having executed orders intrusted to [me]'.

1800 Napoleon concludes the Convention of El Arish with the Ottoman Turks, agreeing a French withdrawal from Egypt.

1805 In the Gulf of Cagliari, trying to intercept the French Fleet: 'You will believe my anxiety. I have neither ate, drank or slept with any comfort since last Sunday'.

1759 Robert Burns, Scotland's national bard, is born at Alloway, Ayrshire.

1782 Albermarle is in collision with the Brilliant, an East Indian store ship, off the Downes. Nelson records: 'At eight in the morning, it blew a hard gale of wind at N.N.W., a large East India Store Ship drove from her anchors, and came aboard us. We have lost our foremast, and bowsprit, mainyard, larboard cathead, and quarter gallery, the ship's head, and stove in two places on the larboard side – all done in five minutes'.

1788 Captain Arthur Phillip, together with 1030 people, including 540 men and 188 women convicts, reach Port Jackson (later re-named Sydney) six days before the French arrive.

1796 Nelson tells Fanny that his captains said on his departure from Genoa: 'You did just as you pleased in Lord Hood's time, the same in Hotham's and again in Jervis' it makes no difference to you who is C-in-C.'

1775 Lord Dartmouth, Cabinet Minister for Colonial Affairs, orders the arrest of Adams and Hancock, hoping to quash the colonial rebellion in America.

1801 Horatia is born at the Hamiltons' house in Piccadilly (some accounts say 29th). The earliest surviving record alluding to the event was from Emma to Mrs Gibson, postmarked 7 February 1801. 'Dear Madame, my cold has been so bad I could not go out today, but tomorrow I will call on you. Write me by the penny post how dear little Miss Horatia is'.

1788 Commencement of Lord North's administration, during the course of which, by fatal misjudgement and obstinacy, His Majesty's colonies in North America were lost.

22nd

23rd

24th

25th

26th

27th

28th

Uniformity in swords was not achieved in Nelson's time. Officers selected them to suit their fighting, ceremonial and dress requirements, including standing for portraits (which often provide evidence of ornate but delicate weapons). It appears that Horatio Nelson, and many other naval officers, favoured an infantry hanger.

An Admiralty Instruction on 4 August 1805 introduced an official pattern sword, but by then presentation swords were *recherché*. Many such swords were presented on behalf of Lloyd's Patriotic Fund and were known as £30, £50, £100 or Trafalgar swords, the difference being the quality of workmanship and embellishment.

Twenty-nine Trafalgar swords were presented, twenty-five to captains and four to lieutenants, all of whom commanded ships. Thirty-nine £100 swords went mainly to captains and commanders but two went to lieutenants, two to army officers and one to a commodore of the Honourable East India Company. The £50 swords were intended for lieutenants but of twenty-eight, fifteen went to Honourable East India Company officers, nine to Royal Marines officers and one to a master. Sixteen £30 swords went to eight midshipmen, four lieutenants of marines and four to mates.

Medals and medallions were in use in Europe in the fifteenth century but made their first appearance in England during the reign of Charles I when he authorised a medal for 'forlorn hopes' soldiers in May 1643.

The House of Commons authorised a medal for the fleet involved in the first Dutch war; Blake's victory off the Texel, in 1653. Blake's medal cost 150 guineas. In 1692 a figure equal to one tenth of all prize money or the proceeds from prizes was approved by parliament to be used for medals and other rewards for officers and seamen.

Following Lord Howe's victory over the French at the Glorious First of June, a naval medal was instituted. Since that time special medals have been struck for significant battles, campaigns or series of campaigns, the latter being the Naval General Service Medal.

Admiral Thomas Graves is credited with building a lifeboat in about 1760 although it is unclear whether the vessel was purpose built or merely an adapted sea boat. The first recorded boat built specifically for the purpose and patented as such was by Lionel Lukin. His craft, a Norwegian yawl, was fitted with cork gunwales, air chambers and a heavy stablising keel. His second craft was more successful and saved a number of lives off the Yorkshire coast. The lifesaving business did not gather momentum until the *Adventure* went down in 1798, a few hundred yards from shore. This disaster led to the announcement of a competition to design a lifeboat and a 2-guinea prize was offered. It was won by William Wouldhave, the parish clerk and built by Henry Greathead, a South Shields boatbuilder. The craft was named *Original* and was in service for forty years.

A mezzotint engraving by William Barnard after the painting by Lemuel Abbott showing Nelson on board Victory *with his sword in hand. Swords at this period were chosen to suit various purposes - both belligerent and ceremonial.*

⚓ 1805 ⚓ Electing to go east, Nelson tells Marsden: 'either the French fleet have put back crippled, or that they are gone to the Eastward, probably to Egypt. Therefore I find no difficulty pursuing the line of conduct I have adopted'.

⚓ 1779 ⚓ Spain asks Britain to cease hostilities following the independence of North America.

⚓ 1803 ⚓ To Sir John Acton, at Naples: 'I am distressed for frigates, which are the eyes of the fleet; for the terrible winter we have had has obliged me to send three into port to be re-fitted: however, I trust we shall fall in with the Enemy, and do the business'.

⚓ 1790 ⚓ The first purpose-built lifeboat is launched on the River Tyne. The first unsinkable lifeboat is patented by Lionel Lukin, a London coachbuilder, on 2 November 1805.

⚓ 1784 ⚓ Nelson gives up his brief attempt to enter politics. He writes to his brother, Rector of Brandon Parva, Norfolk: 'As to you having enlisted under the banners of the Walpoles, you might as well have enlisted under those of my grandmother. They are altogether the merest set of ciphers that ever existed – in public affairs I mean. Mr Pitt, depend upon it, will stand against all opposition'.

⚓ 1788 ⚓ Prince Charles Edward Stewart, the Young Pretender, dies in Rome in exile on the 139th anniversary of the death of his great grandfather Charles I.

29th

30th

31st

A typical frigate (see 30 January). These three-masted ships, fully rigged on each mast, were insufficiently armed (24 to 40 guns) to stand in the line of battle. Their excellent sailing qualities were exploited by Nelson and others for intelligence gathering. Not unnaturally they became known as 'the eyes of the fleet'.

THE FORTUNE OF THE DAY

THE BATTLE OF CAPE ST VINCENT

Derek Allen

'Only History can relate the full story...And I shall write the History.'

Winston Churchill

'February 14th.

A.M. – Fresh breezes and hazy weather. A strange fleet in sight, supposed to be the enemy. At noon, the British fleet began to engage the Spanish fleet, consisting of 27 sail of the line and 10 frigates, brigs, &c.

P.M. – Moderate breezes and hazy weather. The fleet in action with the Spanish fleet. At ½ past 3, one of the enemy's line-of-battle ships struck, and soon after a three-decker. At ½ past 4, a three-decker and a 74 struck [to] the *Captain* very much disabled. At ½ past 5, discontinued the action, and took possession of the enemy's ships and took them in tow.'

Such is the laconic, formal account of the Battle of Cape St Vincent in the Captain's Journal of the frigate HMS *Lively*. Fortunately *Lively* carried passengers that day, among their number a Colonel John Drinkwater, author of a far more circumstantial account of what was in many ways the most important engagement of Horatio Nelson's career. Together with Admiral John Jervis' official dispatch and Nelson's personal account, we are able to reconstruct a narrative of the battle. From this we are better able to assess the relative importance of the victory to the nation, to the Royal Navy, and to Horatio Nelson.

As Jervis said on the eve of the battle: 'A victory is very essential to the English at this moment,' – a sentiment that was equally applicable to the navy. But its particular importance to the young Commodore Nelson is arguably of even greater consequence. Until then he had been highly regarded in his profession, seen by his fellows and peers (as well as the lower decks) as highly motivated, more than competent, zealous and ambitious. He also enjoyed a close understanding with Jervis. But was he, on 13 February, a man of destiny? Was 14 February the opportunity he had been waiting for?

The same question that hangs over Nelson's entire career is particularly apparent at Cape St Vincent: What if? Given the uncertainties of naval warfare Nelson's fortune could have gone either way. But at this date Westminster Abbey was scarcely an option. If the battle had not gone his way, he could have expected at best a court martial, or in death a quiet burial at Burnham Thorpe, or even over the side and into obscure oblivion. The debate will continue over Nelson's unorthodox manoeuvre in wearing out of the line, but the fact remains that he did get away with it, and was indeed commended by Jervis for his skill, enterprise and bravery. In a letter to the First Lord accompanying his official dispatch, Jervis, recognising this moral courage, noted: 'Commodore Nelson contributed very much to the fortune of the day.'

Let us look then at a narrative of events stated as

simply as possible. The year 1796 had not been the most glorious for the Royal Navy. For eighteen months Admiral Jervis had been in command of the Mediterranean fleet and during that time had brought his ships and their crews to a high pitch of efficiency. But the strategic situation had turned against the British: Bonaparte's successes on land in the Italian campaign and the subsequent adherence of Spain to the cause of Revolutionary France meant that the Mediterranean was now a hostile sea. Without adequate bases for resupply it was impossible for the British to maintain a 'fleet in being', and in September Jervis was forced to order a withdrawal through the Straits of Gibraltar and make his base at Lisbon. Britain's constant fear of invasion increased as hostile forces were in control of the coasts all the way from Gibraltar to the Fricsian Islands. Indeed, in December 1796, the French had attempted a descent on Ireland, but without success, in their abortive expedition to Bantry Bay.

So Jervis' task was clear. He must prevent the Spanish fleet from sailing north to join their allies in the Channel. This was indeed the strategic target of the ships under the command of Admiral de Cordoba as they left Cartagena, but they also had a shorter range mission which remained unknown to the British at the time. How differently might the battle have turned out if Jervis had known that four of the Spanish fleet were in fact *urcas* – armed merchantmen – loaded with quicksilver, a vital strategic material necessary in the processing of the silver ore from the Americas, itself a vital prop of the Spanish Treasury.

When the British fleet quit the Mediterranean it had been Commodore Nelson's duty to evacuate British forces from Elba, and so it was that Sir Gilbert Elliot, the former governor of Corsica, and his aide Colonel Drinkwater arrived in the midst of the British fleet on the eve of the battle. Nelson had sailed by night unnoticed right through the Spanish fleet, and his report (along with those of other frigate captains) made it clear that an opportunity for battle was imminent. Strong easterlies had helped the Spaniards through the Straits a week earlier, but had then carried them far out into the Atlantic. So now they had to beat their way back towards Cadiz, the destination of the mercury convoy. In anticipation Jervis gathered his fleet some 11 leagues southwest of

Cape St Vincent. He listened to the reports of reconnaissance with stern satisfaction: the stage was set.

The British fleet numbered fifteen ships of the line and was opposed by twenty-seven Spanish ships. Forming the backbone of each fleet – eight of the British and eighteen of the Spanish – was the two-decked 74-gun ship, the workhorse of eighteenth-century naval warfare. Jervis flew his flag in the 100-gun *Victory*, while Admiral de Cordoba flew his in the *Santissima Trinidad* which, with 136 guns was the largest and most powerful warship of the age, and built, like many of the best Spanish ships, in Havana. Jervis' Mediterranean fleet had been together and at sea, for more than a year, and had become a trained, disciplined fighting force. Despite their lack of recent success, morale was high; in the words of an anonymous seaman they were ready to give the Dons 'their Valentines in style'. Recent storms had deprived Jervis of five of his original fleet: *Courageux*, *Gibraltar*, *Zealous*, *Bombay Castle* and *Saint George*. Fortunately reinforcements from home under Rear-Admiral Parker had just brought the fleet back to its original strength. Among the captains of the fleet were to be found the nucleus of Nelson's 'band of brothers', those officers who would fight alongside him at the Nile and at Trafalgar – Collingwood, Troubridge, Murray, Miller, Foley, Hallowell and Berry.

De Cordoba's ships were well built but were chronically short of trained seamen, partly a result of their habit of manning the ships with large detachments of marine infantry – not sailors at all – and partly because of the losses caused by recurring fever epidemics in Spain's seaports. As Nelson himself observed, the Spaniards could make ships, but could not make men to man them. And there lay the crucial difference between the two fleets. A lack of time at sea brought inevitable results. The Spanish fleet seemed quite unable to manoeuvre together, and on individual ships neither seamanship nor gunnery came close to equalling the standards achieved in the Royal Navy. Although de Cordoba (described by a fellow officer as 'not very bright') had at his disposal nearly twice as many ships, mounting twice as many guns as those of Jervis' command, the lack of trained manpower, and the low morale and discipline of the Spaniards did more than redress the balance.

On the morning of the 14th, coming upon the Spanish fleet sailing in two loose formations, Jervis

Admiral John Jervis, who was granted the title Earl of St Vincent following his success on 14 February 1797.

ordered his squadron to form a single line which he meant to drive between the two masses of Spanish ships. Once through, his ships would turn about and form two groups, one to attack the van and one the rear. Nelson in the *Captain* sailed last but two in the British line. Soon he saw signals hoisted on *Victory* making the order to put about. Jervis had ordered the whole line 'tack in succession', to turn and follow its van into action. Nelson saw that the manoeuvre would give the Spanish time to evade. Thus he ordered his American-born captain, Miller, to wear out of the line and steer directly at the centre of the larger division of the enemy fleet. He knew that this would buy time, but in doing so, not only would he face enormous odds, he would also break the cardinal rule of British naval tactics – never to leave the line without orders.

Captain joined action with seven Spanish ships (among them the *Santissima Trinidad*). *Culloden* (Captain Troubridge) was with him, and later *Excellent* (Captain Collingwood) and others of the squadron. But Nelson fought for over an hour in the very centre of the action, at point-blank range, until nearly all *Captain*'s sails and rigging were gone and her fore topmast shot away. Ammunition stocks grew dangerously low. Aware that he could no longer manoeuvre, Nelson decided on even closer action, and ordered Miller to go alongside the 80-gun *San Nicolas*, herself entangled with the *San Josef.* They boarded, and after brief but fierce hand-to-hand fighting the Spanish capitulated. Nelson ordered Miller to push more men into the *San Nicolas* and turned his attention to the *San Josef*, which quickly surrendered in its turn.

On the morning of 15 February the two fleets were still engaged. As day broke they stood off warily from each other. Neither admiral apparently had any desire to resume hostilities. Jervis had four prizes – always literally of great value to every man in the fleet – to guard, and one of his own ships, the *Captain*, under tow. He was almost as badly outnumbered as he had been the day before, but now he had a victory behind him. If he had known of the mercury shipment convoyed by the Spanish he might have been more aggressive. For de Cordoba, on the other hand, protecting that shipment greatly influenced his assessment of the situation. Of greater weight, though, must have been the loss of four ships and the severe dam-

age to his flagship, the *Santissima Trinidad*. Spanish losses in both men and material had indeed been heavy, but about half the fleet had, for one reason or another, taken no active part in the battle. A council of war – in itself symptomatic of some of the problems a Spanish admiral faced – showed no will to fight on, and eventually it was de Cordoba's ships that broke contact, heading back towards Cadiz.

This account tallies essentially with what arrived by the hand of Captain Robert Calder at the Admiralty on 3 March. Jervis gave an official report of what was a typical encounter battle at sea. The significant news was in the 'list of ships named in the margin – taken', as well as the list of killed and wounded, the heaviest being on *Captain*. Four ships were captured, all ships of the line and two of 112 guns. The great prize of the *Santissima Trinidad* eluded capture, though many in the British fleet believed she had struck, and then re-hoisted her colours. Jervis failed to name any individuals, praising the general gallantry and efficiency of his fleet, but in an accompanying letter to the First Lord he named Troubridge, Collingwood and, in particular, Nelson. Thus far this was an ordinary naval engagement, but something happened that was to make this 'ordinary' battle 'extraordinary'.

Let us look more closely and at a different sort of account, one that pays far more attention to individual contributions. A fortnight after the event, on 27 February, Colonel Drinkwater, by that date off the Scillies but still aboard the *Lively*, addressed his account to 'a friend' (a literary device surely). Drinkwater focused on Nelson's role, and in particular something called his 'Patent Bridge for Boarding First Rates.'

During the action on the 14th, Drinkwater was on *Lively*, stationed with other frigates close to, but not in the midst of the action. Interestingly enough, given his circumstantial account, Drinkwater nowhere claims to have been an actual eye witness – an unlikely claim anyway in the confusion of the day – but employs his secretarial skills to compile in the days and nights following the engagement the *Narrative of the Proceedings of the British Fleet* (first published within the year). His method necessarily brings individuals more to the fore, but what is remarkable is that a long section – almost half – of his work relates to and emphasises the 'Patent

Bridge' episode. By Drinkwater's own account, the genesis of his project had been a conversation with Nelson (with whom he had formed 'a close intimacy' whilst in Corsica) on the morning after the battle. 'I then remarked that, as the *Lively* would bear the glorious news to England, I should feel much obliged by his giving me as many particulars of the proceedings of his ship, the *Captain*, and of his own conduct in the capture of the two ships, as he was disposed to communicate.' Nelson did not apparently need much prompting: 'He good-naturedly replied, "I'll tell you how it happened."' And so, midway through, Drinkwater's account turns quite abruptly from the general to the particular.

'Fortune favours the brave; nor on this occasion was she unmindful of her favourite. Captain Miller so judiciously directed the course of the *Captain*, that she was laid aboard the starboard quarter of the 84 gun ship, her spritsail yard passing over the enemy's poop, and hooking her mizzen shrouds; and the word to board being given, the officers and seamen destined for this duty, headed by Lieutenant Berry, together with the detachment of the 69th Regiment, commanded by Lieutenant

Pearson, then doing duty as marines on board the *Captain*, passed with rapidity on board the enemy's ship; and in a short time the *San Nicolas* was in the possession of her intrepid assailants. The commodore's impatience would not permit him to remain an inactive spectator of this event. He knew the attempt was hazardous; and his presence, he thought, might contribute to its success. He therefore accompanied the party in this attack, passing from the fore chains of his own ship into the enemy's quarter gallery, and thence through the cabin to the quarter deck, where he arrived in time to receive the sword of the dying commander, who was mortally wounded by the boarders. For a few minutes after the officers had submitted, the crew below were firing their lower deck guns: this irregularity, however, was soon corrected, and measures taken for the security of the conquest. But this labour was no sooner achieved, than he found himself engaged in another and more arduous one. The stern of the three decker, his former opponent, was directly amidships on the weather beam of the *San Nicolas*; and, from her poop and galleries, the enemy sorely annoyed with musketry the British on board the

James Fittler's copper engraving after a drawing of the battle by Jahleel Brenton of the Royal Navy.

San Nicolas. The commodore was not long in resolving on the conduct to be observed on this momentous occasion. The alternative that presented itself, was to quit the prize, or advance. Confident in the bravery of his seamen, he determined on the latter. Directing therefore an additional number of men to be sent from the *Captain*, on board the *San Nicolas*, the undaunted commodore headed himself the assailants in this new attack, and success crowned the enterprise. Such, indeed, was the panic occasioned by his preceding conduct, that the British no sooner appeared on the quarter deck of their new opponent, than the commandant advanced, and asking for the British commanding officer, dropped on one knee, and presented to him his sword; making, at the same time, an excuse for the Spanish admiral's not appearing, as he was dangerously wounded. For a moment Commodore Nelson could scarcely persuade himself of this second instance of good fortune; he therefore ordered the Spanish commandant, who had the rank of a Brigadier, to assemble the officers on the quarter deck, and direct steps to be taken instantly for communicating to the crew the surrender of the ship. All the officers immediately appeared; and the commodore found the surrender of the *San Josef* ascertained, by each of them delivering to him his sword. The coxswain of the commodore's barge [William Fearney, like Nelson a native of Burnham Thorpe] had attended the commodore throughout this perilous adventure. To him the commodore gave in charge the swords of the Spanish officers as he received them; and the jolly tar, as they were delivered to him, tucked these honourable trophies under his arm, with all the *sang froid* imaginable.'

Such was Drinkwater's stylish, polished, almost stage-managed account. It is clear that a fortnight after the battle the Nelson legend was already emerging. Nelson's own 'Few Remarks Relative to Myself in the *Captain*, in which my Pendant was flying on the most Glorious Valentine's Day 1797' (in his own hand in the Nelson papers) used almost exactly the same words, and was sent to his family, to the Duke of Clarence, and to his mentor Captain Locker, for 'possible publication'. He adds a slightly self-conscious postscript: 'There is a saying in the Fleet too

Portrait of William Locker, Nelson's captain in the Lowestoffe, *who became a close friend and mentor.*

flattering for me to omit telling -*viz.*, "Nelson's Patent Bridge for boarding First-Rates", alluding to my passing over an Enemy's 80-gun Ship.'

If the victory over the Dons was not that 'glorious and unparalleled' it was certainly timely, and it was certainly regarded as a clear-cut victory at the time: Sir John Jervis received an earldom, whereas the hapless Admiral de Cordoba was arrested and court martialled. The battle restored what the British had always believed to be the proper state of affairs; for the remainder of the Napoleonic Wars the supremacy of the Royal Navy was not to be seriously challenged. But the most important result was surely that it brought Horatio Nelson into the spotlight of history, a role for which he seems to have been well rehearsed.

Parliament's thanks went first, and not surprisingly, to Jervis (Sir Charles Bunbury even suggesting that he take the title 'Salvador del Mundo' after one of the captured ships!). The first proper notice of Nelson's role – evidence perhaps that the 'public relations exercise' was beginning to take effect – appeared in *The Times* on 13 March:

'However incredible it may appear, it is a positive fact, that in the action of the 14 February, Commodore Nelson in the *Captain*, of 74 guns, and Capt. Troubridge, in the *Culloden*, of the same force, turned the whole van of the Spanish Fleet, consisting of three First Rates and four 74 or 80 gun ships.'

In the same issue we find a curious and exotic recipe:

COMMODORE NELSON'S RECEIPT FOR AN OLLA PODRIDA

Take a Spanish First-Rate and an 80 Gun Ship, and after well battering and basting for an hour, keep throwing in your force balls, and be sure to let them be well season'd.

Your fire must never slacken for a single Moment, but must be kept up as brisk as possible during the whole time.

As soon as you perceive your Spaniards to be well stew'd and blended together, you must then throw in your own ship on board of the two decker, lash your Spritsail yard to her mizzen mast, then Jump into her quarter gallery, sword in hand, and let the rest of your boarders follow as they can.

The Moment you appear on the 80 gun ship's quarter-deck the Spaniards will all fly.

You will then only have to take a hop, step and jump from your stepping stone and you will find yourself in the middle of a First-rate's quarter-deck, with all the Spaniards at your feet.

Your Olla Podrida may now be consider'd as completely dish'd, fit to set before His Majesty.

Nelson's New Art of Cookery

One finds corroboration of this pattern by looking at contemporary pictorial evidence. Soon after the battle, on 15 May 1797, a mezzotint engraving of 'Brave Admiral Jervis' was published by Laurie & Whittle, complete with doggerel verse concluding: 'But, all I've know'd and all I've seed Is now out done by Jervis.'

On 4 June 1798 James and Josiah Boydell made available a set of three copper engravings, 'Victory of Cape St Vincent', done by James Fittler, among the foremost engravers of the day, and based on the drawings of Lieutenant Jahiel Brereton, present at the battle on *Barfleur*. Impressive and accurate (as only the discerning eye can see) though they are, they never achieved the popular acclaim which greeted Daniel Orme's 'Admiral Nelson's Reception of the Spanish Admiral's Sword', published on 21 June 1800 (that is, after the crowning achievement of the Battle of the Nile). The whole episode is shown dramatically. The battle is condensed for public consumption to this one image. It has become one of the two enduring snapshots of Nelson's career – the other being set in the *Victory*'s cockpit at Trafalgar.

Naval historians continue to debate whether Nelson anticipated orders, disobeyed orders, or followed the spirit not the letter of his orders when he wore the *Captain* out of line. But at the end of that day all that really mattered, as Jervis realised when he rejected Calder's criticism and embraced Nelson instead, was that the coup had succeeded, and that both he and his protégé would benefit. If Jervis became, apparently at the King's own suggestion, Earl St Vincent, Nelson got his preferred reward when he was made a Knight of the Bath, and also, although by seniority, rear-admiral. In the following weeks Nelson's life was full of the aftermath of victory. He wrote several accounts of the battle for various correspondents,

and received the good wishes of all. He presented the sword of Admiral Winthuysen to the City of Norwich, and was granted the Freedom of the City in return. Characteristically, and perhaps ominously, the only sobering note is to be found in a letter from his wife Fanny, who wrote 'What can I attempt to say to you about Boarding? You have been most wonderfully protected: you have done desperate actions enough. Now may I – indeed I do – beg that you never Board again. *Leave it for captains*.'

The victory, and Nelson's audacious contribution to it, confirmed him as the navy's, and now the nation's, 'Darling Son'. He was now more than a sailor, more than an admiral; he was a hero and his deeds were already legendary. To return to Drinkwater:

'If I may be permitted to hazard an opinion, the whole squadron have gained immortal honour; for the victory of the 14th of February stands, in all its circumstances, first and unparalleled in naval history.'

The whole squadron? Perhaps not, but for one man it may well be seen as the defining moment of his career.

Derek Allen has a longstanding, if amateur, interest in naval and military history of the eighteenth and nineteenth centuries. After graduating from Oxford he worked for a number of years in publishing, and latterly with antique maps and prints. He is now a freelance writer, editor, cataloguer, and picture dealer.

Detail of Daniel Orme's famous painting showing Nelson receiving the Spanish Admiral's sword in surrender on the quarterdeck of the San Josef.

Admiral Jervis embraces Nelson after the battle. In wearing out of the line, Nelson had disobeyed orders, but his admiral recognised the bravery and intuition of his actions.

BENJAMIN FRANKLIN (1706–1790)

Benjamin Franklin was the fifteenth child of a Northamptonshire trader who emigrated with his family to Boston, Massachusetts in about 1685. There he set up a candle and soap making factory. Benjamin was born on 17 January 1706. It was his father's wish that the boy would enter the church, but lack of money to pay for the necessary education forced him instead to seek a position in the printers trade.

At seventeen Benjamin ran away to Philadelphia and by dint of hard work, initiative and utilising his trade he acquired a printing office of his own from where he produced the *Pennsylvania Gazette*. He remained a journalist for twenty years, all the while taking an interest in languages, literature and the sciences, and steadily gaining influence in local affairs. He was chosen clerk of the Pennsylvania General Assembly in 1736 and remained in public life there-after, spending much of his time abroad, particularly in Paris and London. He had in fact gained recognition in Europe through his work with lightning and electricity. In London he applied himself to getting the Stamp Act repealed, winning many friends and the respect of the House. However, after ten years working on the issue of self government for the colonies without success he returned to his homeland to help draft the Declaration of Independence. He made one more trip to Europe in 1776, to solicit help from France where he was acknowledged as a fine diplomat.

In 1787, although exhausted by recent exertions he accepted the office of Chief Executive of Pennsylvania. He continued to work tirelessly for the abolition of slavery and produced his autobiography which received great acclaim. He died on 17 April 1790.

Benjamin Franklin.
(See 6 February.)

A Baxter print of Sir Robert Peel, c.1840.
(See 5 February.)

❦ **1800** ❦ To Lord St Vincent on measures to keep his ships at sea: 'You taught us to keep the seamen healthy without going into port, and to stay at sea for years without a refit. We know not the meaning of the word. The Audacious, Alexander, and others have never seen an arsenal since they have been under my command... Our friend Troubridge is as full of resource as his Culloden is full of incidents; but I am now satisfied that if his ship's bottom were entirely out, he would find means to make her swim'.

❦ *1800* ❦ *The new constitution in France, with Bonaparte as First Consul, is accepted by referendum.*

❦ **1801** ❦ San Joseph, Torbay. To Davison on a meeting with St Vincent and alluding to their prize money suit: 'I hope he says true, but I will not spare him an inch in the point of law, and only hope he will never open the subject. If he does, I am prepared with a broadside, as strong (and backed with justice) as any he can send'.

❦ *1801* ❦ *The first Parliament of the United Kingdom of Great Britain and Ireland assembles.*

❦ **1800** ❦ Nelson arrives at Palermo in Foudroyant but cannot go ashore to the Hamiltons until he has paid his respects to Lord Keith. He writes to Emma: 'I cannot come ashore until I have made my manners to him. Times are changed; but if he does not come ashore directly, I will not wait'.

With head held high: Gillray's portrayal of Pitt's resignation entitled 'Integrity Retiring From Office'.

❦ *1801* ❦ *Pitt resigns as Prime Minister after 17 years in office having fallen out with George III over concessions to Roman Catholics.*

❦ **1805** ❦ Trèville, having sailed on 18 January, is still at large. To Briggs, the British pro-consul at Alexander: 'The governor is now put upon his guard, I hope he will take every means in his power for the defence of Alexander; and in particular, to have vessels ready to sink, to prevent the entrance of the French Fleet into the old Port, until the obstructions were removed, which would give me time to get at them'.

❦ *1783* ❦ *Parliament officially proclaims an end to all hostilities in North America.*

❦ **1785** ❦ Nelson sails into English Harbour, Antigua, and reproaches the captain of Latona for flying his broad pendant. He is later censured by the Admiralty for taking it upon himself, 'To control the exercise of the functions of his appointment'. In practice Nelson was right, for at that time, Moutray was on half pay as the commissioner of the navy at Antigua.

❦ *1788* ❦ *Sir Robert Peel (d. 1850), who first organised the London Police Force and Irish constabulary, is born. He became Prime Minister in 1841.*

❦ **1802** ❦ To Captain Sutton, Amazon, on a variety of matters. He was particularly bitter about the lack of a Copenhagen medal: 'Thank Captain Cochrane for his advice on the thrashing machine...I saw Lord St Vincent yesterday: he looks very unwell. The History of Medals for Copenhagen he has promised me shall be brought before the cabinet council'.

❦ *1778* ❦ *Louis XVI formally recognises the independence of the thirteen American colonies at a ceremonial signing of a treaty with Benjamin Franklin.*

1st

2nd

3rd

4th

5th

6th

The press gang on Tower Hill (see 10 February). Feared and despised, the Impressment Service or press gang roamed the coast and waterways seizing anyone who could not prove exemption by way of trade or status.

The Royal Dockyard at Chatham (detail). (See 7 February.)

🦋 **1793** 🦋 Nelson assumes command of Agamemnon at Chatham. Three days later he tells his brother: 'my ship is without exception, the finest 64 in the service, and has the character of sailing most remarkably well'.

🦋 **1779** 🦋 *William Boyce (b. 1710), composer and 'Master of the Kings Musick' since 1757, dies. His works include the 'Serenata of Solomon' and a collection of Cathedral music.*

🦋 **1801** 🦋 To Lady Hamilton: 'It is your sex that makes us go forth; and seem to tell us – "None but the brave deserve the fair!" and, if we fall, we still live in the hearts of those females who are dear to us. It is your sex that rewards us; it is your sex who cherish our memories; and you, honoured friend, are, believe me, the first, the best, of your sex'.

🦋 **1798** 🦋 *Napoleon sets out to inspect the coast for the best points to embark his forces for the invasion of England by his Armée d'Angleterre. He had presented his plans to the Directory on 12 June 1798.*

🦋 **1804** 🦋 Nelson appoints Rear-Admiral Richard Bickerton to chair a court martial: '[I] do hereby require and direct You to try the said Captain Spelman Swaine, the officers, and Ship's Company, for the loss of His Majesty's late Sloop Raven, on the night of the 5th January 1804'.

🦋 **1801** 🦋 *The Treaty of Lunéville is signed between France and Austria, leaving Britain without any ally against France. Austria recognises the Cisalpine, Batavian and Helvetian republics.*

🦋 **1793** 🦋 From Agamemnon at Chatham, to his brother on manning difficulties: 'Surgeons mates are very scarce, keep that to yourself. I have only got few men, and very hard indeed they are to be got, and without a press I have no idea how our Fleet can be manned'.

🦋 **1763** 🦋 *The Treaty of Paris ends the Seven Years' War; Canada and Senegal are ceded to Britain by France; Florida is ceded to Britain by Spain, but in return Spain obtains all British conquests in Cuba.*

🦋 **1797** 🦋 Nelson, Minèrve, rescues Hardy, who had launched the jolly boat to rescue a man overboard from the sea, in face of two Spanish ships of the line. Colonel Drinkwater's narrative records Nelson's words: 'By God, I'll not lose Hardy. Back the mizzen topsail'.

🦋 **1793** 🦋 *France begins a war on England and Holland. England is not on a war footing following ten years of conflict in America but it is expected to be a short war.*

🦋 **1805** 🦋 To Marsden at the Admiralty: 'the Fleet beat through the Faro – a thing unprecedented in nautical history; but although the danger from the rapidity of the current was great, yet so was the zeal of my pursuit'.

🦋 **1797** 🦋 *The last French invasion of Britain is attempted at Fishguard by 1400 troops commanded by General William Tate. They are soon defeated and repatriated.*

🦋 **1799** 🦋 At Palermo, to St Vincent on the spread of the revolution: 'Our news from Calabria is very bad, as most towns have erected the Tree of Liberty...and in the Island are many discontented people, who have shown themselves in various places, in a manner contrary to Law, and nearly approaching rebellion'.

🦋 **1772** 🦋 *Rioting mars the funeral of Augusta, Dowager Princess of Wales and mother of George III.*

Captain Horatio Nelson RN. An engraving published in August 1797 which manages to convey the charm of Rigaud's original oil portrait of the young and ambitious sea-officer, done between 1777 and 1781 at Locker's request. (See 15 February.)

🦂 1797 🦂 THE BATTLE OF CAPE ST VINCENT

'A few remarks relative to myself in the Captain, in which my pendant was flying on the most glorious Valentine's day 1797. At one P.M., the Captain having passed the sternmost of the enemy's ships which formed their van and part of their centre, consisting of seventeen Sail of the Line, they were on larboard, we on the starboard tack, the Admiral made the signal to 'tack in succession;' but I, perceiving the Spanish Ships all to bear up before the wind, or nearly so, evidently with the intention of forming their line going large, joining their separated Divisions, at the time engaged with some of our centre ships, or flying from us – to prevent either of their schemes from taking effect, I ordered the ship to be wore, and passing between the Diadem and Excellent, at a quarter past one o'clock was engaged with the headmost, and of course leewardmost of the Spanish Division'.

🦂 1791 🦂 The French explorer La Pérouse, who left Botany Bay on 15 March 1788 on the last leg of a circumnavigation expedition, is pronounced lost. His ships L'Astrolabe and La Boussole are believed to have sunk in the Pacific.

🦂 1781 🦂 To William Locker regarding his portrait, painted by John François Rigaud, RA. 'If Mr Rigaud has done the picture send word in the next letter you write to me, and I will enclose you an order upon Mr Paynter'.

🦂 1763 🦂 Prussia, Austria and Saxony conclude the Treaty of Hubertusburg, ending the German wars. Frederick fails to realise his objective which was to gain Saxony.

🦂 1801 🦂 To St Vincent: 'My sole object, and to which all my exertions and abilities tend, is to bring this long war to an honourable termination; to accomplish which, we must all pull in the collar, and, as we have got such a driver who will make the lazy ones pull as much as the willing, I doubt not but we shall get safely, speedily and honourably to our journey's end.'.

🦂 1801 🦂 Sir Humphry Davy is appointed Director of the Laboratory at the New Royal Institution.

🦂 1802 🦂 To Troubridge on raising funds for a monument to Miller, a veteran of St Vincent and the Nile: 'I doubt much if all the Admirals and Captains will subscribe to poor dear Miller's monument; but I have told Davison, that whatever is wanted to make up the sum, I shall pay'.

🦂 1766 🦂 Thomas Robert Malthus (d.1834), theologian, economist and author of 'The Principles of Population', is born.

🦂 1800 🦂 Observing an alarmed midshipman during an engagement with a French 74: 'Charles XII of Sweden ran away from the first shot he heard, though he was afterwards called Great because of his bravery. I therefore hope much from you in the future'.

🦂 1797 🦂 Trinidad is captured by Lieutenant-General Sir Ralph Abercromby and Rear-Admiral Henry Harvey.

🦂 1805 🦂 Nelson, arriving at Malta after chasing Villeneuve, remains alert to operational problems. To Captain John Whitby, Belleisle: 'As an anchor and cable is of great importance, it is my directions that you remain and weigh the anchor, which His Majesty's Ship under your command parted from the night of the 17th Instant; and after having done so, you are to proceed after the Squadron with the utmost possible dispatch'.

🦂 1781 🦂 Necker publishes 'Compte-Rendu', a report on the finances of France. He is accused of 'cooking the books' to show a surplus by ignoring a number of national obligations.

🦂 1797 🦂 Nelson is promoted Rear-Admiral of the Blue with seniority of 1 April and hoists his admiral's flag for the first time. Fanny writes: 'Yesterday's Gazette authorises our good Father and myself to congratulate you on your being a Flag Officer. May it please God your fame and success continue and increase under this promotion.'

🦂 1790 🦂 Emperor Joseph II dies aged 48 and is succeeded by his brother Leopold II, the Iron Duke of Tuscany.

February

14th
15th
16th
17th
18th
19th
20th

The Admiralty building in Whitehall. (See 21 February.)

SIR WILLIAM CORNWALLIS (1744-1819)

Sir William Cornwallis. (See 25 February.)

William Cornwallis (Billy Blue) was a lifelong friend of Nelson. He served throughout the War of American Independence and in 1788 went to India where his brother was governor-general. In 1795, when cruising off Brest he fell in with a vastly superior French fleet under Villaret de Joyeuse and managed a masterly retreat. Later, on the same station he blockaded first Brest in 1801, and then Ushant. This later blockade prevented Admiral Ganteaume from fulfilling his obligation to meet up with Villeneuve's fleet, (although this fleet was being harried by Nelson in the West Indies), thus foiling Napoleon's attempt to launch an invasion of England.

HMS FOUDROYANT

A plaque showing the second ship to take the name HMS Foudroyant (see 27 February), launched in 1798 and still afloat nearly a century later.

There were two naval ships to bear the name during Nelsonís time and a third which originally bore the name *Trincomalee*.

The first was a ship of 88 guns built for the French navy. She was captured by HMS *Monmouth* in 1758 and then took part in Rear-Admiral George Brydges' expedition to Martinique in 1762. She was also used in Keppel's action off Ushant in July 1778 and Sir John Jervis was her commander when, in April 1782, she captured another newly launched French ship, the 74-gun *Pégase*. She was dismantled in Plymouth in 1787.

The second *Foudroyant* was launched in Plymouth in 1798, and in the following year was selected by Nelson to be his flagship although still fitting out. Sadly she was not made ready in time and instead Nelson hoisted his flag in *Vanguard* where it remained until the Battle of the Nile. At Palermo in 1799 Nelson transferred to *Foudroyant* which remained his flagship until he returned to England the following year.

She was refitted, became flagship to Lord Keith, and returned to the Mediterranean. She was present at the capitulation of the French at Alexandria in 1801, later that year to be laid up in Devonport until 1891, spending the last few years as a vessel for gun drills. She beached at Blackpool in June 1897 and was broken up and recycled by local craftsmen.

⚓ **1805** ⚓ To William Marsden at the Admiralty informing him that the sloops Arrow and Acheron have been captured by two French frigates: 'The circumstances of this misfortune can only be attributed to the very long and tedious passage of the convoy which sailed from Malta on the 4th January, and the Enemy having no doubt gained intelligence of them and knowing I was in pursuit of their Fleet had sent two Frigates to the westward to intercept them'.

⚓ *1804* ⚓ *Richard Trevithick, a Cornish engineer, demonstrates the first steam engine to run on rails.*

21st

⚓ **1805** ⚓ To Marsden on the good state of his ships: 'The Fleet under my command is in excellent good health and the Ships, although we have experienced a great deal of bad weather; have received no damage and not a yard or mast sprung or crippled.' Villeneuve, on the same day, to the Minister of Marine on the deplorable state of his ships: 'I declare to you, that Ships of the Line thus equipped, short handed, vessels which lose their masts or sails at every puff of wind'.

⚓ *1784* ⚓ *Captain John Green sails from New York to China to begin Sino-American trade.*

22nd

⚓ **1802** ⚓ To Addington following receipt of a decoration for Copenhagen from the Sultan: 'If I can judge the feelings of others by myself, there can be no honours bestowed upon me by foreigners, that do not reflect ten times on our Sovereign and country'.

⚓ *1792* ⚓ *Sir Joshua Reynolds (b.1723), who became first president of the Royal Academy in 1768, dies.*

23rd

⚓ **1796** ⚓ To His Excellency John Trevor, Minister at Turin, after inspecting the enemy at Toulon: 'I had good opportunities of examining with a seaman's eye, the state of their ships...and I have no doubt in my mind they are fitting for sea...But I think it will be near a month before they are out...Thirteen Sail of the Line and five frigates, except having their sails bent, are perfectly ready....I believe we shall have a battle before the convoy sails'.

⚓ *1783* ⚓ *Following a critical peace treaty debate on 17 February, Parliament votes to discontinue war in America.*

24th

⚓ **1800** ⚓ Nelson gives a letter from the Emperor of Russia to Ball and presents him with the Grand Cross of the Order of St John of Jerusalem and an Honorary Commanderie'.

⚓ *1744* ⚓ *William Cornwallis, a naval contemporary of Nelson, is born. He saw service in America and India.*

25th

⚓ **1800** ⚓ To Lord Minto: 'You my dear friend [will] rejoice to hear that it has been my extraordinary good fortune to capture the Généreux, 74, bearing the flag of Rear-Admiral Perrée.'

⚓ *1797* ⚓ *Paper money in the form of £1 notes are first used by the Bank of England.*

26th

⚓ **1800** ⚓ Nelson, Foudroyant, attempts to recover an anchor previously cut away, but only manages to attach a stream cable on it. He writes to Ball: 'I wish to know precisely whether I may depend on information by guns, signals, &c., if the French ships make any movements, for instance, this night. I only wish to have an opportunity of getting our lost anchor'.

⚓ *1793* ⚓ *Austria and Russia conclude a treaty and agree apportionment of Venetian possessions in the Mediterranean.*

27th

⚓ *1797* ⚓ To Fanny: 'The Spanish War will give us a cottage and a piece of ground, which is all I want.'

⚓ *1780* ⚓ *Tsarina Catherine II appeals to those European countries neutral over America to unite against Britain in a League of Armed Neutrality, because the British navy are attacking ships indiscriminately.*

28th

(No letters have been found on this date by or to Horatio Nelson.)

⚓ *1753* ⚓ *The first leap year day after the adoption of the Gregorian Calendar by Great Britain on 3 September 1752.*

29th

TRIA JUNCTA IN UNO

HORATIO, EMMA AND SIR WILLIAM HAMILTON

Carol Evans

There is no doubt that Horatio Nelson was England's greatest fighting admiral; his perception of naval warfare was new and exciting and the tactics used by him were almost unbeatable. He seems to have had the ability to assess a given situation and react with devastating effect. So then it is strange that a man with these qualities would have such poor judgement when it came to women.

Nelson's mother had died when he was nine years old and soon after her death he was packed off to boarding school where he remained until going to sea with his maternal uncle, Maurice Suckling, at the age of twelve. It is not surprising then, that being deprived of a mother's love and guidance during those formative years, and being brought up almost totally in male company, his judgement and understanding of women was to say the least, limited.

There were several women in Nelson's life who deserve mention. In 1782 he wanted to marry Miss Mary Simpson, daughter of the Provost Marshal of the garrison of Quebec. His friend Alexander Davison persuaded him to drop her. However she was followed not long after by a Miss Andrews: Nelson met her in France in 1783, and again after a short acquaintance wanted to marry her. A little later he had an infatuation for Mrs Mary Moutray, wife of Commissioner Moutray of English Harbour, Antigua.

Another woman not to be left out of the story is Dolly, a whore at Leghorn, with whom he had a relationship while apparently happily married to Fanny. We see from this liaison that Lady Hamilton was not the first woman to be involved in an adulterous affair with Nelson.

Under analysis Nelson's irregular desires predominate but criticism withers in light of his tactical brilliance and pious beliefs. Biographical accounts of Sir William Hamilton and Lady Nelson tend to be accusative while Emma's seem to approve and in some cases applaud her achievements. Of them all, Fanny occupies the high moral ground, never once publicly criticising Nelson or the Hamiltons. Emma on the other hand did all she could to belittle Fanny and alienate her from Nelson's family.

Fanny, Frances Herbert Woolward, daughter of William, a senior judge, was born on Nevis in May 1761. Her father contracted a fatal illness and died when she was twenty. Shortly after, she married Dr Josiah Nisbet but he too died leaving Fanny with a young son. Thus encumbered she joined her uncle, John Herbert, in his Nevis home, Montpelier. It was here that she first met and admired the young captain of His Britannic Majesty's 28-gun ship *Boreas*.

Nelson, besotted by her charm, attention and understanding, saw her as the very epitome of a good naval officer's wife. He proposed, was accepted, and married her on 11 March 1787. One of his naval friends said: 'Yesterday the navy lost one of its greatest ornaments by Nelson's marriage. It is a national loss that such an officer should marry.' The marriage was not a passionate arrangement but domestic affection prevailed and the bond should have endured to the grave. However, it was not to be.

Alexander Pope pronounced there is a 'scoundrelism about persons of low birth' and prima facie evidence of Emy Hart's formative years endorse his opinion, but her circumstances as a child were not those of a scoundrel. Her mother was widowed and left without means two months after giving birth. She moved from the village of Ness, where her husband had worked as a smith, back to her native village of Hawarden, in Flintshire, taking with her little Emy to be brought up by her mother, old Mrs Kidd. Emy's mother, Mary, then disappeared from her daughter's life, leaving the old woman to do her best in rearing the inquisitive and perhaps mischievous child. At the age of thirteen Emy was placed into service with a local doctor, Mr Honoratus Leigh Thomas, as under nursemaid to his children. It is interesting to note that she remained friends with the Thomas family until about 1807.

At the age of fifteen her mother reappeared and wrote asking that Emy be sent to join her in London were she had obtained a position for her. She joined her mother and adopted the name of Emma Hart: her mother's name had also changed and she was now known as Mrs Mary Cadogan. It is said, without foundation, that she had gone through a form of marriage with a William Cadogan at Lausanne in 1768 or 1769. Her mother had obtained a position with the Linley family for Emma. Thomas Linley was a composer and part-owner of Drury Lane Theatre. His

A painting of Emma by George Romney, who, like so many others, was captivated by her beauty and completed many fine portraits of her.

house in Southampton Street, Covent Garden, was the ideal climate for Emma with her inborn love for music and drama. She worked for some time as a maid to the Linleys but left soon after the death of their son, Samuel, a midshipman in the navy. It appears she next took a nursery situation with the family of Dr Budd, at Chatham Place near Blackfriars Bridge. Scandal and rumour now play their part in the tale and we find her engaged to a fruit dealer in St James's Market. That she now progressed or descended to the brothel is the next episode in the legend.

It is said that Emma took up residence in the house of a Mrs Kelly of Arlington Street, who was known locally as 'the Abbess, a devotee of pleasure'. In 1791 she wrote to the artist, George Romney, 'Oh my old friend, for a time I own through distress my virtue was vanquished, but my sense of virtue was not overcome.' In this letter she refers to her poverty and distress, and it would have been around this time that she is said to have performed at the quack Doctor Graham's Temple of Health as the Goddess Hebe Vestina, dressed only in very light draperies (some said no draperies at all). At Mrs Kelly's she would have had the opportunity to meet many of the gay blades of London society and join the world of fashion where a cocktail of extravagance was laid before her; romantic novels, gay parties and a chance to nurture her singing and mimicry talents. Encouraged, she learned to intrigue and beguile.

Her first recorded lover was the dashing Captain John Willet Payne but he foolishly paraded her as a prize and was forced to yield his treasure to the opulent Sir Harry Fetherstonehaugh whom she had met at Drury Lane and who promised to assist her in her ambition to become an actress. Initially she accompanied him at Up Park, his family estate where, it is said, she danced naked on the dining room table at one of the many wild parties held there. Upon conceiving his child, Sir Harry dismissed her without ceremony and packed her off to London with a miserly £5 to see her through her coming trouble.

Not unnaturally she had attracted many admirers. One of the early ones was the aforementioned Romney, who had left his wife and children in the country in order to pursue his career as an artist in London. Overwhelmed by the physical beauty of his new subject, the finest portraits emerged from his brush – intimate, passionate and reflecting a total understanding of the sensitivities of his beautiful young model. But neglect of his regular commissions heralded the foundering of his reputation in society.

Another acquaintance and admirer of hers was the Honourable Charles Greville, whom she had met at Up Park whilst she was Sir Harry's mistress. Greville lived in London and it was to him she turned in her hour of need. She wrote begging for assistance, and Greville, always with an eye for beauty, offered her a position as his housekeeper. Naturally, he gained a highly presentable mistress and the services of Emma's mother as cook and housemaid. Emma fell in love with her new master, who went to considerable trouble to teach her monogamous ideals, improve her writing skills and develop her musical abilities. Unfortunately, during the four years they were together his finances diminished and retrenchment was forced upon him. He also wished to marry well, and to do this he had to be rid of Emma.

By chance Sir William Hamilton, Ambassador to the Court at Naples and also Greville's uncle, was in London. It was two years since the death of his wife, and a perfect opportunity presented itself to Greville. He suggested that Hamilton take Emma off his hands. At first Sir William was not impressed, thinking himself to old for the young and nubile 'tea maker of Edgeware Row'. However, following lengthy correspondence he at last succumbed and allowed Emma and her mother to join him in Naples. After some time the truth about the arrangement dawned on Emma. She was horrified, and pleaded with Charles to visit her at the earliest opportunity. After several years of pleading, she at last heard from Greville that he had no intention of joining her, and he advised her to go to his uncle's bed. Never thinking the old man would marry her, Greville believed that his inheritance would remain secure.

Sir William Hamilton, brought up almost as a foster brother to the King of England, led an honest life within the context of a vile and corrupt society. He immersed himself in his passion for volcanoes, vases and anything marketable as an antiquity and used his position at court to advance his 'hobbies'. He was not a favourite of the Neapolitan Queen. Maria Carolina's allegiance was, not unnaturally, with her sister in France. She and King Ferdinand tolerated Emma, whose beauty they admired, but who was

not, as Sir William's mistress, allowed to attend court. In 1791 Sir William returned to London on business and took the opportunity to marry Emma, on 6 September at Old Marylebone Church. Upon their return to Naples Emma, now able to attend court, became a firm favourite of the Queen. Following the execution of Louis XVI and Marie Antoinette, and now threatened by French and republican sympathisers, the King and Queen sought British assistance through Sir William and the new Lady Hamilton.

Lord Hood despatched Nelson (in the *Agamemnon*) to Naples to request the good offices of its government. There was an immediate and reciprocal friendship between Sir William and Nelson at their first meeting. Nelson lost no time in explaining that if he lived he would be at the very top of his profession. This was relayed to Emma along with the news that Nelson was 'a little man who could not boast of being very handsome, but this man, who is an English Naval Officer, Captain Nelson, would become the greatest man that England ever produced...he will one day astonish the world'. The first meeting between Nelson and Emma was brief and unremarkable. Nelson, writing to his wife, reported that Lady Hamilton was 'a young woman of amiable manners, and who does honour to the station to which she is raised'. It would be nearly five years before they were to meet again, and that meeting would be very different.

On 22 September 1798 Nelson returned to Naples as the Victor of the Nile. By now Lady Hamilton, elevated above her class and somewhat insensitive to the difference between right and wrong, clearly recognised the opportunity unfolding before her. Sir William was sixty-eight, Nelson forty and a celebrity, and she was thirty-three and the centre of attraction. Whether her relationship with Nelson started as a charade is unclear, but start it did and would only end with his death in 1805.

From this, the second meeting between Emma and Nelson, Fanny never stood a chance. She loved her husband, who as we know was no celibate when away from her. Lord St Vincent once said of him: 'he could not resist the temptations of the luscious Neapolitan Dames'. How then could he resist a temptress whose body was barely concealed by thin muslin dresses, who wore no drawers, stays or petticoats, for 'they are uncomfortable and unfashionable'.

The following years saw a catalogue of humiliations for his devoted wife. His early letters mentioned a woman who was 'a credit to her sex'. Gradually the two were given equal status: 'what can I say of her and Sir William's goodness to me? They are in fact with the exception of you and my dear father the dearest friends I have in the world'.

Criticism of his stepson Josiah followed, often not without due cause it must be said, and then the rumours started to reach England. Fanny offered to visit him in Naples, but was refused. His response was to demand some prints, and a cap and handkerchief for Lady Hamilton, and obediently she carried out this galling instruction. In 1800, after Nelson was ordered home, the *tria juncta in uno* left Naples, travelled across Europe and finally landed at Yarmouth. Fanny had been informed that they were on the way and Nelson had particularly requested her to await him at their home – Roundwood, near Ipswich. Fanny however, thought differently, and had made her way to London. Nelson and the Hamiltons had the discomfort of following her without stopping for refreshment.

Lord and Lady Nelson were reunited at Nerot's Hotel, St James Street, on Saturday, 8 November 1800. Her reception is said to have been extremely cold and mortifying to his feelings. They dined together with the Hamiltons and immediately the signs of their estrangement were evident. Over the

Portrait of Frances 'Fanny' Nelson whose quiet, unassuming nature was no match for the sensual and engaging personality of Emma Hamilton.

next few days of processions, parades and parties, Nelson took care to avoid Fanny. Their last appearance together in public was on 24 November when they saw *Pizarro* at Drury Lane. Fanny fainted at the end of the third act; Emma showing latent compassion, assisted her, while Nelson according to the *Morning Post*, remained where he was to the end. After much uneasiness and recrimination on both sides, Nelson took his final leave of Lady Nelson on 13 January 1801, and soon after left London for Plymouth. On quitting her, he emphatically said: 'I call God to witness there is nothing in you or by you or by your conduct I wish otherwise'. He was accompanied to Southampton by his brother, The Reverend William Nelson, and from that place wrote the following note: 'My dear Fanny, we arrived heartily tired; and with the kindest regards to my father and all the family, believe me your affectionate, Nelson.'

Procuring Josiah a command of the frigate *Thalia* was Nelson's last act of kindness towards his wife and stepson, who had once possessed his heart entirely. After 4 March 1801 when Nelson advised his wife of this appointment, he never addressed her directly again. Communication was held through his agent Davison, who paid her a quarterly allowance of £400 settled upon her by Nelson.

Fanny, dowager Vicountess Nelson died in May 1831. Her tombstone at Littleham churchyard Exmouth, gives her age as seventy-three. After her separation from Nelson she spent the remainder of her life in furnished houses in London, Bath, Brighton and the West Country, varying her residence with the seasons. Occasionally she travelled abroad, once to Lyons and once, surprisingly, to Switzerland, to go boating with Lord Byron on Lake Geneva. Prince William remained in touch with Fanny even after ascending to the throne as King William IV. It was he who long ago in Nevis congratulated Nelson at his wedding for carrying off the principal favourite of the island.

Sir William's death on Wednesday, 6 April 1803 left Emma with half a chance to marry Nelson, but divorce from Fanny was out of the question. Sir William was laid to rest with his first wife at Slebech Church, Pembrokeshire. Nelson did not attend his friend's funeral, but remained in London. From this time until the eve of the Battle of Trafalgar, Lady Hamilton presided over Lord Nelson's household at Merton. Many writers have endeavoured to present Emma as a paragon of virtue and goodness, and as a woman who had claims which deserved the recognition of her country. There is no doubt that she did assist with the victualling of the Mediterranean fleet before the Battle of the Nile, but not to any great extent. On the whole she had little cause for complaint as to the provision that was made for her, both by her husband and by Nelson.

After Trafalgar her fall from grace was rapid. Character flaws emerged, an example of which was the swooning during the 'Death of Nelson' in the opera *Thirty Thousand*. The first time may have been genuine but several repeat performances were clearly for effect.

By now spurned by Nelson's family (whom she had so studiously cultivated, and turned against Fanny) and ignored by her country, she found herself in increasing financial difficulty. On 14 January 1810, Emma received a bitter blow: her long-ailing mother died. Throughout Emma's glories, her sorrows and anxieties she had been with her, always ready to assist, always ready to act on Emma's behalf, and in her best interest. Later that year her old friend the Duke of Queensbury also died, and with him her hopes for financial help. Her misfortunes accelerated, and despite help from Davison, and some of Nelson's old friends she went to debtors prison in 1813 for ten months. Her estate was sequestrated for the benefit of her creditors. Alderman Smith secured her release and she immediately repaired to Calais, and the country her lover had fought against for so long became her safe haven. It was in Calais on 15 January 1815, that Emma Lady Hamilton died. Surrounded by strangers, oppressed by poverty, and with only the company of Horatia her child by Nelson to console her during her last moments, she left this sad world. With her death the curtain fell on one of the truly great romantic stories of the age.

Carol Evans was educated in Liverpool, and studied Social History and English Literature. Her main interest is genealogy. She has written many articles for journals and local history societies, dealing mainly with the eighteenth and nineteenth centuries. She is married to Keith Evans of the Nelson Society and The 1805 Club. They live in Liverpool, were she runs a family history research facility. Carol derives her interest in Nelson and Emma from her husband's involvement in naval history. She is at present researching into the early life of Emma and her family in Cheshire and Flintshire, and on completion, hopes to publish her findings.

Merton Place in Surrey, Nelson's home between 1801 and 1805. Rustic and secluded, yet conveniently situated for the commuter into town, Nelson had scarcely the time nor the opportunity to enjoy the place whilst duty called.

THE BOSTON MASSACRE

British redcoats attempt to break up a mob outside the customs house, which eventually leads to the death of five civilians, later to be known as the Boston Massacre.

The American Revolution may have begun on Independence Day, 4 July 1776, at Lexington Green on 19 April 1775, or perhaps on 5 March 1770, the date of the Boston Massacre. Defining the date or trigger is not easy. In simple terms the new nation had outgrown the concept of colonialism for trade. Absent landlords had neither the power nor resources to protect their interests, or raise revenues from them. Given these weaknesses a colonial breakaway was inevitable, but to the English merchants and Parliament, striving to make good a debt of £130 million, incurred by wars earlier in the century, it was a disaster.

Parliament passed Grenville's Revenue Act of 1764 which, in its preamble claimed: 'It is just and necessary that a revenue be raised... in America for defraying the expenses of defending, protecting and securing the same.' Samuel Adams, an outspoken Boston radical saw it differently and at Faneuil Hall on 24 May 1764, told the townsfolk: 'No parts of His Majesty's dominions can be taxed without consent...every part has a right to be represented in the supreme or some subordinate legislature...'. In other words no taxation without representation = Independence.

In 1765 Grenville proposed replacing the Sugar Act (the Revenue Act) by a new Stamp Act. This measure actually halved the tariff on sugar but imposed harsh measures elsewhere and signalled the intent actually to collect the dues. Opposition was spontaneous, violent and widespread. On the night of 14 August 1765, a mob levelled the stamp office building and ransacked Stamp Master Andrew Oliver's house. Governor Francis Bernard lost control as political muscle shifted to New York and its Congress. Samuel Adams addressed the House and referred to the Stamp Act as a landmark in the history of America as it united the loyal conservative south and revolutionary radical north who now expressed their anti-tax views with a single voice.

General Thomas Gage, in charge of British troops now being sheltered and supplied in American towns following the Quartering Act of 1765, warned Parliament of the strength of feeling uniting the colonies. Parliament's response was to suspend the New York legislature whereupon patriots in Boston announced a boycott of British goods. Diplomacy faltered and the fuse was ignited when HMS *Romney* seized the *Liberty* on suspicion of tax evasion. Customs commissioners, remembering the Stamp Act riots, fled to safety on board *Romney* and advised Gage in New York of the disorder 'even open revolt'. Months of legal wrangling followed during which time British redcoats reinforced Boston as a show of force. The British were outnumbered sixteen to one, subjected to insults, taunts and stone throwing. One evening a mob attacked customs worker Ebenezer Richard's house he brandished a musket and when his door was knocked down fired into the mob mortally wounding eleven year old Christopher Snider.

Two thousand people attended Snider's funeral under the Liberty Tree. Adams seized the opportunity and used his versatile oratory skills to convince the crowd that it was the British, not Richard, who were to blame for the boy's death.

A few days later on 5 March 1770 Private Hugh White was on sentry duty outside the custom house. Several youths taunted him he butted one and they ran off. As the news spread, a mob of about 200 descended on him. Private White, frightened and confused, called for help. The captain of the day, Thomas Preston, fearing escalation into a pitched battle called out a patrol of only seven men to rescue White. They reached the hapless sentry, formed a ring around him and attempted to withdraw. The crowd pressed forward stopping any movement by the patrol while Preston pleaded with them to disperse; they would not and began pelting the 'lobsterbacks' with clubs, one was struck and as he fell to the ground his musket discharged. More shots rang out without orders from Preston, killing a total of five civilians and wounding six.

It was a 'massacre' Samuel Adams proclaimed.

1801 Reflecting on Sir Hyde Parker's lack of enthusiasm to engage the Danes: 'Our friend here is a little nervous about dark nights and fields of ice, but we must brace up; these are not times for nervous systems.'

1792 The Holy Roman Emperor Leopold II suddenly dies, aged 44, and is succeeded by his son Francis who will reign as the last Holy Roman Emperor until 1806, then as the first Austrian Emperor, Francis I, until 1835.

1st

1799 In a state of depression, possibly pining for Lady Hamilton: 'My only wish is to sink with honour into the grave, and when that shall please God, I shall meet death with a smile. Not that I am insensible to the honours and riches my King and Country have heaped upon me, so much more than any officer could deserve; yet I am ready to quit this world of trouble, and envy none but those of the estate six feet by two'.

1781 The Congress in the United States assembles and unites in ratifying the Articles of the Confederation.

2nd

1796 To the Duke of Clarence: 'It is evident the French are preparing for battle. It is said the campaign will open against Italy with 80,000 men; if the Enemy's fleet should be able to cover the landing of 20,000 men between Port Especia and Leghorn, where I have always been of the opinion they would attempt it, I know of nothing to prevent their fully possessing the rich mine of Italy'.

1792 The Scottish architect Robert Adam dies (b. 1728). He transformed Palladian Neo-classicism in England.

3rd

1801 Nelson writes his last recorded letter to Fanny from the St George: 'Josiah is to have another Ship and go aboard if the Thalia cannot soon be got ready. I have done all I can for him....Living I have done all in my power for you, and if dead you will find I have done the same, therefore my only wish is to be left to myself, and wishing you every happiness Believe that I am Your affectionate Nelson & Bronte.'

1797 Vice-President John Adams, who succeeded George Washington on 7 December 1796, is sworn into office.

4th

1786 Having received instructions from Admiral Hughes that he was not to enforce the Navigation Acts: 'I must either disobey my orders or disobey Acts of Parliament, which the Admiral was disobeying. I determined upon the former, trusting to the uprightness of my intention, and believing that my country would not allow me to be ruined by protecting her commerce'.

1770 The Boston Massacre, leading to the War of Independence, takes place. Five civilians are killed.

5th

1801 St George, off Yarmouth, prior to sailing for Copenhagen. Nelson writes a will: twenty thousand pounds, if and when he had it, was to be put into public funds to provide £1,000 a year for Fanny; three thousand pounds in trust for Emma, together with three diamond boxes and the picture of the King of Naples'. But there was no mention of Horatia or Josiah.

1791 Bangalore is besieged by Cornwallis and taken by storm on 21 March.

6th

1799 To Earl Spencer, from Vanguard, Palermo: 'A few days past, I was presented in due form with the Freedom of the City of Palermo, in a gold box, and brought upon a silver salver. I have endeavoured so to conduct myself as to meet the approbation of all classes in this Country'.

1797 'The Times' advertises that Hair Powder Tax certificates are to be made available. This was one of several revenue initiatives to pay for the War.

7th

1805 To Ball, praising the Captain-General of Andalusia for the return of Captain Layman, ex Raven: 'The Marquis of Solano has been so great to these unfortunate people, and his sending them to me, I believe without the absolute condition of their being Prisoners [of war] that I cannot sufficiently return his kindness'.

1801 In face of French opposition, Sir William Sidney Smith, Tigre, lands troops in Aboukir Bay. The Emperor Napoleon referred to Smith as the man who had robbed him of his destiny.

8th

SIR WILLIAM HERSCHEL (1738-1822)

Born Frederich Wilhelm at Hanover on 15 November 1738, Herschel followed in the footsteps of his father as an army musician, playing in the Hanoverian Guard until 1757. He then moved to Bath, England where he became an organist and teacher of music. In his leisure time he indulged in his passion for observing the heavens, constructing both 20-foot and 40-foot telescopes at his home in Slough which showed volcanic mountains on the moon. His discovery of Uranus on 13 March 1781 won him the Copely Medal at the Royal Society and a professorship at the age of forty-three. Known as the father of sidereal astronomy, his discoveries were profound and prolific. Two primary discoveries were the movement of the solar system through space and evidence that binary stars move around a common centre of gravity (substantiating Newton's theory of gravitation). In 1785 he introduced the disc theory of the stellar system. He postulated that gravity was the means of evolution of matter and hypothesised that nebulae are composed of stars, laying before the Royal Society a catalogue of 500 nebulae and star clusters. Returning to Uranus he showed that it rotates in retrograde motion – as does Venus – and found it to have two moons. In his later work he found infrared radiation. Herschel was made King's Astronomer by George III, and knighted in 1816. He died at Slough on 25 August 1822.

(Further reading *The Scientific Papers of Sir William Herschel*, edited by J L E Dreyer (1912).

The 40-foot telescope erected by Herschel at Slough. He used this forty-eight-mirrored reflecting telescope to study the Milky Way and nebulae.

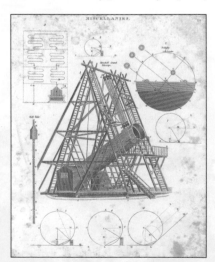

JOSEPHINE ROSE TASCHER DE LA PAGERIE (1763-1814)

Josephine was born in Martinique on 23 June 1763. She married Alexandre, Vicomte de Beauharnais in 1779, and had two children by him before they became estranged. He went to the guillotine in 1794 while she began moving in fashionable Parisian society. She met Napoleon Bonaparte and married him on 9 March 1796. She was crowned Empress by Napoleon in 1804, but her failure to produce a male heir brought about the annulment of their marriage in 1810. She retired to Malmaison, living in grand style until her death on 29 May 1814.

JOHN BYNG (1704-1757)

Byng was the fourth son of Viscount Torrington. He rose rapidly to flag rank but his career came to an abrupt end after his failure to relieve Minorca which was under siege by the French in 1756. He was delayed in Gibraltar and on arrival found the British to be holding out in Port Mahon.

Byng fought an indecisive action and after four days returned to Gibraltar leaving the garrison to its fate. He was court martialled and having been found guilty of lack of resolution, was shot on the quarter-deck of *Monarch* on 14 March 1757. This was a face-saving act by the government of the day and brought strong condemnation from many. It prompted the remark: 'Dans ce pays ci il est bon de teur de temps en temps un amiral pour encourager les autres.'

TREATY OF AMIENS

The Treaty of Amiens was agreed on the 25 March 1802 and signed two days later by Britain, France, Spain and the Botavian Republic (Holland). It marked the end of the French Revolutionary Wars and forced Britain to cede many of its acquisitions from previous conflicts – among them Malta. Failure to withdraw from Malta was cited by Napoleon the following year for the breakdown of the treaty, and in May 1803 hostilities resumed. The ensuing conflict known as the Napoleonic Wars continued until 1815.

🦑 **1805** 🦑 To Emma, eighteen years to the day after marrying Fanny: 'Nothing can be more miserable, or unhappy, than your poor Nelson.' Referring to the sinking of Raven and loss of dispatches: 'You will conceive my disappointment!...I have much fear that they may have fallen into the hands of the Dons'.

🦑 *1796* 🦑 *Napoleon Bonaparte marries Josephine de Beauharnais.*

🦑 **1795** 🦑 To Fanny: 'To his [God's] will do I resign myself. My character and good name are in my own keeping. Life with disgrace is dreadful. A glorious death is to be envied; and if anything happens to me, recollect that death is a debt we must all pay, and whether now, or in a few years hence, can be of little consequence'.

🦑 *1804* 🦑 *Sidmouth resigns and is succeeded as prime minister by William Pitt, who returns to office for the last time.*

🦑 **1804** 🦑 On keeping his crew healthy and free from boredom: 'sometimes by looking at Toulon, Ville Franche, Barcelona and Rosas; then running round Minorca, Majorca, Sardinia, and Corsica; and two or three times anchoring for a few days, and sending a ship to the last place for onions, which I find the best thing that can be given to seamen'.

🦑 *1793* 🦑 *A rebellion against the French Republic breaks out in the Vendée. The rebels inflict defeat on the Revolutionary Army on 20 March 1793, but are finally and violently crushed on 27 April 1797.*

🦑 **1800** 🦑 Off Malta, to Davison on prize money: 'There cannot, in my opinion, be the smallest doubt of my having an undoubted right to share for all things taken, from Lord Keith's quitting this command till his resuming it, as Commander-in-Chief....Right is right. I only want justice, and that I will try to obtain at the expense of everything I am worth.'

🦑 *1778* 🦑 *Captain Lindsey sails Victory from Portsmouth for the first time.*

🦑 **1795** 🦑 Vice-Admiral William Hotham, Britannia, and Nelson, Agamemnon, engage a French fleet under Rear-Admiral Pierre Martin, Sans Culotte, off Genoa. Ça Ira, and Censeur, are taken. From Agamemnon's log: 'At a quarter before eleven A.M., being within an hundred yards of the *Ça Ira's* stern, I ordered the helm to be put a-starboard, gave her a whole broadside, each gun double-shotted. Scarcely a shot appeared to miss.'

🦑 *1758* 🦑 *Haley's comet reaches its perihelion. Twenty-three years later Sir William Herschel, looking through a home-made telescope at Bath, discovers Uranus. It was originally called Georgium Sidus in honour of the King.*

🦑 **1805** 🦑 To Marsden regarding an Order in Council: 'I have received you letter...authorising an increase to be made to the salaries of the Secretaries to Flag Officers; also, that no Secretary is to be allowed more than one Clerk as an assistant, and that no Purser of any of His Majesty's Ships in Commission shall be allowed to officiate at the same time as Secretary to a Flag Officer.'

🦑 *1757* 🦑 *Admiral John Byng is executed on board Monarch by a firing squad of marines.*

🦑 **1783** 🦑 From Albermarle's log, off Porto Plate: 'At 4 came up with the chase – found her to be a Flag of Truce from Brest, bound to Cape François with the preliminary Articles of Peace.'

🦑 *1803* 🦑 *Britain contravenes the Treaty of Amiens by demanding the right to stay in Malta.*

🦑 **1801** 🦑 To Davison on the plans to negotiate with the Danes: 'I have not yet seen my Commander-in-chief, and have had no official communication whatever. All I have gathered of our plans, I disapprove most exceedingly, honour may arise from them, good cannot'.

🦑 *1759* 🦑 *Dr Johnson on the subject of a sailor's life: 'No man will be a sailor who has contrivance enough to get himself into a jail; for being in a ship is being in a jail, with a chance of being drowned.'*

9th

10th

11th

12th

13th

14th

15th

16th

THE CODE NAPOLEON

Napoleon, when First Consul of France, appointed a commission headed by Jean Jaques Regis de Cambaceres to draw up, in precise terminology, a uniform national code of law. It was probably the most radical reform in Europe since Henry II's Common Law. After four years in the making it was published in 1804 as the Code Civil and replaced the then extant law in France which had survived since Roman times.

The Code was widely adopted in Europe, parts of the United States and the province of Quebec, and many of its principles remain in being.

Lord Nelson was entitled to wear four decorations - those of the orders of the Bath, St Ferdinand and Merit, the Crescent, and St Joachim. The four orders that he invariably wore were embroidered on the breast of every coat, the Order of the Bath being uppermost.
(See 17 March.)

Sir William Sidney Smith (see 18 March), the man who Napoleon said robbed him of his destiny.

1797 To Nelson from the Admiralty: 'I have His Majesty's commands to acquaint you, that in order to mark his Royal approbation of your successful and gallant exertions on several occasions, His Majesty has been pleased to signify his intentions of conferring on you the Most Honourable Order of the Bath'.

1799 Queen Charlotte, Keith's flagship, blows up at Leghorn killing 673 of her crew. Keith was ashore at the time.

17th

1799 To Captain Sir William Sidney Smith, Tigre: 'Captain Troubridge tells me it was your intention to send into Alexandria, that all French ships might pass to France – now, as this is in direct opposition to my opinion, which is, never to suffer any one individual Frenchman to quit Egypt – I must therefore strictly charge and command you, never to give any French ship or man leave to quit Egypt'.

1766 British Parliament repeals the Stamp Act which it had passed on 22 March, the previous year.

18th

1804 On the health of his ships and ships' companies during the blockade of Toulon: 'A small sum, well laid out, will keep fleets healthy; but it requires large sums to make a sickly fleet healthy, besides the immense loss of personal services. Health cannot be dearly bought at any price – if the fleet is never sickly'.

1802 Napoleon introduces the Legion d'Honneur to replace the old suppressed orders of knighthood.

19th

1800 Recuperating in Palermo: 'As yet it is too soon to form an opinion whether I ever can be cured of my complaint....At present I see but glimmering hopes, and probably my career of service is at an end, unless the French fleet shall come into the Mediterranean, when nothing shall prevent my dying at my post....Do not fret at anything. I wish I never had, but my return to Syracuse in 1798 broke my heart, which on any extraordinary anxiety now shows itself, be that feeling pain or pleasure'.

1767 Firmin Abauzit, the Swiss scholar who contributed to the translation of the New Testament into French, dies.

20th

1800 Nelson at Palermo in Foudroyant writes a memorandum in his order book: 'By my Patent of Creation, I find that my family name of Nelson has been lengthened by the words, "of the Nile". Therefore, in future my signature will be, Bronte Nelson of the Nile'.

1804 The Code Napoleon, combining radical Roman Law reforms, is promulgated. It unifies legal practice in France.

21st

1799 On learning that the French are negotiating with the Turks to recover their army from Egypt: 'No, to Egypt they went with their own consent, and there they shall remain whilst Nelson commands the detached squadron; for, never, never will he consent to the return of one ship or Frenchman.'

1794 Sir Charles Grey and Vice-Admiral Sir John Jervis, Boyne, capture Fort Bourbon and Martinique.

22nd

1784 Informing Locker he is to transport Lady Hughes, wife of the commander-in-chief on that station, to the Leeward Islands: 'I understand [Boreas] is going to the Leeward Islands; and I am asked to carry Lady Hughes and her family, a very modest request, I think: but I cannot refuse, as I am to be under the command of this Gentleman, so I must put up with the inconvenience and expense, two things not exactly to my wish'.

1798 Samuel Taylor Coleridge, poet, philosopher and Shakespearean critic, completes 'The Rime of the Ancient Mariner'. His other works include 'Biographia Literaria' and 'Aids to Reflection'.

23rd

1784 Nelson assumes command of Boreas. From the ship's log: 'Came alongside Hoy with the guns and all the Gunner's stores; employed getting them on board. Came on board Captain Nelson and superseded Captain Wells'.

1801 Tzar Paul I of Russia is murdered by nobles. Had the news reached Hyde Parker a few days earlier the Battle of Copenhagen might never have been fought.

24th

JOHN WESLEY (1703-1791)

John Wesley was a son of the Reverend Samuel Wesley, Vicar of Epworth in Lincolnshire. Educated at Charterhouse and Oxford where he was ordained and became a Fellow of Lincoln College he became a leading debater in a society whose discourse was predominantly over religious matters, dubbed Methodists. From here, Oglethorpe invited him to lead a mission to Georgia. It was not a success; Wesley could not reason with the colonists.

On his return from Georgia in 1736 where he had witnessed the refuge for the poor and distressed, John Wesley took up evangelism. His ideal was the preservation of order, particularly among the working class who had been abandoned by the church, and where it had been disrupted by industrial reforms. His style of radicalism and religious revival led to Methodism. By 1784, having spent most of his time in scenes of squalor and human suffering he had established a church outside of the Anglican fold. Fifty years as a preacher, sometimes preaching twice a day and often in the face of violent mobs, slowly transformed attitudes as he and his brother Charles built a huge following, giving hope and a feeling of purpose where before there had been despair.

SIR RALPH ABERCROMBY (1734-1801)

Abercromby demonstrated his brilliance during the Duke of York's disastrous campaign of 1799 in Holland, winning the admiration of the Dutch. He again showed great leadership in Alexandria in 1801 where Nelson had already cut off Napoleon's expeditionary force. Abercromby lauched his assault from boats, charged the French and drove them towards the city. He was injured in the fighting which lasted for several days and died a few days after being carried to Keith's flagship.

The Peace of Amiens (see 27 March) was seized upon with something of an air of desperation by the British public who had suffered the consequences of war for eight years or more. Nelson, however, was cynical of its real substance, and viewed it as little more than a temporary truce. Courtesy of William Latey.

The death of Sir Ralph Abercomby, who, as commander of the expedition to the Mediterranean, had effected the successful landing at Aboukir Bay, but was mortally wounded in the ensuing battle. (See 28 March.)

1795 Following his engagement with the French, 12-14 March: 'Fortune in the late affair has favoured me in a most extraordinary manner, by giving me an opportunity which seldom offers of being the only Line-of-Battle ship who got singly into action on the 13th, when I had the honour of engaging the Ça Ira, absolutely large enough to take Agamemnon in her hold. I never saw such a ship before....I cannot account for what I saw: whole broadsides within half pistol-shot missing my little ship, whilst ours were in the fullest effect'.

1774 *Boston sea port is shut by the British Parliament until restitution is made to the East India Company for the tea lost in the harbour waters.*

25th

1794 Off Bastia to his brother: 'I am to command the Seamen landed from the Fleet. I feel for the honour of my country, and had rather be beat than not make the attack. If we do not try we never can be successful. I own I have no fears for the final issue; it will be conquest, certain we will deserve it'.

1799 *Irish rebel prisoners including Thomas Addis Emmet (elder brother of the more famous Robert) and Russell arrive to be interned in Fort George in Dublin.*

26th

1794 Off Bastia, to Sir William Hamilton while waiting to begin the campaign: 'What would the immortal Wolfe have done? As he did, beat the enemy if he perished in the attempt'.

1802 *The Marquis of Cornwall, England; Joseph Bonaparte, France; Azura, Spain and Schimmelpennink for Holland sign the Treaty of Amiens which was brokered on 1 October 1801, by Hawksbury and Otto.*

27th

1800 To Sir Thomas Troubridge following his blockade of Valetta: 'You know my dear friend, that I highly approve and admire your public conduct; but for you to fret yourself to death, because you believe that all the world are not so honest as yourself, is useless – for you cannot reform it, were you an angel; and makes all people sorry to see you torment yourself'.

Sir Thomas Troubridge.

1801 *Sir Ralph Abercromby dies in Admiral Keith's flagship from wounds received at Alexandria.*

28th

1794 To his brother: 'You ask, by what interest did I get a ship? I answer, having served with credit was my recommendation to Lord Howe, First Lord of the Admiralty. Anything in reason that I can ask, I am sure of obtaining from his justice'.

1788 *Charles Wesley, English hymn writer and evangelist, composer of numerous hymns such as 'Love Divine, All Loves Excelling', dies.*

29th

1804 On nutrition for the sick, to Captain Sir William Bolton HM Sloop Childers: 'Doctor Snipe, Physician to the Fleet...recommended Macaroni as a light, wholesome, and nourishing food....you are hereby required and directed to order the Purser [at Naples] to purchase a thousand pounds of the best large pipe Macaroni for the use of the sick and convalescent Seamen on board the different Ships'.

1746 *Francisco José de Goya y Lucientes (d. 1828) is born of peasant stock at Fuendetodos, near Saragosa.*

30th

1800 On the Franco Turkish treaty, allowing Napoleon's vanquished troops to leave Egypt: 'I ever had it to be impossible to permit that any army to return to Europe, but as prisoners of war, and in that case, not to France.... One Ally cannot have the power of getting rid of an enemy's vanquished army, by sending them with arms in their hands to fight against a friend'.

1774 *The Boston Port Bill demanding damages following the 'tea party' is passed to bring the American colonies to order.*

31st

DOWNRIGHT FIGHTING

THE BATTLE OF COPENHAGEN

Hans Christian Bjerg

Portrait of Admiral Sir Hyde Parker. Nelson found his hesitancy and indecision in the days leading up to the battle immensely frustrating and during the fighting itself he would disobey Parker's orders.

'The Battle of Copenhagen was, I must allow, hard fought,' wrote Nelson, 'but our success was complete.' In the historical perspective, this statement is essentially correct, and the name 'Copenhagen' is rightfully engraved on the base of Nelson's Column in Trafalgar Square; but it also hints at why the battle is a remarkable event in the history of Denmark and in the annals of its navy.

The roots of the quarrel which led eventually to battle lay in Britain's declared 'command of the sea' versus the neutral country's insistence that their merchantmen were, even in the turbulent years of the Revolutionary War, and despite their cargo, untouchable. Furthermore, as the war continued into the late 1790s, any pragmatism that still attached itself to the situation was dissolved by Britain's now more aggressive attitude towards so-called neutral shipping. In Denmark this policy was met with equal belligerence. Resistance to the British was led by Crown Prince Frederick, whose tendency was to direct the policy of his Foreign Secretary. Frederick it was who inspired businessmen, and likewise decorated many Danish naval officers in their resistance to the searching of the cargoes of convoys under Danish colours by British warships.

The crisis came on 25 July 1800 when a British squadron met a Danish convoy of six merchantmen under the escort of the frigate *Freya* in the English Channel and insisted on searching for contraband of war. The two commanders were under contrary orders; a fight was inevitable. After a four-hour struggle *Freya* struck her colours, and the convoy was taken to the Downs to be searched. It was as a result of this incident that Lord Whitworth was despatched to Copenhagen with a fleet of nineteen sail of the line to reinforce the British message. In consequence, the Danish Government was obliged to abandon the armed protection of convoys as of 29 August 1800.

Relations between Britain and Russia also cooled during 1800, just as those between the Tsar and Napoleon improved. In December 1800, the Tsar proposed that Denmark-Norway, Sweden and Prussia should renew the Treaty of Armed Neutrality first endorsed in 1780. This presented the Danish Government with a significant dilemma: to refuse to join the Armed Neutrality – and so keep its agreement with Great Britain – meant becoming an enemy of the two great powers on the continent, i.e. France and Russia. Denmark chose to join the Armed Neutrality.

When the news of this agreement reached London in January 1801, the British Government answered by placing an embargo on all Russian, Swedish and Danish ships in all British ports. Orders to this effect were prepared for the Royal Navy. The main target was Russia, and a fleet was gathered in Yarmouth bound for the Baltic Sea. Command of this fleet was entrusted to Admiral Sir Hyde Parker with Vice-Admiral Nelson as his second-in-command. This was a much considered combination, and was, supposedly, well suited to the situation which demanded a measure of 'political hesitation' as well as precise naval tactics.

From the British point of view there was less and less room for diplomatic applications, so the navy took over. To quote Nelson again: 'A fleet of British ships of war are the best negotiators in Europe, they always speak to be understood, and generally gain their point'.

To enter the Baltic Sea it is first necessary to pass the Approaches – protected by Danish sea power. With this very much in mind, and with a copy of the 1800 agreement in his portfolio, Sir Nicholas Vansittart was (in vain) sent to Copenhagen in February.

Thus, the British fleet, consisting of fifteen – later increased to eighteen – sail of the line, including two Fourth Rates, five frigates, four sloops, eight bomb vessels, two fireships, as well as a number of gun-brigs and cutters, left Yarmouth on 12 March 1801. They reached a position just north of the Sound on the 22nd of the same month. The Danish Government had been aware of the risk of an attack by a British fleet forcing its way into the Baltic Sea since January, and now put into operation their planned defence.

In the 1780s a commission had proposed the improvement of the seaward fortification of Copenhagen. It included building both a number of bomb-barges as well as new sea forts in order to deter any direct bombardment of the Danish capital from the sea, but very few items of the proposal had been accomplished when the enemy sailed over the horizon in 1801. At the last moment, the Danish government began to fortify the Trekroner Fort which covered the northern entrance to the harbour of Copenhagen, and in similar haste were ten ships of the line equipped. The Danes' intention was to close the eastern side by means of a row of so-called 'blockships' – obsolete ships of the line, unrigged and without internal fittings, but otherwise fully armed. These vessels were towed into position and hog-tied.

The southern part of the Danish defence line was its most vulnerable point with only weak defences in support of its blockships.

On 23 March, Vansittart reported to the British fleet as follows: at the Danish court he had demanded confirmation of the agreement of 1800 regarding the British 'right' to search convoys for contraband of war, and furthermore the free passage of the British fleet through the Danish Straights. Both demands were rejected. Sir Hyde Parker had now only to await a favourable wind to go down the Sound and prepare to overcome the Castle of Kronborg in order to pass the narrow gauntlet between the Danish and Swedish fortifications.

As aforementioned, for tactical reasons, the best angle to attack the weak Danish defence was from the south, but Hyde Parker was not entirely convinced that his fleet should waste time attacking the Danish navy in Copenhagen, and should instead continue directly to the main task, namely, the Russian fleet lying in the Baltic. He had not, however, decided whether his best route lay in going down the Sound, or through the Great Belt and south of Zealand. This hesitation irritated Nelson almost beyond measure. His one intent was to attack the fleets in the Baltic one by one before they could unite.

Eventually, Hyde Parker made his decision and the British fleet passed the Kronborg close to the Swedish coast on 30 March and came to anchor 5 miles north of Copenhagen. The only damage inflicted from the resulting duel of guns was that done by a British missile landing on the roof of their own consul in Elsinore!

East of Trekroner Battery however, the Sound was divided by the Middle Ground into two north-south going channels. The Danish navy, under the command of Captain Olfert Fischer, had, as we have seen, placed their blockships to cover the southern

Plan of the Battle of Copenhagen showing the treacherous Middle Ground and other shoals that were an additional hazard to Nelson and his ships.

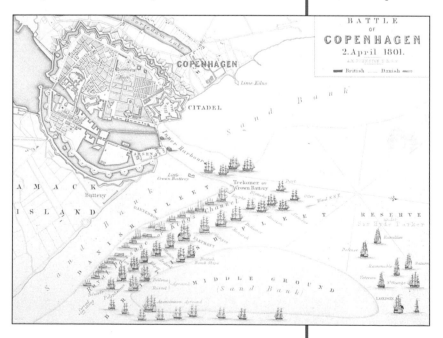

Pocock's painting of the Battle of Copenhagen illustrates, amongst other things, the lack of room to manoeuvre during the fighting.

entrance of the harbour of Copenhagen in the western channel known as Kongedybet (The King's Deep); this line consisting of ten blockships and ten lighter floating batteries.

After a clandestine inspection, Nelson, at least, was convinced that the best way to attack was from the south. With this in mind, he urged Hyde Parker that ten sail of the line – commanded by himself (the Hero of the Nile) – be despatched to the east of the Middle Ground shoal. The remainder of the fleet, lying north of the line, should be used to prevent any movement of the Danish fleet that might prove useful to the support of the relatively weak southern position. A squadron of frigates, south of Parker's fleet, was ordered to keep the Danes occupied towards the north; its given purpose was to capture or destroy as many of the blockships as possible, and thus enable the bomb vessels to gain positions where they might open the bombardment of Copenhagen. Nelson reckoned he could destroy the Danish defences within an hour. Eventually, Parker accepted the plan and gave Nelson twelve sail of the line.

In the days leading up to 2 April there was great activity in Copenhagen. In March, thick ice had assisted in the building of defences and the equipping of ships. Lack of manpower was more than compensated for by a tremendous spirit of patriotism, and voluntary enlistment more than met the requirement. In fact, about 25 per cent of the Danish crews were volunteers with, therefore, no previous combat experience.

The Danish defence line, south of the Trekroner Battery, consisted of two ships of the line, seven blockships, one frigate, and eight different types of defence-barges. Nelson's task therefore (with just twelve ships under his command), was to destroy or otherwise disable eighteen ships under the cover of the Battery's 66 guns.

Between 9.45 and 10.15am on 2 April, Nelson's squadron got under way and headed north in the Kongedybet eventually forming a line parallel with the Danes. At this moment, he no doubt had in mind the shoals of Aboukir. The wind had shifted to the south-southeast, assisting his passage, but here, with no pilot to guide them, during the turn south of the Middle Ground three British ships went aground, thus greatly reducing his fighting capability. It was necessary therefore to call upon the northern squadron of frigates under Captain Riou to approach the Danish line more closely than was at first anticipated – under the circumstances, a dangerous task for frigates.

The first shot of battle came at 10.30. Even though the crews of the British ships were well drilled and were experienced in battle compared to the Danish crews, many of whom were 'street volunteers' and thus untrained, the battle soon became far tougher than Nelson ever appears to have expected. 'Here', he was later to write, 'was no manoeuvring: it was downright fighting.' After two hours of brutal slogging, a couple of Danish ships were put out of action whilst others had surrendered. The Danish line was punctured.

By about 1.00pm, the situation, at least as it was seen from Parker's flagship, appeared alarming. The same wind which had favoured Nelson's squadron in the morning now prevented Hyde Parker from going to his aid. Furthermore, had not Nelson promised to deal with the Danes within the hour? Even after two and a half hours of fighting the battle was unfinished.

At 1.30pm, Hyde Parker, worried by the situation as he perceived it, ordered that the signal 'Discontinue the Action' be hoist. Nelson's first reaction on sight of the flags was to reassure himself that his own signal 'Close Action' was still flying. He then turned to his flag-captain on HMS *Elephant*, and putting his telescope up to his blind eye remarked laconically to him – and to posterity – 'You know, Foley, I have only one eye – I have a right to be blind sometimes. I really do not see the signal.'

Captain Riou saw the signal clear enough and began to withdraw. Shortly afterwards, a cannonball cut him in two.

Nelson's attitude at Copenhagen is a classic example of the rule that disobedience under special circumstances can be justified. He was in a comparatively favourable position, though the danger still remained of his ships being squeezed between the Danish line and the Middle Ground. Moreover, the existing wind offered a retreat to the north only – past the still largely intact Trekroner Battery; hardly an option.

At the same time as Hyde Parker hoisted his signal, the centre of the Danish line was being neutralised. Olfert Fischer, the now wounded Danish commander-in-chief shifted his flag to the *Trekroner*.

Looking at the situation around 2.00pm from Nelson's point of view it is worth remembering that the principle task, according to the accepted tactical plan, was not to destroy the Danish navy, but to place the bombardment vessels in a position where they could launch an assault on Copenhagen - or at least threaten to do so in order to force the Danes into the abandonment of the Treaty of Armed Neutrality. Similarly, a lot of the Danish vessels, which may by this time have surrendered, still posed an obstacle to the placement of the British bomb vessels. And Nelson still faced the problem of removing his fleet from the Kongedybet with the wind against him.

It was at this moment that Nelson chose to play his trump card – or was it all a bluff? He hoisted the flag of truce, a signal that he wanted to open communication with Olfert Fischer. He wrote as follows:

'To the brothers of Englishmen, the Danes, Lord Nelson has directions to spare Denmark, when no longer resisting; but if firing is continued on the part of Denmark, Lord Nelson will be obliged to set fire to all floating batteries he has taken, without having the power of saving the brave Danes who have defended them.'

It is worth noting the document itself, written in haste and under fire, is blotted, but equally at Lord Nelson's insistence, it bears his seal, as if to give the impression of a situation entirely under control. The content and meaning of the letter have been discussed ever since. Nelson insisted till his death that he wrote it out of humanity, though even among friends it was difficult for him to gain a hearing. In Denmark it has always been considered a cynical bluff which only succeeded because it was delivered directly into the hand of the Crown Prince – observing from the shore – and not to Fischer who had a much more accurate grasp of the situation. But what did the letter mean? The Danish fire had slackened, their centre was smashed, but at this time Nelson had received no surrenders. Moreover, to put into position his own bombardment vessels he would

have had to move or destroy the Danes with little time or consideration for the Danish crews even if they had struck their colours.

Without consulting Fischer, the Crown Prince accepted the cease fire. We know that at the same time he received news of the assassination on 11 March of Tsar Paul. The League of Armed Neutrality dissolved with his death. Today we know that Sweden had intended to send a squadron of ships from Karlskrona to help the Danes, but strong contrary winds prevented the vessels from even leaving harbour. By 2.45pm the action was practically over and it had faded out by 3.15pm. An armistice was negotiated and signed on 9 April 1801. This armistice was to continue uninterrupted for fourteen weeks, during which period the Dane's participation in the Treaty of Armed Neutrality was formally suspended. The final dissolution of the treaty came in October the same year.

Copenhagen was Nelson's most severe action. The British lost 253 killed (more than at the Nile) and 688 wounded. The Danes had 790 killed, many of them volunteers, and 900 wounded. Two thousand were taken prisoners of war, and twelve ships (most of which proved beyond repair) were captured.

'The French', Nelson was to say later with regard to Copenhagen, 'fought bravely, but they could not have stood for one hour the fight which the Danes had supported for four.'

Hans Christian Bjerg (Dr Bjerg) was born in 1944, and was educated at the University of Copenhagen. He specialised in naval and military history, and since 1964 has been a member of the Board of the Naval Historical Society in Denmark. In 1967, he founded the Review of Naval History, and was editor until 1978.

In 1974, he became historical consultant to the Royal Danish Navy, and from 1975 has been a lecturer at the Academy of the Royal Danish Navy in Copenhagen. In the same year he published the *Bibliography of Danish Naval History*. Other published works include *Naval Technological Development in Denmark* and – as co-author – a comprehensive work on *Danish warships 1690-1860*. Dr Bjerg's current work includes a translation of A T Mahan's *The Influence of Sea Power on History, 1660-1783* which has never been published in Denmark.

Nelson's famous disregard of Hyde Parker's signal to disengage – 'I have a right to be blind sometimes' – as portrayed in a postcard design published c.1905.

One of the most enduring and best-known images of Admiral Lord Nelson by John Hoppner (see 4 April), an engraving of which was published to coincide with Nelson's funeral in early January 1806.

❧ **1801** ❧ The fleet moves to a position within 2 miles of Copenhagen. On a council called by Sir Hyde Parker: 'Now we are sure of fighting, I am sent for. When it was a joke I was kept in the background; tomorrow will, I hope, be a proud day for England'.

❧ *1794* ❧ *Danton goes to the guillotine. He said: 'I prefer to be guillotined than to guillotine.' He also said to Robespierre: 'You will follow me.'*

❧ 1801 ❧ THE BATTLE OF COPENHAGEN

Remarking on a shot which went through the mainmast rigging: 'It is warm work, and this day may be the last to any of us at a moment – but, mark, you, I would not be elsewhere for thousands'.

❧ *1805* ❧ *Hans Christian Andersen (d. 1875), master of the fairy tale, is born in a slum near Copenhagen.*

❧ **1800** ❧ Remarking on the capture of the 'escapees' from the Nile: 'I thank God I was not present, for it would finish me could I have taken a sprig of these brave men's laurels: They are, and I glory in them, my darling children, served in my school, and all of us caught our professional zeal and fire from the great and good Earl of St Vincent'.

❧ *1798* ❧ *Frederick Augustus, the second son of George III, The Grand Old Duke of York is appointed commander-in-chief of Great Britain.*

❧ **1800** ❧ From Palermo to Sir Thomas Troubridge when the last four French ships had been captured: 'My task is done, my health is finished, and, probably, my retreat for ever fixed, unless another French fleet is placed for me to look after'.

❧ *1758* ❧ *John Hoppner is born (d. 1810). He became a chorister in the Chapel Royal and exhibited in the Royal Academy from 1780.*

❧ **1799** ❧ To Blackwood, Penelope: 'Is there a sympathy which ties men together in the bonds of friendship without having a personal knowledge of each other? If so, I was your friend and acquaintance before I saw you. Your conduct and character on the late glorious occasion [French attack on Naples] stamp your fame beyond the reach of envy'.

❧ *1790* ❧ *Sirius, acting as supply ship to the First Fleet is totally destroyed on a reef off Norfolk Island, Australia, thus stranding officers, guards and convicts alike.*

❧ **1797** ❧ On hearing that battle honours had been awarded for Cape St Vincent: 'I beg you will thank all our friends for their kind congratulations; and I must be delighted, when from the King to the peasant, all are willing to do me honour. But I will partake of nothing but what shall include Collingwood and Troubridge. We are the only three glorious ships who made great exertions on that glorious day: the others did their duty, and some not exactly to my satisfaction. We ought to have had the Santissima Trinidad and the Soberano, seventy-four. They belonged to us by conquest, and only wanted some good fellow to get alongside them, and they were ours'.

❧ *1803* ❧ *Sir William Hamilton dies in Emma's arms, in Piccadilly, aged 72.*

❧ **1805** ❧ To Captain Sotherton, Excellent, showing frustration at the loss of the French fleet: 'Don't keep Amazon a moment longer than my orders to Captain Parker; and if Termagant is still at Naples, send her to me; for I want all the vessels I have under my command to send information. I am entirely adrift by my Frigates losing sight of the French Fleet so soon after their coming out of Port'.

❧ *1770* ❧ *William Wordsworth (d. 1850) is born at Cockermouth. He earned a degree at Cambridge in 1791. He became a supporter of the Girondins, but in 1797 settled in Somerset where he concentrated on writing poetry.*

1st

2nd

3rd

4th

5th

6th

7th

BASTIA

Vice Admiral Lord Hood, commanding a fleet of twenty-one sail of the line, was charged with the defence of Toulon. Nelson, newly arrived in the Mediterranean was sent to Naples to seek reinforcements and obtained a promise of 4000 men from King Ferdinand. These, together with 750 from Gibraltar, were insufficient to prevent the Revolutionary Army under Lieutenant-Colonel Bonaparte forcing Hood to withdraw. Hood turned his attention to San Fiorenzo in Corsica where he was welcomed by Pasqual Paoli, the nationalist leader and lobbyist for independence from the French.

The town was taken after a number of assaults ensured a British foothold on the island from which to launch the second phase, an attack on the northern capital, Bastia. Dundas and Moore made initial attempts but were repulsed whereupon Hood was advised that the action should be continued as a blockade by the navy. Hood was unimpressed and landed Nelson and Colonel Villettes with 1200 troops 3 miles to the north of Bastia; meanwhile he anchored his ships in the bay but out of range of the shore batteries. Villettes marched on the town while Nelson landed guns and dragged them to within range of Bastia.

Shortly before midnight on 9 April the French began their counter-offensive, firing at the British position, but they did not launch an infantry attack and a relative stalemate ensued. On the morning of the 11th Hood offered surrender terms to the French but this was rejected unequivocally by General Gentili and of course provoked a new onslaught by the British. Unfortunately the range was too great and the defences too strong for any tangible effect. There were two results: disagreement between the navy and army as to each others effectiveness and, by chance, the gradual starvation of the city which in effect induced its capitulation.

Having won Bastia for Hood, a generous letter of commendation was sent to Nelson. Naturally he took great pride in his achievement but it was starvation through blockade, and not strictly Nelson's land assault which brought about the capitulation.

Homann Heir's chart of the Straits of Gibraltar, c.1756. (See 12 April.)

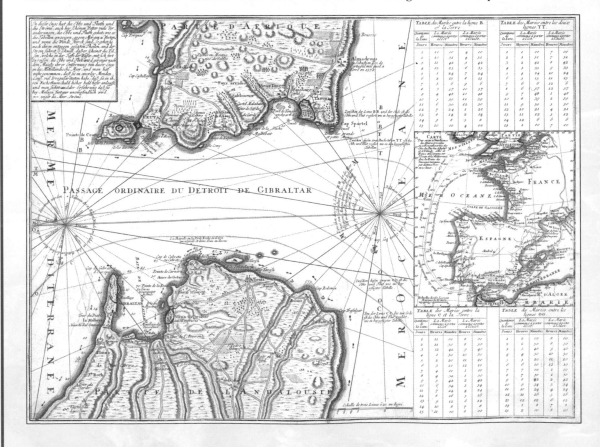

1801 To a young lieutenant who had expressed a dim view at Copenhagen on 2 April: 'At such a moment, the delivery of anything like a desponding opinion unasked was highly reprehensible, and deserved much more censure than Captain Foley gave you'.

1795 George IV marries Caroline, daughter of Charles Duke of Brunswick-Wolfenbultel.

1801 During peace negotiations after Copenhagen one of the Danes hinted at a renewal of hostilities: 'Renew hostilities! Tell them we are ready at a moment – ready to bombard this very night'.

1801 Armistice is agreed between the Danish Government and Sir Hyde Parker.

1797 After St Vincent: 'The Spaniards threaten us they will come out, and take their revenge: the sooner the better; but I will not believe it till I see it; and if they do, what will mines of Mexico or Peru signify, compared with the honour I doubt not we shall gain by fighting an angry Don? They will have thirty sail of the line, we twenty or twenty-two; but fear we shall have a peace before they are ready to come out. What a sad thing that will be'.

1778 William Hazlitt (d. 1830), English critic and essayist, and reporter for the 'Morning Chronicle', is born.

1784 Nelson has difficulty in proceeding to sea and runs aground. From Boreas' log: 'At 7 weighed: in canting Ship got stern way: let go the anchor again and the Ship got on shore. P.M. at ½ past 3 weighed and came to sail'.

1770 George Canning is born. He became foreign secretary in Portland's administration, 1807, president of the India Board in 1820, governor-general of India in 1822 and prime minister in 1827, but died on 8 August of that year.

1795 Hotham, after a brush with the French on 14 March 1795, which he did not follow up, said to Nelson: 'We must be content we have done very well.' Nelson writes to Fanny: 'Had I been supported I should certainly have brought the Sans Culottes to battle, a most glorious prospect. A brave man runs no more risk than a coward'.

1781 Admiral Darby relieves the starving Gibraltar amid heavy bombardment from the Spanish batteries.

1794 From his journal on preparations to attack Bastia: 'We began on the 13th of April a battery for three 24 pounders close to Torga Tower, which stands on the sea-side, 1230 yards from the Town battery, and 1600 from the Citadel'.

1797 A telegraph message arrives at the Admiralty from Portsmouth. Its terse message reads: 'Mutiny brewing in Spithead'. More a semaphore than an electric telegraph in the modern sense, it nevertheless managed to cover the 70 miles in something like three minutes.

1777 To his brother William at Christ College, Cambridge: 'I passed my Degree as Master of Arts on the 9th Instant, [passed the Lieutenant's examination] and received my Commission on the following day for a fine Frigate of 32 guns' (Lowestoffe, Captain Locker).

1759 The composer, George Frederick Handel, dies, aged 74.

8th

9th

10th

11th

12th

13th

14th

FOR THE BENEFIT OF
Mr. Stanton, jun. and Mr. F. Stanton.
Who respectfully solicit the Patronage of the Public.

THEATRE, STAFFORD.

On TUESDAY Evening, FEBRUARY 7th, 1837,
Will be performed a new interesting Nautical Drama, (never acted here) called The

Mutiny at the Nore.

Richard Parker, Mr. WALTON.—Captain Arlington, Mr. MASTERMAN.
Jack Adams, Mr. CHESTER.—Timothy Bubble, Mr. HOPE,—Dickey Chicken, Mr. PHILLIPS.
William Parker, (Parker's Child,) Master PHILLIPS.
Lieut. Davis, Mr. F. STANTON.—Bill Riley, Mr. STANTON, jun.—Tom Allen, Mr. ECCLES.
Sailors, and Marines, by Supernumeraries.
Mary Parker, Miss STANTON.———Molly Brown, Miss H. STANTON.
Dame Goose, Mrs. ROWLANDS.

In the course of the Drama, the following Scenery, Painted expressly for this occasion, by Mr. Stanton. jun.
Timothy Bubble's FARM(on the ISLE of GRAIN——INSIDE the FARM HOUSE.
Quarter Deck of the Sandwich.
Revolt of the Crew—Perilous Situation of Parker's Child—Intrepidity of British Sailors..
SUBMISSION TO THEIR OFFICERS.
INN on the ISLAND—INTERIOR VIEW.
Parker betrayed——taken Prisoner——and Death of Captain Arlington.
Cabin of the Sandwich.——Deck of the Sandwich.
EXECUTION OF WILLIAM PARKER.

END OF THE PLAY,
A Favorite SONG, by Mrs. PHILLIP.
And by particular Desire, Mr. PHILLIPS will Sing
"The NERVOUS FAMILY."

The whole to conclude, with the Operatic Drama, of

MASANIELLO;
Or, The Dumb Girl of Portici.

Alphonso, Son of the Duke of Arcos, Mr. WALTON.
Lorenzo, Captain of the Guards, Mr. MASTERMAN.
Masaniello, (Thomaso Aniello,) Mr. STANTON, jun.
Guiseppo Aniello, his Cousin, (with a Song) Mr. PHILLIPS.—Borella, Mr. CHESTER.
Giaccomon, Mr. F. STANTON.————Jocoso, Mr. ECCLES.————Serjeant, Mr. HOPE.
Soldiers, Fishermen, Conspirators, &c. by numerous Supernumeraries.
Princess Elvira, Miss H STANTON.
Fenella, the Dumb Girl of Portici, (Sister to Masaniello,) Miss STANTON.
Briella, Wife to the Serjeant, Mrs. WOOD.
Fishermen's Wives, Ladies of the Court, Dancers Children, Chorus Singers, &c. &c.
Mrs. ROWLANDS, Miss E. STANTON, Mrs. PHILLIPS, Misses and Master WOOD
PHILLIPS and ECCLES.

The whole to conclude with the Irruption of Mount Vesuvius.

BOXES, 3s.——PIT, 2s.——GALLERY, 1s.

Tickets may be had of Messrs. H. and F. STANTON, at Mrs. Yates's Green-gate Street, and of
Mr. MORGAN, Bookseller; where Places for the Boxes may be taken.

MORGAN, PRINTER, STAFFORD.

*The Nore mutiny entered the national consciousness, as
this nautical drama, forty years on, suggests.*

MUTINY

There were two great British naval mutinies during Nelson's life. The first was at Spithead in 1797 when the Channel fleet refused to go to sea during the Revolutionary War with France until the seamen's demands relating to pay and conditions of naval service had been fulfilled. Admiral Hood (Viscount Bridport), at first pacified the seamen in his flagship, but a few days later he was unable to control the fleet. Lord Howe was called in to do so after which Hood took the fleet to sea to blockade Brest.

Unusually, no ringleaders were hanged; in fact there were no courts martial, since it was considered the men were justified in their claims.

During the same year mutiny broke out in HMS *Sandwich* in the fleet at the Nore. The ringleader was Richard Parker, a former midshipman who had chosen to rejoin the navy rather than serve a long prison sentence. The grievances were the same as those of the Spithead fleet which, because they had been met to the satisfaction of that fleet, were unnecessary. Parker managed to persuade several of Admiral Duncan's North Sea fleet to join him. He arranged the ships in two lines and opened fire on any trying to escape. However, one by one they worked their way out such that the mutiny collapsed. Parker, together with twenty-four seamen known to be the ringleaders were brought before a court martial and hanged from the yardarm, the customary punishment for mutiny.

In December 1801 another mutiny broke out in the Bantry Bay squadron under Admiral Mitchell. Twenty-two men were brought to trial on board *Gladiator* in January 1802. Seventeen were condemned to death, of whom eleven were executed on board *Majestic*, *Centaur*, *Formidable*, *Térméraire*, and *L'Achille*; the others were sentenced to receive 200 lashes.

Mutinies were not confined to the British – the Toulon fleet mutinied on 1 December 1789 and the Brest fleet on 17 September 1790. Following the massacre of mutineers 45,000 people marched in protest against the French authorities.

1805 The Admiralty accuses Nelson of allowing Captain Mouat to impress men from transports but Nelson returns a copy of his general order prohibiting such impressment. To Marsden: 'I conceive Captain Mouat's application to the Transport Board improper, as it implies a doubt of my putting a stop to the evil he complained of, and tending to give much trouble where none was necessary'.

1797 Mutiny begins at Spithead, British sailors in Queen Charlotte demand better conditions.

15th

1796 To Jervis, the French now ready to sail from Toulon: 'I cannot believe the French Squadron will venture out of Toulon to come this road; but it shows what mischief may ensue, should Admiral Man proceed to the West Indies, and Richery come here. If you should leave the coast with two sixty-fours, it may be unpleasant; but with the addition of a Seventy-four, if we cannot act offensively, I have no fear that six Frenchmen will hurt us'.

1763 The Earl of Bute is forced to resign, deemed to be not only incapable, but worse than that, by popular verdict, unfit to be prime minister of England.

16th

1794 To Pollard, his agent at Leghorn, off Bastia: 'We want many good things; some porter, either a cask or bottled. I hope soon to have the pleasure of writing to you from Bastia'.

1790 Benjamin Franklin, discoverer of the Gulf Stream, inventor of the lightning conductor, president of the Pennsylvania Society for the Abolition of Slavery, dies in Philadelphia. His funeral is attended by more than 20,000 people.

17th

1793 To his brother: 'I understand from second-hand that we are to carry out the West India Convoy. To me it is perfectly indifferent to what corner of the world we go: with a good Ship, and Ship's company we can come to no harm'.

1775 The American patriot Paul Revere makes his famous ride from Charlestown to Lexington to warn of the advancing British troops.

18th

1805 To Ball after the enemy had sailed for the West Indies but contrary winds prevent a chase: 'My good fortune seems flown away I cannot get a fair wind, or even a side wind. Dead foul, dead foul! But my mind is fully made up what to do when I leave the Straits, supposing there is no certain information of the enemy's destination'.

1775 A clash at Lexington between British troops and colonials begins the American War of Independence. Eight years later to the day the American Congress proclaims victory.

19th

1805 To Fox: 'Broken-hearted as I am, Sir, at the escape of the Toulon Fleet, yet it cannot prevent me thinking of all points intrusted to my care, amongst which is Gibraltar'.

1792 France declares war on Leopold of Austria, the King of Bohemia and Hungary, but the attack on the Austrian Netherlands fails.

20th

1794 From Journal C: 'The Torga battery opened at daylight on the Town battery and Camponella, and apparently with good effect. The Enemy kept up a most heavy fire on us the whole day, with shell and shot, from the citadel, Town, Stafforella, Camponella, a square tower, and the two batteries newly raised under Stafforella. Brigadier-General D'Aubant came on the heights from St Fiorenzo, with all the Staff and Field Officers of that Army, and a guard of fifty Corsicans'.

1782 Friedrich Wilhelm August Froebel (d. 1852), the great German educator and economist is born.

21st

COMPTE DE PIERRE CHARLES JEAN BAPTISTE SILVESTRE VILLENEUVE (1763-1806)

Nelson's French counterpart at Trafalgar was born at Valensoles on 31 December 1763. Having joined the French navy and adopted Republican principles, he rose quickly to the rank of captain in 1793 and then admiral in 1796.

He was given the rear division under Admiral Brueys in 1798 and saw action at the Nile. In this battle the van and centre of Brueys fleet suffered at the hands of Nelson but Villeneuve's rear division was only lightly engaged. Having seen the destruction early in the morning of 2 August Villeneuve, in his flagship *Guillaume Tell,* with *Généreux* and two frigates set sail and escaped. They were the sole remnants of the fleet which had carried Napoleon's troops to Egypt.

Villeneuve was later given command of the Toulon squadron which formed part of Napoleon's 'grand design'. The strategy was for the Toulon, Brest, Ferrol and Rochefort squadrons to combine in the West Indies, return in strength to defeat the British Channel fleet and pave the way for the Armée d'Angleterre to be ferried into the southern counties. Nelson, however, through relentless pursuit across the Atlantic, in the West Indies and back across the Atlantic prevented the formation of this battlefleet.

Having fled before Nelson's fleet, Villeneuve was intercepted by Sir Robert Calder off Finisterre. They fought an indecisive action during which Villeneuve lost two ships before breaking off the action and heading for Cadiz in the belief that a superior British fleet lay to the north between himself and Brest.

Despite having orders to sail, Villeneuve at first refused to do so in face of the blockading force of Sir Cuthbert Collingwood and later Nelson, and in the belief that his ships were no match for the British. Finally on 19 October 1805, while his successor Admiral Rosily was heading for Cadiz, Villeneuve sailed. Two days later his combined French and Spanish fleet was destroyed. Villeneuve was captured and taken to England as a prisoner. He was released and returned to France where he died from stab wounds in an hotel in Rennes. A farewell letter had been left to his wife but the question as to whether his death was suicide or murder is still unresolved.

Vice-Admiral Pierre Villeneuve.

1801 On the Danish armistice and his duty towards his prisoners: 'God forbid I should destroy a non-resisting Dane! When they became my prisoners I became their protector.'

1806 Villeneuve is found stabbed to death in a locked room; a suicide note to his wife is found by him.

1801 To Davison: 'You will, at a proper time, and before my arrival in England, signify to Lady N. that I expect, and for which I have made such a very liberal allowance to her, to be left to myself, and without any inquiries from her; for sooner than live the unhappy life I did when I last came to England, I would stay abroad for ever. My mind is fixed as fate; therefore you will send my determination in any way you may judge proper.'

Hogarth's portrait of the cross-eyed John Wilkes, holding aloft the bonnet of Liberty.

1763 The notorious 'Number 45' of the North Briton John Wilkes seditious paper is published.

1795 On red hot shot to the Duke of Clarence: 'I hope, and believe, if we only get three sail from England, that we shall prevent this fleet of the enemy doing further service in the Mediterranean, notwithstanding the red-hot shot and combustibles, of which they have had a fair trial and found them useless. They believe that we should give them no quarter; and it was with some difficulty we found the combustibles, which are fixed in a skeleton like a carcass; they turn liquid, and water will not extinguish it.'

1743 Edmund Cartwright (d.1823), a Lancashire rector and inventor of the power loom is born. In 1785 he patented his design, but it did not become commercial until he opened a factory in Pollockshaws near Glasgow in 1801.

1801 On his law suit against St Vincent over prize money: 'This day comes on my trial with the Great Earl. May the 'just' gain it.'

1800 William Cowper (b.1731), poet and hymn writer, dies at East Dereham.

1796 To Jervis on the French advance towards Sardinia: 'If the King of Sardinia does not make peace, I should hope that such conduct of the French would rouse the whole nation to arms. As to my going to Naples, I need only say, the Neapolitans would not like the interference of a foreigner, especially Mr Fortiguerra, who fancies himself equal to any Officer in Europe.'

1802 In contravention of the Treaty of Amiens, Bonaparte occupies Flushing. Britain issues an ultimatum and he withdraws on 12 May 1803.

1794 From Journal C: 'We began the battery on the ridge for two 18-pound carronades, and one 12-pounder on the spot where Captain Clarke was wounded; 250 yards from Camponella, 900 yards from the Citadel, 700 yards from the town. The labour of getting up guns to this battery was a work of the greatest difficulty, and which never, in my opinion, would have been accomplished by any other than British seamen.'

1791 Samuel Finley Breese Morse (d.1872), inventor of the electric telegraph system which bears his name, is born. The first signals were passed between Washington and Baltimore on 24 May 1844.

Romanticised in film and the subject of lingering debate as to its cause, this mutiny and the sequel, the voyage of *Pandora*, make remarkable reading and give an extraordinary insight into the hardships of seafaring that prevailed during the epoch even by ships dedicated to discovery and the development of trade.

Bounty, originally *Betha*, a 250-ton vessel was built in Hull in 1784 as a merchant ship. She was acquired, on behalf of a group of merchants and planters, by the Admiralty, armed as a transport and fitted out to carry breadfruit seedlings from Tahiti to the West Indies as a source of food for slaves working the sugar plantations.

Command was given to William Bligh who had learned the art of navigation as master of *Resolution* during Cook's second voyage of discovery. With a crew of about forty-five he departed Spithead in December 1787 and after a passage of ten months, logging 26,000 miles, he arrived at Tahiti. During the voyage his crew experienced his strict disciplinarian nature and the severe punishments he inflicted. Opinions no doubt softened during the five months of near paradise spent collecting the seedlings and fraternising with the local population, who adopted a more than friendly attitude towards the British seamen. Within three weeks of returning to sea they 'mutinied'.

On 28 April 1789, when the ship was off Tofau, Fletcher Christian, who had earlier attempted to leave the ship by make-shift raft off Tonga, and about half of the crew, in an act of piracy, took the ship and cast Bligh, together with eighteen loyal crew members adrift in the ship's launch – an open boat only 18 feet long. They eventually reached Timor after a voyage of 3618 miles losing only one man during the ordeal. Meanwhile the mutineers sailed via Tahiti, where they embarked a number of native women, to the Pitcairn islands where they ran *Bounty* ashore and burned her.

Bligh made his way back to the Admiralty and reported his loss whereupon HMS *Pandora* was dispatched to recover the mutineers. Fourteen were captured at Tahiti but during the passage home *Pandora* was wrecked on the Great Barrier Reef with the loss of four prisoners drowned. Another astonish-

ing open boat episode ensued, but this time at the end of a long and arduous voyage rather than on setting out. Eventually the survivors of *Pandora* and ten prisoners made their way home; a court martial was convened and three prisoners hanged.

Bligh returned to sea and was master of one of Duncan's fleet at Camperdown on 11 October 1797, where he demonstrated his outstanding courage during a particularly bloody battle. He further distinguished himself at Copenhagen in 1801. He was appointed governor of New South Wales, but again his inability to get on with people surfaced and following a quarrel over rum traffic he was arrested and sent home. He rose to vice-admiral in 1813.

(Bligh's biography is by G Mackaness and a short account of *Pandora* is by Geoffrey Rawson.)

Detail of a watercolour portrait of William Bligh by Hazel Kelly. Courtesy of Tim Waters.

⚓ **1803** ⚓ To Captain Sutton on fitting out Victory: 'A barge I like much better than a Cutter for my ease, and I have wrote to the Comptroller about the cabin' (it was done to the San Josef).

⚓ *1789* ⚓ *Mutiny on the Bounty off Tofua in the Friendly Islands. William Bligh and 18 of his crew are set adrift in an open boat. Fletcher Christian returned to the Pitcairn Islands where he landed on 23 June 1790.*

⚓ **1793** ⚓ To Fanny from Agamemnon: 'We arrived at Spithead last night, and this morning I got my orders to go to sea until the 4th of May. We are all well: indeed, nobody can be ill with my Ship's Company they are so fine a set. Don't mind what newspapers say about us. God bless you'.

⚓ *1802* ⚓ *The marines are given the new title Royal Marines by George III, for honour, courage and loyalty.*

⚓ **1797** ⚓ Patrolling off Cape de Gatte, to the Duke of Clarence: 'In October I intend to ask permission to return to England until February, should the war still continue; and when it is considered that I have been four years and nine months without one moment's repose for body or mind, I trust credit will be given me that I do not sham.'

⚓ *1789* ⚓ *Following the first national election in the United States, held on 7 January 1789, George Washington is sworn into office as first president of the United States.*

George Washington (see 30 April) is portrayed here as the commander-in-chief of the Continental Army of America.

THE STATION FOR HONOUR

NELSON AND THE NAVIGATION ACTS

Jimmy Pack

American independence and the slave trade were familiar topics to Nelson but his views were not entirely shared by his contemporaries or masters. Nor were his methods. Even as a fledgling officer he was quite capable of carrying out instructions to the letter, based on his own interpretation. A typical subject was the Navigation Act of 1661 which, so far as Nelson was concerned, was being flaunted by the Americans, ignored by his seniors – many of whom had been suborned by rich American trading families – much to the advantage of the French and Spanish who remained powerful forces in the Western Atlantic and with whom Britain seemed to be at endless war. An account of Nelson's command of *Boreas* illustrates both his skills as a navigator and an independent approach in his formative years, both of which have been scrutinised endlessly.

For the war, Britain needed strategic bases in the Western Atlantic. The island of Tortola had already proved its worth and Governor Shirley conveyed to London its advantages as a cruising ground for privateers. London now looked again at neighbouring St John, which also could be of strategic significance in future conflicts. Shirley was ordered to arrange a report on the island and he told George Nibbs, President of Tortola, to prepare it. Nibbs wrote that there was a battery of six small cannon at Cruz Bay, that the riding for ships was bad there, but that at the eastern end of the island, at Coral Bay, there was 'one of the best harbours in the West Indies'.

Six months or so after this report reached England, Captain Horatio Nelson sailed for the West Indies in HMS *Boreas*. He was forced to sit out the hurricane season in Barbados, but then stood immediately north for the Virgins with orders to undertake the examination of Coral Bay and to gather information about the wood and water there.

On 23 November 1784, Nelson wrote to William Locker:

> 'I am on my way to examine a Harbour said to be situated in the Island of St John's, capable, it is supposed, to contain a Fleet of Men-of-War during the hurricane seasons. It is odd this fine harbour, if such a one there is, should not have been made use of long ago; but there is an order from the Admiralty to send a Frigate to examine it: it is said here to belong to the Danes; if so, they will not let me survey it.'

Coral Bay, which has three inner harbours – Coral Harbour, Hurricane Hole and Round Bay – is today recognised by yachtsmen as an invaluable haven from storms. Nelson's original chart is now tucked away in the Admiralty records of the Public Records Office in London. It shows that Nelson gave his own names to these three inner sanctuaries. Evidently, the Danes did not oppose this survey, which confirmed the bay to be an excellent anchorage at all times. There was only one anxious moment when *Boreas* struck a rock on approaching the bay, but subsequent inspection revealed no notable dam-

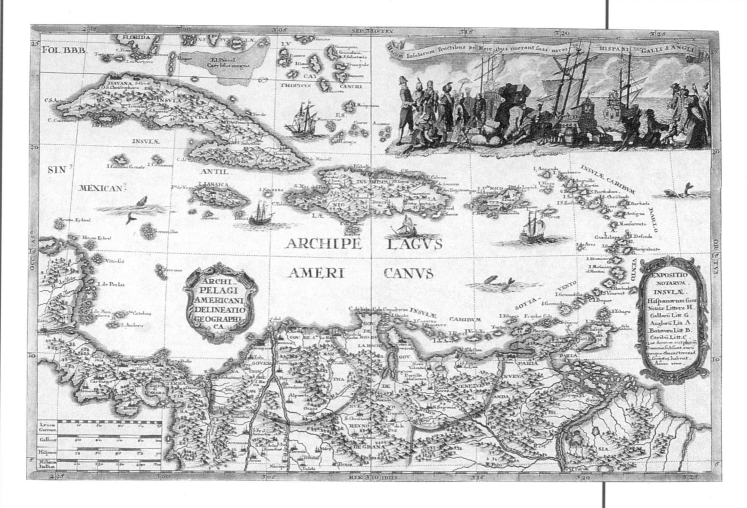

A chart of the West Indies c.1700. Courtesy of Alice Carlsson.

age. Sir Richard Hughes, the naval commander-in-chief in the area, reported to the Secretary of the Admiralty:

'You will be pleased to acquaint the Lords that conformable to their directions, I sent the *Boreas* to reconnoitre and Survey the Large Harbour laying at the East end of St Johns, one of the Virgin Islands; She is return'd from the performance of that service, and, I have herewith forwarded for their Lordships inspection, the Draught of that Harbour, taken by Captain Nelson, together with his Account and Remarks, on its Capabilities in all respects, by which it seems to have answered the Description given of it, to Lord Sydney through the hands of Governor Shirley. The Island of St Johns is, nevertheless, at present in possession of the Danes, and acknowledged to be under their Government and Protection.'

Nelson's 1784 voyage to the Virgins covered more than the survey of Coral Bay, important though it was. On 22 October Admiral Hughes had ordered Nelson in the *Boreas* and Wilfred Collingwood in the *Rattler* to cover St Kitts, Monserrat, Nevis and the Virgin Islands. The task of Royal Navy ships in the West Indies was not an easy one. The American War of Independence had ended the year before, but when Nelson took command of the *Boreas*, at the age of twenty-six, relations between Britain and her former colonies were still delicate to say the least. High on the list of issues were the Navigation Acts, instituted by Britain in 1661. These Acts insisted that colonial trade could only take place in British vessels manned by British crews with British ports as their destination. Britain's merchant navy flourished as a result and the nation's wealth was maintained by a continuing favourable balance of trade. Another vital by-product was the ever-increasing flow of prime seamen to maintain supremacy in the maritime wars.

As Britain's colonies had developed, particularly those in North America and the British West Indies, the Acts became anachronistic and were resisted. Although, by 1763, British warships were stationed in the West Indies to enforce legal trade under the Acts, it was an almost impossible task. Vested interests ensured there was many a nod and wink. In the Virgins, where Danish and British possessions were in such close proximity, every conceivable artifice was employed to circumvent them. St Croix was a notable example, where a number of established American traders had their other foot well planted. They maintained a regular seaborne traffic, not only in provisions and lumber, but in many other illegal items.

Once the United States gained independence, the privilege of trading in the West Indies no longer existed. But, it could hardly be expected that a mutual dependence favoured by geographical considerations, could terminate overnight. Sympathy for the American cause had been manifest in the West Indies even while the war was on. Obtaining necessities from England simply to satisfy British projectionist policies was both expensive and time consuming. American shipyards were now building ships which were seaworthy and cheap, and if their products were arriving in Danish, Dutch and French islands, it was unrealistic to assume the British islands would not take advantage.

The British authorities had not always pressed their own enquiries too hard, so long as a dubious wartime practice seemed useful to the cause. Tortola, in particular, was handily placed. Governor Shirley frankly admitted to London (although not until the war was over):

'...the remote Leeward situation of the Island made it very convenient for the inhabitants of the Neighbouring Islands, as well as French, as those taken from us and in their Possessions, to convey their Produce thither, where, by some means or other, it was converted into British produce, and shipped from thence in British Bottoms to Ports of Great Britain and Ireland. Such a practice at that time made it a place of considerable consequence, as Eighty or sometimes One Hundred Top-sail vessels have been known to sail from there in the space of a year,

valuably laden and destined to an English Market which added greatly to his Majesty's Revenue.'

With peace, a hundred vessels a year shrank to a mere ten, carrying no more than 4000 hogsheads of sugar, and there was no incentive for the government in Britain to treat Tortola with any particular consideration. The special interests of the British Virgin Islands were lost in the wider policy. The late war had reinforced British determination to make the colonies serve the trade and financial interests of the home country. It had also an extra edge of bitterness and resentment against attempts by the newly independent Americans to interfere with British monopolies in the area. If they wanted to be a foreign country they must take the consequences. As early as 2 July 1783, an order in council allowed trade between America and British West Indian ports only if 'the goods imported or exported were carried in British or colonial ships'. Certain vital food provisions were banned from carriage, even by this method, and the intended effect was to close British West Indian trade to United States shipping altogether.

Not every British official and officer in the West

Indies pursued his government's policy with vigour. Nelson's attention was drawn to the burgeoning American seaborne warships to enforce the Acts. Hughes vacillated, and their opposing interpretation led to discord. Nelson had already shown his character two years previously when he was serving as commander of the frigate *Albemarle* on the North American station. The war was almost over and naval operations had virtually ceased apart from in the West Indies. Nelson requested a transfer to that fleet, even though his station was a profitable one for prize money. His commanding officer pointed this out to him, not wishing to lose an outstanding officer. Nelson replied: 'Yes, But the West Indies is the station for honour.'

Writing home a short time later, Nelson again showed his selfless motivation. 'Money', he said, speaking of the North American station, 'is the great object here, nothing else is attended to.'

A few months later, he reported:

'I have closed the war without a fortune; but I trust, and, from the attention that has been paid to me, believe, that there is not a speck on my character. True Honour, I hope, predominates in my mind far above riches.'

This insight into the man explains why he was not prepared to see the Navigation Acts ignored only in the breach while British West Indian merchants, local officials and planters, encouraged American trade for their own gain. Admiral Hughes, fully aware of his government's policy, yielded to pressure to let sleeping dogs lie. Only by Nelson's confronting him with a copy of the Acts did the Admiral consent to the Americans being considered, as the Acts specified, 'Foreigners, and excluded from all commerce with the islands in these seas'.

Initially, Nelson treated offending American vessels with kid gloves. Then, in 1785, matters took a more serious turn. Custom house officials allowed American ships to trade under British flags and to obtain British registers, while the local vice-admiralty courts were far from helpful, despite accumulating evidence of illegal trafficking. The islanders did everything they could to prevent Nelson and his colleagues, the Collingwood brothers, from carrying out what they considered to be their duty.

Nelson and the Collingwoods tightened the screw, concentrating on places where the violations were most flagrant. The Royal Navy was most active at St Kitts and Nevis, where Nelson seized four vessels in two days. The British Virgin Islands were left largely to their own devices – some of which were hardly legal. In October 1785, Governor Shirley promised London he would do all in his power to enforce the law. 'If any foreign sugars and rum are imported into the British West India Islands,' he wrote, 'I should apprehend such practices must take place chiefly at Dominica and Tortola, on account of the particular situation of these Islands.'

Nelson's duties, however, were to give him yet one more opportunity to scrutinise the local scene at Tortola. Admiral Hughes returned to England in August 1786 without relief, leaving Nelson as the senior officer on station and with increasing responsibilities. The most important of these was to assume the role of a seagoing chamberlain for His Royal Highness Prince William Henry, who arrived in November, commanding the frigate *Pegasus*.

Nelson wrote to the Admiralty from Nevis on 15 March 1787:

'I have attended His Royal Highness since our sailing, to Monserrat, Nevis, and St Christopher's, and shall sail for the Virgins on Monday the 19th instant, from whence, after calling at English Harbour, Antigua for a few days, I shall attend His Royal Highness to Grenada, which will finish the tour.'

William was the third son of George III, who had been sent into the navy at an early age and whom Nelson had known as a midshipman in 1782. Now, five years later, the Prince had passed successfully through the stages of promotion to lieutenant and post-captain and was at the pinnacle of his short naval career.

Despite Prince William's somewhat unstable character (his father would die insane), which led to many shortcomings, he had become a competent and professional sailor, and his relationship with Nelson was one of friendship and respect. No better mentor could have been found for the Prince during the ensuing six months. One historian wrote that the Prince, 'went into the navy and though he had to

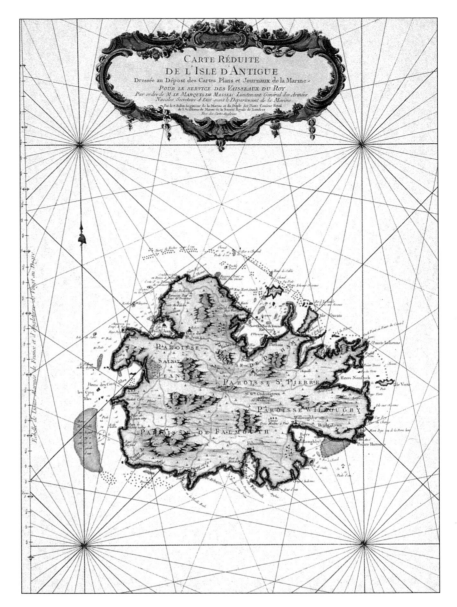

leave the service, he spent the rest of his life roaring around on an imaginary quarterdeck, using dreadful language even on solemn occasions'.

But, he was also a man of considerable discernment who was quick to appreciate Nelson's genius and contagious enthusiasm. Of Nelson, the Prince later wrote:

'It was at this era...that I particularly observed the greatness of Nelson's superior mind. The manner in which he enforced the spirit of the Navigation Act, first drew my attention to the commercial interests of my country. We visited the different islands together; and as much as the manoeuvres of the fleets can be described off the headlands of islands, we fought over again the principal naval actions in the American War.'

Visiting the British Leeward Islands was a happy interlude in the lives of both men, but when it came to official calls and the inevitable social entanglements onshore, Nelson kept in the background as protocol demanded. The one notable exception to this state of affairs was the occasion of Nelson's marriage to Frances Nisbet on 11 March 1787, when it could be said that the Prince was in every sense playing the supporting role in giving away the bride – although he made Nelson postpone the wedding until he could be there to perform this duty.

The visit to Tortola that followed Nevis in the itinerary was understandably a sober affair for Nelson – perhaps a tedious duty after his recent wedding. On the short passage to the Virgins, he wrote his customary letter to his old friend, Captain William Locker:

'...my time since November, has been entirely taken up with attending the Prince in his tour round these Islands. However, except Grenada, this is the last, when I shall repair to English Harbour, and fit *Boreas* for a voyage to England. Happy shall I be when that time arrives: no man has had more illness or trouble on a Station than I have experienced; but let me lay the balance on the other side – I am married to an amiable woman, that far makes amends for everything: indeed till I married her I never knew happiness.'

The logs of *Boreas* and *Pegasus* recount in identical fashion – and with the usual spare language of the navy – the bare bones of Tortola's royal and distinguished occasion. They report that on Wednesday, 21 March, Virgin Gorda lay to the northwest and was passed some 8 leagues away; the following day, they pursued their course through Round Rock Passage, leaving Ginger Island to port and sailed into the Sir Francis Drake Channel; and, on the afternoon of 23rd, they arrived in company in the anchorage of Old Road, Tortola, where they secured. *Pegasus'* log records the mooring as the east point of the bay, east 1½ miles distant; the west point, west by north, 1 mile away; and the old fort, north by west of the town 1½ miles away.

The Danes graced the visit by sending a warship, the *Count Bernsdorff*, from St Thomas, and salutes of guns were exchanged between her and *Boreas*. Governor Shirley, who was at Tortola for the Royal visit, was also awarded a thirteen-gun salute when he paid a visit aboard the *Pegasus*. Prince William Henry was given a twenty-one-gun salute by *Boreas*. Nelson writing orders from his ship while at anchor, gave explicit instructions to the *Pegasus*:

'It is my directions that you fire twenty one Guns to salute His Royal Highness Prince William Henry, beginning after *Boreas* has finished.'

The Prince, meanwhile, was concerned that his own ship make the right impression. A few days before arrival in the Virgins, he issued special instructions as to alertness and neatness: 'The young gentlemen whose turn it is to go with me in the barge, is to be perfectly cleaned ready by Seven Bells in the morning'. Nothing is recorded of the festivities ashore, but it was said of the Prince during his tour that 'he could dance or make love till three in the morning, return on board and be on deck at seven, spick and span, complaining furiously about the turn out of his officers'.

The visit lasted five days. Aboard *Boreas*, Nelson was busy with ship's business, writing orders for the court martial of a seaman for insubordination towards the boatswain. He also – assuming his role as senior officer – gave new sailing orders to Prince William Henry to head for Nevis and await his arrival there. On Wednesday, 28 March, the two ships made their departure. It was Nelson's last visit to the Virgin Islands. On 7 June, *Boreas* sailed for England.

Captain A J (Jimmy) Pack (1914-1995) Jimmy's distinguished naval career began in 1932. It included service in the battleship HMS *Malaya*, the cruiser HMS *Carlisle* and the carrier HMS *Illustrious* and theatres including the Mediterranean, the Far East and the South Atlantic. As a member of the supply and secretarial branch he was bound to join an admiral's staff. He did; and served a prolonged spell of thirteen years as secretary to Admiral of the Fleet, Sir Charles Lambe. He was appointed curator of the old Victory Museum when it was run under the auspices of the Society for Nautical Research from 1965 until 1972 after which he masterminded the undertaking by the Ministry of Defence of the museum and its collections. He became its first director and was awarded an OBE in 1979 for his services to the museum. One of Jimmy's best loved works was *Nelson's Blood*, the story of naval rum. This essay was to be part of a comprehensive work on the life of Nelson, the manuscript of which is now held by the Royal Naval Museum.

VISCOUNTESS NELSON (1761-1831)

Born Frances Herbert Woolward to William Woolward, a senior judge, and sister to John Richardson Herbert, who became president of the local council of Nevis. Four months after the death of her father, Francis married Dr Josiah Nisbet on 28 June 1779. Within months of the wedding Dr Nisbet became ill and the couple returned to England where their son Josiah was born. Dr Nisbet died in 1781 and Fanny's uncle, John Herbert (himself a widower), invited her and Josiah to his home, Montpelier, a rambling white-pillared colonial mansion – the largest house in Nevis.

Nelson, *Boreas* and his friend Prince William, *Pegasus*, were stationed at English Harbour, Antigua, where Nelson met Fanny. A few months later he proposed to the young widow and was accepted. The wedding was conducted by the Rector of St John and St Thomas on Sunday, 11 March 1787 in the opulent setting of the principal reception room of Montpelier.

In May 1787 Nelson sailed for England. His new wife and stepson accompanied by John Herbert and his daughter followed in greater comfort in a West Indiaman. During the summer of 1788 they moved to his father's rectory. After years of unemployment, at the reopening of hostilities with France in 1793, Nelson was appointed to *Agamemnon*. Fanny was left in the care of his father and sisters at Burnham Thorpe where she kept up an affectionate correspondence with her husband. Josiah sailed with him as a midshipman.

Fanny nursed Nelson tenderly during the months of convalescence after losing his arm at Tenerife, and before he returned to service in the Mediterranean he bought Roundwood, a house near Ipswich.

Back on station, Fanny tried to visit Nelson but he refused her. By 1799 he was living with Sir William and Lady Hamilton in Palermo, having made no real attempt to camouflage his affair with Emma. Evacuating Italy, the trio travelled through Europe as a group, landing in Yarmouth in November, 1800. Nelson was reunited with Fanny at Nerot's Hotel in King Street where she was waiting for him with his father. The obligation of sleeping under his own roof in the uneasy circumstances of his return in the company of the Hamiltons was thus removed.

Lady Nelson had sterling qualities which bound the Nelson family to her. They were especially beholden to her for her attentive care of the Reverend Nelson. A frail invalid aged eighty in 1800, Lady Nelson had shown herself equally useful and kind towards the family – the children of Nelson's sisters and particularly those of his elder brother (the Reverend William Nelson) whom she constantly entertained in London in school holidays. At the age of forty, Josiah married a godchild of Fanny's. She stayed for long periods with her son and his wife in the Champs Elysées.

Following her husband's death, Fanny, dowager Viscountess Nelson spent the remainder of her life in furnished houses in London, Bath, Brighton or the West Country, varying her residence with the seasons. Occasionally she travelled abroad, once to Lyons and once, surprisingly, to Switzerland to go boating with Lord Byron on Lake Geneva. Prince William remained in touch with Fanny even after he ascended to the throne as King William IV. It was he who long ago in Nevis had congratulated Nelson on carrying off the principal favourite of the Island.

After ten years of marriage Josiah died of pleurisy in August 1830. Fanny did not recover from this blow; she died on 4 May 1831, in Harley Street, London.

Beryl Hardy Nisbett JP

Diomed (see 4 May), at 15 hands and 3 inches ran against horses owned by the Dukes of Cumberland and Bolton among others, and won for Sir Charles 1850 guineas. It was the number and quality of subscribers that guaranteed the future success of the Derby.

1794 To Fanny prior to the attack on Corsica: 'Only recollect that a brave man dies but once, a coward all his life long. We cannot escape death; and should it happen to me in this place, remember, it is the will of Him, in whose hands are the issues of life and death'.

1813 Southey's 'Life of Nelson' is first published. He was also a poet, writing 'The Inchcape Rock' and 'Lord William'.

1803 To Sir William Scott, campaigning on behalf of ordinary seamen: 'Something should be attempted at these times to make our seamen, at the din of war, fly to our Navy, instead of flying from it'.

1798 King George reviews the fleet at Spithead a year after the North Sea fleet mutinied.

1804 To Lord Hobart on the strategic value of Sardinia: 'Having in former letters, stated its immense importance, I only now presume to bring the subject forward to Your Lordship's most serious consideration. The question is not, shall the King of Sardinia keep it? That is out of the question; he cannot, for any length of time. If France possesses it, Sicily is not safe an hour'.

1790 Stanislaus II, King of Poland, creates a constitution which provides for an hereditary monarchy and separates executive and legislative judicial powers.

1831 Vicountess Fanny Nelson dies in London aged 70. On this day in 1786, Nelson had written to her: 'Duty is the great business of a sea officer. All private consideration must give way to it however painful it is.'

1780 The first Derby, a race for three year olds instituted by the 12th Earl of Derby, is run at Epsom and is won by Sir Charles Bunbury's horse, Diomed.

1801 Nelson, in the Baltic following Copenhagen, receives his appointment as commander-in-chief of the Baltic. To Addington: 'My health is gone, and although I should be happy to try and hold out a month or six weeks longer, yet death is no respecter of persons. I own, at present, I should not wish to die a natural death'.

1789 The États Généraux is summoned by Louis XVI. It comprises 368 ecclesiastics, 285 nobles, 621 deputies & tiers état. Their hopes were no sooner realised than dashed.

1788 On exposing gross frauds in the West Indies: 'That thing called honour, is now alas! thought of no more. My integrity cannot be mended, I hope; but my fortune, God knows, has grown worse for the service; so much for serving my country. I have invariably laid down, and followed close, a plan of what ought to be uppermost in the breast of an officer: that it is much better to serve an ungrateful country, than to give up his own fame'.

1758 Maximilien Robespierre is born. He insisted the Convention approve the existence of a Supreme Being and the immortality of the Soul, and called for the abolition of the death penalty. He went to the guillotine in 1794.

1798 To Orion, Alexander and Vanguard: 'It being of the very greatest importance that the squadron should not be separated, it is my positive orders that no temptation is to induce a line-of-battle ship to separate from me, except the almost certainty of bringing a line-of-battle ship of the enemy to action; but in common cases, if the weather is such as to risk separation, or the approach of night, it is my directions you will leave off chase, and rejoin me, even without waiting for the signal of recall, unless I make the signal to continue the pursuit'.

1765 HMS Victory is floated up in the Old Single Dock, Chatham.

1801 Summarising his situation in the Baltic: 'I look upon the Northern League to be like a tree, of which Paul [Russia] was the trunk, and Sweden and Denmark the branches. If I can get at the trunk, and hew it down, the branches fall of course; but I may lop the branches and yet not be able to fell the tree, and my power must be weaker when strength is required'.

1797 Able-seamen are awarded their first pay rise since 1 January 1653, when it was set at 24 shillings per month.

JOHN HARRISON (1693-1776)

John Harrison was born at Foulby, Yorkshire on 24 March 1693. He began a career in carpentry and taught himself mathematics and, while working as an estate carpenter, he constructed, with his brother James, a number of long base clocks. They employed a number of new techniques including the first bimetallic pendulum which overcame linear expansion variations caused by changes in temperature. Several of his timepieces were remarkably accurate and led him to consider diverse applications.

In 1714 an Act of Parliament set up a Commission for the Discovery of Longitude at Sea, known as the Board of Longitude. It had long been realised that an accurate determination of the time difference between the sun passing overhead at the Greenwich meridian and overhead at the position of the observer would enable that observer to calculate the longitudinal distance from the Greenwich meridian to the observation position. Latitude, determined by the sun's declination had never been a problem, thus with both latitude and longitude the mariner could 'fix' his position.

Sir Isaac Newton and Edmund Halley were early advisors to the government. On their advice the Board was set up and an offer of reward (£20,000) for solving the problem was declared. Early research was based on the known fact that the sun subtends an arc of 15° each hour, thus the link with time was axiomatic. The accuracy was set at no more than a 30-mile error for the standard passage to the West Indies, a voyage of about six weeks.

Harrison's first attempt to secure the prize was with a chronometer which he named H-1 and built between 1728 and 1735. It was elaborate and massive, weighing 72 pounds; mostly brass, a material easily crafted, robust and elegant, but although it performed admirably on a round trip to Lisbon, it was discounted by the Admiralty as the conditions set by the prize fund required it to be assessed during a passage to the West Indies.

In 1730, during the construction of H-1, Harrison went to the Royal Observatory at Greenwich seeking an audience with Dr Edmund Halley, Astronomer Royal. Halley, unable to help, directed Harrison to George Graham, the acclaimed scientific instrument maker of the day and a fellow of the Royal Society. Graham, suitably impressed by Harrison's drawings made a generous loan to subsidise further work. H-2, which took two years to construct, was even larger but very robust, standing up to much deliberate abuse, but Harrison wished to make further improvements and began a twenty-year labour of love building H-3. It won the Copley Gold Medal in 1749 but not the Longitude Prize.

Finally, H-4 was produced; a 'tiny', 3-pound watch which he presented to the Board in 1760. His son William took it to the West Indies in 1762, during which time it lost only five seconds on the outward journey, but secured only £1500 of the Prize Fund because *all the test conditions had not been met.* A second test in 1764 easily fulfilled the requirements to win the reward. On one return journey to Barbados Harrison's chronometer lost only fifteen seconds but the Admiralty awarded only half the prize stating that they required more proof of its 'general utility at sea', and demanded a full description and two replicas.

Harrison was embittered by this parsimonious attitude and began a long struggle to gain his reward which was finally granted by Parliament in 1773 following intervention by the King.

Watchmakers began to copy Harrison's design and one by Larcum Kendall was used by Cook on his second voyage of discovery in the Pacific. On sighting land following his circumnavigation his calculated position was only 8 miles in error, a remarkable tribute to the pioneering work in this field by Harrison.

John Harrison died in Red Lion Square, London, soon after Cook's return and was buried in Hampstead on 2 April 1776.

Gillray's graphic depiction of the so-called 'filthy practice' of Jenner's smallpox innoculation. (See 14 May.)

1805 To his sister, Mrs Bolton: 'God knows where I may be on July first, and, therefore, I send you a bill for one hundred pounds; and when I get home I hope to be able to keep Tom at College without one farthing's expense to Mr Bolton'. Tom, his nephew, later became the second Earl Nelson.

1805 The German playwright Johann Christoph Friedrich von Schiller (b. 1708), who wrote 'William Tell' and 'An die Freude' (Ode to Joy) later incorporated in Beethoven's Ninth Symphony, dies at Weimar.

9th

1805 To Ball on his brave decision to quit his station: 'My lot is cast, and I am going to the West Indies.' On 23 August the West India merchants unanimously agreed: 'That the prompt determination of Lord Nelson to quit the Mediterranean in search of the French Fleet; his sagacity in judging of, and ascertaining their course, have been very instrumental to the safety of the West India Islands in general'.

1768 Hand spinners and weavers break into the home of James Hargreaves and smash his machinery.

10th

1805 To Viscount Sidmouth, following a long blockade, and resolved to sail for the West Indies in pursuit of Villeneuve: 'I this day steer for the West Indies. My lot seems to have been hard, and the enemy most fortunate; but it may turn – patience and perseverance will do much'.

1778 William Pitt the Elder, 'Earl of Chatham, The Great Commoner', dies at Hayes.

11th

1803 To Sutton: 'The d–d Pilots have run Raisonnable aground: take great care of scant winds and sands'.

1797 The British North Sea fleet begin the mutiny at the Nore in Sandwich.

12th

1799 Nelson is guarding Sicily and Naples but fears the French are at sea. He ponders his options: 'What a state I am in! If I go, I risk Sicily, and what is now safe on the Continent; for we know, from experience, that more depends on opinion than on acts themselves. As I stay, my heart is breaking'.

1764 Harrison's fourth chronometer test in Tartar easily fulfils the accuracy criteria set by the Admiralty.

13th

1805 Relentlessly pursuing Villeneuve's superior force, which on this day has reached Martinique: 'It will not be fancied I am on a party of pleasure running after eighteen sail of the line with ten, and that to the West Indies'.

1796 Edward Jenner successfully introduces the vaccination which leads to the eradication of smallpox in Britain. It is introduced on 21 June 1799.

14th

1803 To George Rose, on the Irish Pension: 'I was with Mr Addington this morning; and as we conversed on the subject of the extension of my Annuity, and also the extraordinary thing of my not receiving the Irish Pension, as was done for Lords St Vincent and Duncan – I have to beg of you, to tell Mr Addington, that it was a mistake'.

1800 The premiere of Mozart's opera 'Le Nozze di Figaro' is interrupted by an attempt by James Hatfield on the life of King George III. There had been a previous attempt on his life earlier that day!

15th

1805 To Emma: 'As it is my desire to take my adopted daughter, Horatia Nelson Thompson, from under the care of Mrs Gibson, and to place her under your guardianship, in order that she may be properly educated and brought up, I have, therefore, most earnestly to entreat that you will undertake this charge'.

1770 The French Dauphin, later Louis XVI, marries Marie Antoinette at Versailles.

16th

1803 To Sutton: 'If I can get my things on board Victory pray lose no time: If you can get twelve good sheep, some hay, and fowls and corn, it will do no harm, for I may yet go out on the Victory'.

1792 A group of New York merchants set up the New York stock exchange on Wall Street.

17th

The coffin presented to Nelson by Captain Ben Hallowell (see 23 May). Nelson was indeed laid to rest in this coffin in 1806.

Endeavour, *on which Cook sailed to observe the transit of Venus (see 25 May) is shown here safely careened at the mouth of the river, later to bear her name, in Queensland, where extensive repairs were carried out.*

1803 To Sir Evan Nepean on being recalled to duty as a result of England's declaration of war against France: 'I have arrived here at one o'clock this afternoon, and have hoisted my Flag on board His Majesty's Ship Victory. Captain Sutton informs me she will be in every respect ready for sea on Friday morning'.

1804 Napoleon is proclaimed Emperor by the French Senate; a plebiscite ratifies his elevation.

1801 Negotiating the release by Russia of British merchant ships: 'I hope it is all right: but seamen are but bad negotiators – for we put the matter to issue in five minutes, what diplomatic forms would be five months doing'.

1798 The French fleet sails from Toulon. Thirty-five thousand men embark: many meet their fate at Aboukir Bay.

1797 To James Simpson, consul of the USA, who seeks an escort for a convoy of twelve ships at Malaga: 'I shall immediately grant the protection you have requested, by sending a Frigate, who shall protect them close to the Coast of Barbary. In thus freely granting the protection of the British Flag to the subjects of the United States, I am sure of fulfilling the wishes of my Sovereign, and I hope of strengthening the harmony between the two nations'.

1768 Dolphin returns to England after a two-year round the world voyage. She failed to find a southern continent, but did discover Tahiti.

1794 Troops under Lieutenant-Colonel Villettes and seamen under Captain Nelson capture Bastia after a thirty-seven day siege. To Lord Hood: 'Sent Captain Young ashore – on the morning of the 21st who soon returned to the Victory with two Officers and two of the Administrative Bodies, settled the Articles of Capitulation which were signed the following morning'.

1780 Elizabeth Fry (d.1845), prison reformer and reliever of the destitute, is born near Norwich.

1799 To Lady Hamilton, knowing of the deteriorating situation at Malta and concerned about its governor. 'Ball has not joined: I am under the greatest apprehension that he has quitted Malta on the first report of the French, and has either been surprised, or taken the route via Messina. Although the first would be unpleasant for England, yet the last would be equally distressing for me. Altogether I am not pleasantly situated'.

1790 The Assembly in Paris passes a law giving itself and the king the right to declare war.

1799 Ben Hallowell presents Nelson with a coffin made from the mainmast of L'Orient: 'Herewith I send you a coffin made of part of L'Orient's Main Mast, that when you are tired of Life you may be buried in one of Your own Trophies – but may that period be far distant, is the sincere wish of your obedient and much obliged servant'.

1798 Believing a French invasion is imminent Irish nationalists engage in the first battle in the Irish Rebellion at Kilcullen. General Dundas is defeated by a large body of insurgent Irish.

1796 To Sir John Jervis: 'I have felt, and do feel, Sir, every degree of sensibility and gratitude for your kind and flattering attention, in directing me to hoist a distinguishing pennant; but useful, is nearly, if not quite at an end, I assure you I shall have no regret in striking it; for it will afford me an opportunity of serving nearer your flag, and of endeavouring to show, by my attention in a subordinate station, that I was not unworthy of commanding'.

1764 James Otis, a Boston lawyer, in his 'No taxation without representation' speech, denounces British taxes.

1804 To Troubridge on whether embarked soldiers should hold authority over captains of ships, if senior: 'Let them once gain the step of being independent of the navy on board ship, and they will soon have the other, and command us...the King himself cannot do away the Act of Parliament. Although my career is nearly run, yet it would embitter my future days and expiring moments, to hear of our Navy being sacrificed to the Army'.

1768 Lieutenant James Cook on Endeavour sails for the Pacific to observe Venus crossing the sun.

PITT THE YOUNGER (1759-1806)

c⸻✦⸻ɔ

With 'The firm hand on the tiller....', William Pitt steers the ship of the Constitution clear of the Rocks of Democracy, topped by a cap of Liberty to port, and the Whirlpool of Arbitrary Power on the starboard tack. Pursued all the while by Charles Fox and fellow Jacobin sympathisers, he makes for the Safe Haven of Public Happiness. By James Gillray, 1793.

When Pitt came down from Cambridge; where he was influenced by Wilberforces' belief in free trade, he quickly adopted the politics of the Whigs and took his seat in parliament opposing the Tory North's administration.

North and the King had blundered into war with the American colonies and, after an unsuccessful Fox-North coalition an election was called. Pitt, at twenty-four was returned and immediately set about economic reform. Although he was popular, diligent and honest he was defeated on almost every major issue including economic reform, India, the slave trade and taxation. Later, his sinking fund would fail, not because it was badly framed but because the quiescent state over a twenty-two year period, was war rather than peace. Pitt's problems did not stop there: he brought Hastings to trial, more to deflect parliamentary scrutiny from himself than to persecute the Governor of India, and brought outrage over the Regency Bill.

There was, however, one subject which united the country. Pitt had received a report that the navy was in a bad way; not a single ship fit for service without repair, while the dockyards were hotbeds of inefficiency and corruption. His wisdom was in appointing Admiral Howe as First Lord of the Admiralty, who, in five years from 1783, built the fleet that was later to make heroes of many British admirals.

During his early tenure in office Pitt was able to achieve a settlement for India which lasted until the mutiny of 1857, his Canada act lasted until the Rebellion of 1839 and his despatch of the First Fleet to Australia can be considered the most fortunate of colonial adventures. In short he had given England ten years of peace, but within a year of his speech in 1792 prophesying fifteen years of peace for Britain, he took the country into one of the longest wars in modern history declaring: 'England will never consent that France shall arrogate the power of annulling at her pleasure, and under the pretended natural right, of which she makes herself the only judge, the political system of Europe, established by solemn treaties and guaranteed by the consent of all the powers.'

The war began badly for Pitt, the only success being Howe's Glorious First of June. Elsewhere allies were deserting Britain, who was forced to withdraw from the Mediterranean in 1797. By now Bonaparte was being proclaimed a brilliant general with virtually the whole of Europe capitulating to him. Again naval success, this time at St Vincent relieved the gloom. It was followed by mutinies and again by a glorious victory at Camperdown. Bonaparte turned to Egypt but again the navy defeated his fleet at Aboukir Bay forcing him to abandon his dream of a French Mediterranean. Copenhagen was Pitt's next problem, The cannons of Hyde Parker and Nelson spoke for him but shortly afterwards Pitt resigned, not because of the wars but through disagreement with the King on the Irish Catholic problem. He was out of office for three years. Addington agreed terms at Amiens but when that failed times were too serious for Pitt to languish in retirement. As he returned to office Napoleon proclaimed himself Emperor, an invasion was feared, and Lord St Vincent was moved to utter the most famous naval phrase of the wars: 'I do not say, my Lords, that the French cannot come. I only say, they cannot come by sea.'

Following the success at Trafalgar, Pitt thought the matter of Europe was settled. 'England has saved herself by her exertions; and will, as I trust, save Europe by her example.' But Napoleon annihilated the armies of Austria and Russia at Austerlitz, Pitt, on hearing the news offered his famous phrase: 'Roll up the map, it will not be wanted these ten years.'

The blow was too much for him. His last words were: 'My country, how I leave my country.'

26th

1798 The King of Sardinia, fearing French reprisals, refuses entry into St Peters by Nelson's storm-battered ships. Nelson enters and carries out reparations: 'When I reflect that my most gracious Sovereign is the oldest (I believe), and certainly the most faithful, ally which His Majesty of Sardinia ever had, I could feel the sorrow which it must have been to His Majesty to have given such an order and for your Excellency, who has to direct its execution'.

1790 The Assembly force Louis XVI to relinquish all assets of the Crown to the nation. The crown jewels are stolen on 17 September 1792.

27th

1797 A prophetic letter to Davison, marked Theseus: 'changed from Captain this day. We are at anchor looking at the Dons, who say they will come out on the 29th or 1st of June and settle our business. They expect seven Ships of the French from Toulon, and four Spanish Ships of the Line from Carthegena, which will make their force at least forty, perhaps forty-five Sail of the Line. We are twenty-two'.

1792 The Assembly in Paris orders the deportation of all priests who refuse to swear allegiance to the Church's civil constitution. This day is 'Oak Apple' day in England, 'A day of joy by the Church and King people, who to testify to their loyalty put up oak branches at their doors.'

29th

1799 Off Trapani to Jervis: 'Troubridge and Hallowell are now with me, and we wish we could fly for the honour of battle to your aid: this must be the last Campaign, for in Italy at this moment, except those in Mantua and Ancona, I am confident there is not a Frenchman; they are, thank God, going to the Devil as fast as we can wish. Peace, peace, blessed peace we shall now have, I am sure of it'.

1759 William Pitt the Younger is born at Hayes.

28th

1804 To Marsden at the Admiralty: 'You will please acquaint Admiralty, that Victory, on her passage to the Mediterranean, captured the Ambuscade French Frigate, manned her, and directed her to Gibraltar. On her way there, she fell in with and captured the Marie Thèrese, a French Merchantman, and carried her with her to that place. On arrival the Revolutionaire and Bittern laid a claim as joint captors'. A dispute on prize entitlement follows.

1765 Patrick Henry protests against the Stamp Act in the House of Burgesses. It is repealed by the British Government on 18 March 1766.

30th

1796 Agamemnon, Gulf of Genoa, to Jervis: 'Mr Trevor seems to think a Spanish war is almost unavoidable, and that the French, after all their protestations, will take possession of Leghorn. My mind is clear, if they have force to penetrate further into Italy, they will possess themselves of Leghorn'.

1795 Parliament makes a large contribution to the debts of the bankrupt Prince of Wales following his marriage to Princess Carolina of Brunswick.

31st

1798 To the Earl of St Vincent reporting on the damage suffered by Vanguard: 'That the accidents which have happened to the Vanguard were just punishment for my consummate vanity, I most humbly acknowledge, and kiss the rod which chastised me. I hope it has made me a better officer, as I hope it has made me a better man'.

1792 The Prince of Wales makes his maiden speech to the House of Lords nine years after taking his seat. His subject is seditious publications.

Tinkers, Poets, Whores and Scoundrels

THE ITALIAN CONNECTION

Tom Pocock

Lady Hamilton welcomes the victors of the Battle of the Nile into the port of Naples on 22 September 1798.

I n the mythology of the Mediterranean, Italy and Sicily can be seen as the Siren Rocks to an eighteenth-century Ulysses, Horatio Nelson. It was not just that Emma Hamilton was herself his siren, but that the siren song of all things Italian beguiled him and conjured up the least admirable qualities in his complex character which threatened the wreck of all his promise.

Captain Nelson, as he then was, first appeared off Naples in 1793 on a mission from the commander-in-chief, Admiral Lord Hood, to persuade King Ferdinand IV of the Two Sicilies – that is, Southern Italy and Sicily – to send troops to support the British, Spanish and royalist French in the defence of Toulon against the armies of Revolutionary France.

Never had the young man from Norfolk seen such a city. Famous for its beauty, wealth and culture throughout Europe, Naples lay languorously around the bay of the same name beneath the black, volcanic heights of Versuvius. Going ashore, he was taken to the Palazzo Reale, an even grander version of Holkham Hall in Norfolk, which was the most imposing mansion he had yet seen and was itself modelled in the style of the Italian architect Palladio.

Received by the King himself, Nelson was hugely flattered, for he revered royalty with a superstitious fervour. This stemmed, perhaps, from a 'religious experience' he had undergone when recovering from malaria as a midshipman. Plunged into depression over his imagined lack of professional patronage, he had suddenly felt a surge of optimism at the thought that his King was his patron. In his unsophisticated eyes, all royalty was touched by the divine.

There he also met the British ambassador, the lively-minded, intelligent connoisseur, Sir William Hamilton, and his beautiful wife, Emma. Returning to sea, his mission successfully accomplished, he had been left with an indelible image of exotic and, indeed, erotic, splendour.

There is no evidence that Nelson had yet fallen in love with Lady Hamilton, although it does seem in the light of letters they exchanged that there was an electric charge of mutual attraction. But this did not prevent Nelson, while visiting Leghorn the following year from having an affair with an opera singer, Adelaide Correglia. This was noted with distaste by his friend Captain Thomas Fremantle, who noted: 'He makes himself ridiculous with that woman.' Nelson hinted, rather disingenuously, that his involvement was a form of intelligence gathering but it was more than that because, some months later, he was writing to the British agent in that port, asking him to pay her rent on his behalf.

Nelson's return to Naples in 1798 as the victor of the Battle of the Nile, when Emma fell, swooning into his one remaining arm, is one of the most theatrical scenes in history, combining the comic with the heroic. Emma wafted him ashore to the luxury of the Palazzo Sessa, her husband's embassy, and there he quickly fell in love with her. In a letter to Lord St Vincent, he confessed, 'I am writing opposite Lady Hamilton, therefore you will not be surprised at the glorious jumble of this letter.'

Lady Hamilton knew just how to manage Nelson, constantly reassuring him of his immortal fame. For his fortieth birthday, soon after his arrival, she invited eighty guests to dinner, eight hundred to supper and nearly two thousand to a ball at which Emma herself sang a hymn to Nelson to the tune of the National Anthem. He was an insecure man, partly because of his mixed social background – a wife related to the Norfolk aristocracy but he himself coming from a relatively poor, middle-class family – and partly because, although he had become a friend of King George's son, the Duke of Clarence, the King himself was said to have taken a dislike to him, this perhaps prompting his over-reverence towards King Ferdinand and his queen.

The Neapolitan sovereign and his consort were a grotesque couple; proud, mercurial, comic, cruel, generous, libidinous and hysterical in turn; he, absorbed in blood-sports on an Ancient Roman scale; she, alternately wildly temperamental and devout, sometimes 'screeching like an eagle' with rage and sometimes writing prayers on scraps of paper and eating them, or stuffing them into her stays, as a means of transmitting them to the Almighty.

The Queen had greeted the news of the victory with hysteria. As Lady Hamilton said: 'She fainted, cried, kissed and embraced every person near her, exclaiming, "Ho, brave Nelson... Oh, Nelson, Nelson, what do we not owe you! Oh, Victor, saviour of Italy. Oh, that my swollen heart could now tell him personally what we owe to him!"' She now had the chance to put these sentiments into practice and soon he was a welcome guest at the Palazzo Reale.

Nelson was aware that the monarch was surrounded by a corrupt court. It was, he wrote, 'a country of fiddlers and poets, whores and scoundrels', and he further noted: 'Naples is a dangerous place.' It was; not only to himself and his marriage but to the Allied cause because, amongst the riffraff he so despised, were liberal idealists and intellectuals who hated their boorish King and believed that the future lay in republicanism as proclamated by the French Revolution; and the French army was already established south of Rome.

Later that year Nelson was one of those who rashly urged the King to lead his army against the French. In the event, the Neapolitans took Rome but as soon as the French bothered to counterattack, they swept all before them. As the King fled in panic to Naples, its citizens began to rebel. But this was not a rising of an oppressed working class, because amongst this section of the population the King was surprisingly popular. He was seen as a simple hard drinking, hard swearing Jack-the-lad, who went to sea with the fishermen and sold his catch alongside them in the markets. This was essentially a middle-class rebellion, led by the liberal intelligencia, who despised the King and dreamed of an idealised republic.

With the French at the gates and insurgency within, the royal family feared for their lives and did not look for a saviour in vain. In the melodramatic *coup de main*, Nelson landed from his squadron at night, led his men with drawn cutlasses into the Palazzo Reale and through secret passages to the royal apartments, from which they spirited the royal party down to the waterside and by boat to the waiting ships. It was only safety of a sort, however, because the squadron then sailed to Palermo through the worst Mediterranean storm Nelson had ever known, an infant prince dying of seasickness and exhaustion in Emma's arms.

At Palermo, the King was content with his hunt-

Silhouette of Nelson's father, the Reverend Edmund Nelson. Nelson's insecurity may have stemmed from his mixed social background: related to aristocracy through marriage, yet himself the son of a comparatively poor parson.

The Victor of the Nile: a portrait of Horatio Nelson done at Palermo by an unknown artist.

ing and shooting and even Nelson seems to have been temporarily swallowed by the louche life into which Emma led him. Curiously, the Admiral was less genteel than his simple sailors: when Hamilton told a party of them that they had saved the Kingdom of the Two Sicilies, they just replied, 'Very glad of it, sir, very glad of it'. And when the King held out a hand for Nelson's servant Tom Allen to kiss, the robust Norfolkman shook it firmly and said, 'How d'ye do, Mr King.' Nelson, on the other hand, while aware of the royal shortcomings, allowed himself to be swept along by his loved one in their train. He sat beside Emma at the card table until late into the night, drinking champagne until, as he put it, 'My health is such that, without a great alteration, I venture to say a very short space of time will send me to that bourne from whence none return.'

The months following the Battle of the Nile saw an apparent change in Nelson's character and the upright parson's son became hard to recognise. He was beginning his affair with Lady Hamilton and to this flouting of the moral standards he was about to add uncharacteristic cruelty. It has been suggested that the blow on the forehead he suffered in the action at Aboukir Bay may have damaged the frontal lobes of his brain with consequent, and, perhaps, temporary, brain damage leading to the loosening of inhibitions and impaired judgement. Both were to be displayed in two tragedies: one on a tiny scale involving just two individuals, himself and his wife; the other one on a grand scale, involving thousands.

From the moment his naval career had faltered with his retirement on half pay to Norfolk with his new wife in 1787, his marriage had been slowly disintegrating. The couple were ill-suited and certainly Fanny Nelson had no idea of how to cope with her volatile, vain, brave, and insecure but brilliant husband. Relations improved when she nursed him after the loss of his arm at Tenerife in 1797, but, when he returned to the Mediterranean in the following year, the ties were not strong enough to withstand a long separation, particularly when Emma Hamilton had exactly the degree of enthusiasm, sexuality, materialism and humour to enchant him. As the affair with Adelaide Correglia had demonstrated, Nelson had followed the custom of leaving his marriage vows at Gibraltar yet he remained a parson's son and the guilt was there, however deeply sublimated, or ratio-

nalised. His attempt at the latter prompted him to find Fanny not only irritating in her inefficiency over packing his gear for forwarding, but in fussing over the risks he had to take and, indeed, of being the mother of his stepson Josiah, with whom he had fallen out over his attentions to their hostess in Naples. Unwilling to admit his own guilt, it was easier to blame her for the failure of their marriage.

The other example of this uncharacteristic behaviour was about to unfurl in the spectacularly tranquil setting of the Bay of Naples. Just as King Ferdinand's vainglorious march on Rome, which Nelson had so rashly encouraged, was a total disaster, so his counteroffensive after the loss of his capital was a triumph. While remaining in Palermo himself, the King had assigned the task of re-conquest to a forceful and wily prelate, Cardinal Ruffo, who was popular among his subjects in southern Italy, able to rouse both monarchists and the religious and also to appeal to those who joined his banner for the prospect of plundering Naples. So successful was Ruffo, that when Nelson's squadron anchored in the Bay of Naples on 24 June 1799, the city seemed to have fallen.

The rebels, abandoned by the French army, had shut themselves into three great castles of Naples – two on the waterfront and one on the hill above the city – but agreed to surrender under a general amnesty and the option to be evacuated to France. Ruffo had signed these terms and was awaiting the arrival of the British, followed, at a safe distance, by the King. But Nelson was in no mood to show mercy towards those he saw as traitors, and allies of the hated French. Declaring that the Cardinal had no authority to negotiate on behalf of the monarch, he tore up the truce and handed over the helpless rebels and their families to the mercy of the King's judges and executioners.

What followed is remembered as a stain on Britain's and Nelson's reputation for decency and justice. The royal courts, encouraged by the King and Queen, began passing sentences of death, or savage imprisonment, on almost all those connected with the foundation of what they had called the Parthenopean, or Vesuvian, Republic: not only political agitators, but the intellectual idealists and writers, both men and women, who had envisaged a new dawn in the overthrow of the Bourbon monarchy.

Emma Hamilton, who had accompanied the Queen to Naples, also encouraged this vengeance, although Sir William, aghast at finding some of his most intelligent friends amongst the condemned, was appalled. Nelson himself has been blamed for handing over the republicans' senior naval officer, Prince Carraciolo, to a royalist court martial which ordered him to be hanged immediately. This brutal behaviour needs to, of course, be seen in context.

Hindsight always distorts the climate in which wartime decisions are taken. Nelson, with his memories of the atrocities committed by the vengeful revolutionaries after the fall of Toulon, hated the French and all who offered them support. King Ferdinand was an invaluable ally, whom he had narrowly saved from extinction and was now restoring to him his capital, one of the prime naval and mercantile bases of the Mediterranean. Add to this his need to be seen by his mistress, Emma Hamilton, as the masterful saviour of Italy and to gain yet more glory in the eyes of his own countrymen. Add to that the state of his health: the late nights; the unaccustomed rich and liverish food and the alcohol, which had been his diet in Palermo; also, perhaps, the effects of the blow to the head in Aboukir Bay. All this seemed to distort his judgement; but, even while he was handing over the flower of the Neapolitan intelligentsia to the royal hangman, the familiar, humane admiral reprieved one of his own men under sentence of death.

This, of course, was the period when Nelson began disregarding instructions from his superiors. Three times during that July, he ignored orders from Admiral Lord Keith, the commander-in-chief in the Mediterranean, to join him in Minorca, which was thought to be in danger of attack, concluding: 'I have no scruple in deciding that it is better to save the Kingdom of Naples and risk Minorca...'.

Finally Lord Spencer, the First Lord of the Admiralty, recalled Nelson to London. Tactfully putting down the admiral's 'inactivity' to his health, Lord Spencer wrote memorably: 'You will be more likely to recover your health and strength in England than in an inactive situation at a foreign court, however pleasing the respect and gratitude shown to you for your services may be.' So, taking their time, Nelson and the Hamiltons made their slow return via the friendly courts of Europe, arriving in London at the end of 1800 for the inevitable breakup with his wife, and the beginning of a new chapter in his life.

When he returned to Italian waters during the long watch on the French fleet at Toulon, which led to the final campaign of Trafalgar, the King and Queen were still there but the Hamiltons, of course, were not. On first re-entering the Bay, he wrote to Emma: 'Close to Capri, the view of Vasuvios calls so many circumstances to mind that it almost overpowers my feelings', and he mused on, 'dear Naples, if it is what it was.' But, of course it was not.

Thereafter, Nelson seems to have regained the humanity and sense of purpose that had faltered at Naples and Palermo, even if this involved continued self-dilution over his behaviour towards is wife. All are agreed that his genius as a leader touched sublime heights as the climax was approaching off Cape Trafalgar and that Nelson's greatness was thereafter fixed in both British history and mythology. But his Italian years – most notably the two years following the Battle of the Nile – remained an integral part of the legend. He was seduced by Italy and those he met there. His weaknesses displayed at Naples and Sicily throw into sharper relief the strengths he showed elsewhere. From that time he could be seen by his fellow countrymen as both Superman and Everyman, the vulnerable, fallible but ultimately triumphant hero.

Tom Pocock is the author of fifteen books, mostly historical biographies. Five are about Nelson and his time – his *Horatio Nelson* was runner-up for the Whitbread Biography Prize of 1987 – and he has been described in the *Daily Telegraph* as 'our greatest authority on the Admiral'. He has also written Nelson's biographical entry for the *Encyclopaedia Britannica* and has given lectures about him at the National Maritime Museum.

Born in 1925 into an old naval family with roots in Nelson's Norfolk, he was a Fleet Street journalist for many years and reported on nine wars from the final year of the Second World War to Northern Ireland. He is married, has two daughters and lives in London.

Lady Emma Hamilton. Amidst the surroundings of an extravagant Neapolitan court, Nelson was entirely seduced by her voluptuous charms.

THE GLORIOUS FIRST OF JUNE

France needed grain. It was being supplied by the Americans in convoys protected by the Brest fleet under Rear-Admiral Villaret-Joyeuse, an able but relatively junior officer whose promotion had been accelerated by the guillotine. His flag was in *Montagne*, ex *Cote d'Or*, considered the finest man-of-war afloat.

Admiral 'Black Dick' Howe aboard *Queen Charlotte* commanded the British fleet, notably equal in size to the French fleet, though slightly under-gunned but with more men. The two admirals' orders were also similar: protect home trade, disrupt that of the enemy and destroy the enemy fleet.

Black Dick never smiled unless he was engaged with the enemy. The French, too, relished the prospect of an encounter and perhaps some prizes. They had well found ships, trained men and were in confident mood following their army's success at Valmy and Jemappes. This was the scenario to the west of Ushant in late May 1794 as an American grain convoy approached France.

On 28 May the fleets met, but a general action did not develop. Again on the 29th, exchanges were made but nothing was decided. During the next two days no shots were fired while both fleets manoeu-vred in search of an advantage. None had been achieved in the foggy conditions until shortly before sunset when they were a mere 5 miles apart. Now, in failing light, Howe declined a battle before morning.

At 8.12am on 1 June, *Queen Charlotte* signalled each ship to steer for and independently engage the ship opposite her. Howe's plan was to bear down on the enemy, break its line in as many places as possible and secure the leeward position, thus preventing the enemy fleeing downwind. Such a tactic carried the initial penalty of exposing Howe's ships to greater enemy fire during the approach. In passing through the line, however, he could rake along their decks firing each cannon in sequence and, once the lee position had been obtained, he could dictate the engagement.

Battle was joined at 9.24am after which time the British inexorably gained the upper hand. By the outcome, and over the five days, they suffered 290 killed against 3000 Frenchmen; they had captured six ships and severely disabled five more – a truly great sea battle and highly commendable in naval terms. But great as it was it could have been better. Eleven ships captured would indeed have ranked against Nelson's endeavours at the Nile or Trafalgar and it is worth wondering what the outcome would have been if he had been the commander-in-chief. Would he have allowed the disabled ships to escape and more significantly, would he have prevented the convoy of grain from reaching France.

Howe on board the Queen Charlotte as Captain Neville of the Queen's Regiment is led away mortally wounded. The contemporary facetious toast was: 'May the French ever know <u>Howe</u> to be master of the sea.'

1784 Boreas, experiencing difficulty getting to her anchorage, solicits help from Resource. From her log: 'At noon out boats and towed the Ship. Shortened sail. Made the signal with a gun for assistance. Came on board a boat from the Resource. At 4pm came to in Funchal Roads'.

1794 *The Glorious First of June. Lord Howe, Queen Charlotte, defeats the Brest fleet under Rear-Admiral Villaret-Joyeuse, Montagne, off Ushant in the first truly oceanic battle.*

1st

1788 To Prince William, on cruising with the home squadron: 'The actions of all officers, however brilliant, are wonderfully obscured by serving at a distance, for the capture of a privateer makes more noise taken in the Channel, than a frigate or even ship of the line, afar off'.

1780 *The Lord George Gordon 'No Popery' riots, against the Roman Catholics Relief Act of 1778, break out in London.*

2nd

1795 By taking a French prize, Nelson obtains valuable intelligence. To Jervis: 'I have an account of the exact force of the Enemy the 6th February, sent to General Buonaparte: it consists, including the garrisons of Toulon and the whole Coast, 65,000 men. [it] is not as great as I believed; and if the report is true, of the peasantry taking arms, it yet gives me hopes that the Army of the Enemy may repent their advance into Italy'.

1769 *The transit of Venus, which Endeavour set sail to observe on 26 August 1768, occurs. It is a phenomenon which only happens once every hundred years.*

3rd

1805 To Marsden, from Carlisle Bay, Barbados: 'There is not a doubt in any of the admirals' minds, but that Tobago and Trinidada are the Enemy's objects'. Prior to pursuit he embarks Sir William Myers and 2000 troops.

1805 *The Horse Guards at Buckingham Palace troop the colour for the first time.*

4th

1796 To Jervis after taking a vessel with Austrian troops on board: 'they are, Sir, as fine healthy-looking men as I ever saw, the oldest of one hundred and fifty-two is thirty-four years of age. I think, till we have an opportunity of sending them to General Beaulieu, they would add strength to our Ships, five Ships, thirty each'.

1779 *The explorer Alexander Von Humboldt sails from Spain for South America on an expedition to open up Venezuela, Colombia and Peru.*

5th

1804 To Emma. Victory's log had recorded a salute at Toulon for the declaration of Emperor: 'What a capricious Nation those French must be! However, I think, it must, in any way, be advantageous to England. There ends, for a century, all Republics!'

1797 *Napoleon founds the Ligurian Republic in Genoa which is annexed to France. It is ratified by the constitutional assembly on 10 June.*

6th

1779 To Locker, from Badger, off St Anne's. The Glasgow, Captain Thomas Lloyd, was lost by fire when a cask of rum ignited: 'I suppose before this you have heard of the fate of the poor Glasgow. Indeed it was a shocking sight. She anchored at half-past three, and at six was in flames, owing to the steward attempting to steal rum out of the after-hold'.

1778 *George Bryan Brummell (d. 1840), better known as Beau Brummell, leader of fashion, is born in London. Following a brief spell in the army, he inherited a fortune. His fashion tast led him to be known as the arbiter of elegance. He died in the pauper lunatic asylum in Caen.*

7th

GEORGE LOUIS STEPHENSON
(1781-1848)

George Stephenson, father of the steam railway, was born at Wylam near Newcastle in 1781. He became assistant to his father at Dewley colliery where he developed an interest in clocks which he repaired in his spare time. He studied James Watt and Newcomen (his father operated a Newcomen steam pump), and went on to become an enginewright at Killingworth Mine in 1812, where he became known as the 'engine doctor'. The following year he achieved sponsorship to build a steam locomotive, *Blücher* which made its successful trial run on 25 July 1814. In 1815 he patented a steam blast which gave more efficient draft to boilers and invented a safety lamp, bringing him into controversy with Sir Humphry Davy regarding originality. His main work was devoted to steam railways. His first public railway opened in 1825 and ran from Stockton to Darlington. He improved on Blenkinsop's third rail ratchet system and by 1829 had achieved 36 miles per hour with *Rocket*. Stephenson became President of the Institute of Engineers in 1847 and died at Tapton House near Chesterfield on 12 August 1848, leaving his son Robert, by his first wife, to continue his engineering work.

JOHN CONSTABLE (1776-1837)

John Constable was born at East Bergholt in Suffolk. His father was a miller, owning both water and wind mills which were to feature so prominently in his son's works. Mr Constable wanted his son to enter the church but the boy had no aptitude for bookwork, nor any desire to follow his father as a miller. When John was twenty-three his father relented and allowed him to go to London to study at the Royal Academy. His first ambition was as a portrait painter but he in fact was destined to become the founder of the 'School of Faithful Landscape'.

Captain Bligh and his company reach Timor after their extraordinary voyage in Bounty's *longboat. (See 12 June.)*

⚓ 1795 ⚓ Lord Hood is ordered by the Admiralty to strike his flag on 2 May 1795. 'Then came accounts of Lord Hood's resignation. Oh, miserable Board of Admiralty! They have forced the first officer in our service away from his command. The late Board may have lost a few merchant vessels by their neglect; this Board has risked a whole fleet of men-of-war'.

⚓ 1781 ⚓ *George Louis Stephenson, builder of the Rocket steam engine, is born at Wylam on Tyne.*

⚓ 1801 ⚓ On being asked by merchant businessman Hercules Ross to be godfather to his son: 'The blessing of peace, must first shed its benign rays over us, and under the present Ruler of France I see but little prospect of that happy event. Buonaparte's power exists by war, and as France must in time be tired of it, I think his life will be cut short'.

⚓ 1798 ⚓ *Napoleon requests permission to enter Malta, is refused by the Knights of St John, but forces an entry.*

⚓ 1805 ⚓ To Simon Taylor in Jamaica: 'I have been, and shall die, a firm friend to our present Colonial system. I was bred, as you know, in the good old school, and taught to appreciate the value of our West India possessions; and neither in the field, nor in the senate, shall their just rights be infringed, whilst I have an arm to fight in their defence, or a tongue to launch my voice'.

⚓ 1768 ⚓ *British customs officers seize the sloop Liberty at Boston; four years later to the day, American Patriots attack and destroy the British Customs sloop Gaspee.*

⚓ 1798 ⚓ To Lord St Vincent, acknowledging his orders to pursue the Toulon Fleet: 'You may be assured that I will fight them the moment I can reach their fleet, be they at anchor, or under sail'.

⚓ 1776 ⚓ *The English artist John Constable is born.*

⚓ 1794 ⚓ Nelson is wounded in the right eye during the siege of Calvi and can only determine darkness from light. From Journal C: 'At daylight on the 12th, the Enemy opened fire from the town and San Francesco, which, in an extraordinary manner, seldom missed our battery; and at seven o'clock, I was much bruised in the face and eyes by sand from works struck by the shot'.

⚓ 1789 ⚓ *Captain Bligh reaches Timor after navigating 3600 miles of open ocean in Bounty's longboat.*

⚓ 1796 ⚓ To Fanny on leaving the worn out Agamemnon and joining Captain: 'You will see, my dear Fanny, by the date of this letter, that I have at last left poor old Agamemnon. Whether it is right or wrong, time must determine'.

⚓ 1795 ⚓ *Thomas Arnold (d.1842), educationalist, is born at Cowes. He became headmaster of Rugby School.*

⚓ 1803 ⚓ To His Highness the Capitan Pacha: 'The restless ambition of the Person who, for the misfortune of mankind, still rules in the Government in France, has called me forth from my repose once more to arms. I trust that the Ottoman Empire will be allowed to remain tranquil, and not again be unjustly invaded; but should any attempt be made by the French to carry such an object into execution, I am instructed to use every means to prevent it'.

⚓ 1800 ⚓ *Battle of Marengo. Napoleon narrowly but brilliantly defeats Baron von Meles of Austria and regains Northern Italy.*

8th

9th

10th

11th

12th

13th

14th

The race for India began when Vasco da Gama discovered an ocean route around the Cape of Good Hope in 1498. Portugal, Holland and France vied for trade. Britain, through the English East India Company, joined the fray in 1600 and soon established trading posts at Madras, Bombay and Fort William (now Calcutta).

In 1707, following the death of Emperor Aurungzebe the Mughal Empire collapsed. Five Hindu princes, forming the Maharatta Confederacy began dealing in war and plunder and soon the whole of India succumbed to change, revolution and violence. The stabilising influence came from Europe through its commitment to trade.

France successfully exploited native quarrels, bringing the Carnatic and the Deccan under their influence but threatened to extinguish British interest in 1744 when war broke out between the two nations – Joseph François Dupleix, as governor-general, taking Madras. (To his chagrin it was handed back to the British in exchange for Louisbourg at the Treaty of Aix-la-Chapelle.) Robert Clive began the retaliation. He stormed and successfully held Arcat in 1751 and brought about a change of mood. His victory at Plassey in 1757 began the overthrow of the French, whose fate was determined at the Treaty of Paris. On Clive's suggestion, a clause was inserted forbidding the French to keep armed forces in India. Thus, the foundations for huge expansion by the East India Company were laid.

Periodically the Nawabs rose, resenting the English trading company's power without responsibility, neglect of the native population and unfettered corruption. Lord North recognised that the trading company had outgrown its capacity – or even desire to govern, and framed the Regulating Act which introduced a new style of administration. Warren Hastings became governor-general and succeeded in keeping the equilibrium, despite the exertions of Hyder Ali, one of many of the new princes who wished to be rid of the shackles of European control. Hastings prevented India going the way of the American colonies, but the outbreak of the Maritime Wars with France (1778-83) and surrender of Burgoyne brought new pressures, and Admiral Suffren to the bay of Bengal. Suffren, one of the most aggressive of French admirals was quick to enlist the support of Hyder Ali, once again jeopardising British existence on the sub continent.

With parliamentary difficulties compounded by the madness of King George, a British political solution seemed remote but the world scale importance of India was recognised by both Nelson and Napoleon. Nelson recognised that protection of the burgeoning imperial expansion in trade stretched naval resources to breaking point, but he never lost sight of its value throughout his blockading years in the Mediterranean. Napoleon and the revolutionaries recognised that a thinly spread British navy would undoubtedly leave holes for exploitation, be they in the West Indies, Mediterranean, English Channel or further afield. He made every effort to stir up the natives and it fell upon the Marquis Wellesley to suppress them and effect sweeping annexations to vastly expand British India.

Defeat of Hyder Ali by Sir Eyre Coote.

1797 In a letter to Fanny soon after the Nore Mutiny: 'A few nights ago a paper was dropped on the quarterdeck, of which this is a copy: "Success attend Admiral Nelson! God bless Captain Miller! We thank them for the officers they have placed over us. We are happy and comfortable, and will shed every drop of blood in our veins to support them, and the name of Theseus shall be immortalised as high as the Captain's ship's company".'

1805 *In Piccadilly the first shop to be lighted by gas, an invention by William Murdoch, is reported in the 'Morning Post' as a wonderful event.*

1805 Nelson surmises Gravina and Villeneuve have gone east. He tells his captains: 'If we meet them, we shall find them not less than eighteen, I rather think twenty, sail of the line, and therefore do not be surprised if I should not fall on them immediately; we won't part without a battle'.

1779 *Spain, taking advantage of the British defeat at Saratoga, follows France in declaring war on Britain, and besieges Gibraltar. The Dutch follow suit in declaring war on Britain in 1780.*

1798 To Sir William Hamilton from the Bay of Naples, searching for the French Fleet but concerned at the advance of the French Army: 'If the Enemy have Malta, it is only as a safe harbour for their Fleet, and Sicily will fall the moment the King's Fleet withdraw from the coast of Sicily: therefore we must have the free use of Sicily, to enable us to starve the French in Malta'.

The Battle of Bunker Hill.

1775 *The Battle of Bunker Hill near Boston is fought between Loyalists and Patriots. The Loyalists win but suffer 1150 casualties.*

1795 Off Minorca. 'The French say they will fight us again, provided we are not more than two or three ships superior; I can hardly believe they are such fools; pray God they may'.

1784 *George III creates New Brunswick, a new province in Canada, to take loyalist British settlers from the US.*

1799 From Sir John Acton to Sir William Hamilton following Nelson's request to go into Naples 'to bring affairs in that city to a happy conclusion': 'I beg of you my dear Sir, to present their Majesties' most sensible gratitude for this repeated comforting declaration. All their trust is in Lord Nelson certainly, and the safety of both Kingdoms'.

1769 *Hyder Ali of Mysore compels the British at Madras to sign a treaty of mutual assistance.*

1796 To his brother: 'Opportunities have been frequently offered me, and I have never lost one of distinguishing myself, not only as a gallant man, but as having a head; for, of the numerous plans I have laid, not one has failed, nor of opinions given, has one been in the event wrong. It is this latter which has perhaps established my character more than the others'.

1789 *The Tennis Court Oath signals the beginning of the French Revolution. Riots follow rumours that the nobility intend to collect the nation's grain and ship it abroad. Jaques Necker had ordered its requisition for fair distribution.*

15th
16th
17th
18th
19th
20th

Robert Clive was born on 29 September 1725. He first went to India as a clerk for the British East India Company in 1743 and four years later took a commission in the Company's army. He fought against Joseph François Dupleix during the capture of Arcot in 1751 and within two years had earned an appointment as lieutenant governor of Fort St David, near Madras. He was sent to retake Calcutta following its fall to the newab of Bengal. Further success at Plassey led to his becoming the British governor until his return to England in 1760; two years later he was made Baron Clive of Plassey.

Clive returned to India as governor of Bengal in 1765 and applied himself to the task of curbing financial corruption – from which, incidentally, he had benefited in previous years. His next return to England saw the same charges levelled against him. His trial lasted for six years until finally he was acquitted. But by this time he had become an opium addict, and this, together with the strain of his trial, led him to commit suicide on 22 November 1774.

Engrav'd from the Original Picture painted by Callet Painter to the late King

LOUIS XVI

Born Aug.ᵗ 23 1754, and, beheaded Jan.ʸ 21, 1793.

Portrait of King Louis XVI (see 25 June).

Robert Clive. (See 23 June.)

1802 Nelson refuses an invitation to the City of London because the usual appreciation has been refused to those who fought under him at Copenhagen: 'I should feel much mortified when I reflected on the noble support I that day received, at any honour which could separate me from them, for I am bold to say, that they deserve every honour and favour which a grateful country can bestow'.

1798 General Gerrard Lake defeats Irish rebels at Vinegar Hill, enters Wexford and so ends the Irish rebellion.

1796 To the French Minister at Genoa: 'Generous nations are above rendering any other damage to individuals than such as the known Laws of War prescribe. In a vessel lately taken by my squadron was found an imperial full of clothes belonging to a general officer of artillery. I therefore send you the clothes as taken and some papers which may be useful to the officer, and have to request you will have the goodness to forward them'.

1772 The James Somerset case is heard. The Lord Chief Justice ruled: 'as soon as any slave sets foot in England he becomes free.' There were more than 10,000 slaves in England at this time.

1796 Nelson tells Jervis that the King of Sardinia and France has signed a treaty and General Beaulieu and the peasants have killed 15,000 Frenchmen: 'Pray God it be true'.

1757 Lord Clive defeats the Bengalese at Plassey, the battle secures India for the British Empire.

1790 Exasperated at being on the beach: 'My not being appointed to a ship is so very mortifying, that I cannot find words to express what I feel on the occasion.' Later he writes to the Admiralty: 'If your Lordships should be pleased to appoint me to a cockle boat I shall feel grateful'.

1763 Josephine, who marries Napoleon in 1796 and is crowned Empress in 1804, is born in Martinique.

1803 Nelson returns from Malta in Amphion to Cpris in the Bay of Naples and awaits the arrival of Maidstone with news of the French advances. To Hugh Elliot: 'If the French assemble a greater number of Troops than usual at Brindisi, Otranto and Tarento, then I think not a moment should be lost to secure Sicily'.

1791 Louis XVI, Marie Antionette and their children are apprehended at Varennes and returned to Paris by National Guardsmen. The King's powers are temporarily suspended by the Assembly.

1800 On leaving Foudroyant his barge crew write to Nelson: 'It is with extreme grief that we find you are about to leave us. We have been along with you in every engagement Your Lordship has been in, both by Sea and Land; and most humbly beg of your Lordship to permit us to go to England, as your Boat's crew, in any Ship or Vessel, or in any way that may seem most pleasing to Your Lordship'.

1794 Within a month of Howe's great victory, the French, in the Battle of Fleurus, defeat a British fleet in the English Channel. They force the Duke of Coburg to withdraw from Belgium.

1794 From Corsica on the subject of prize money: 'I hope those who are to get so much money will make proper use of it. Had I attended less than I have done to the service of my country, I might have made some too: however, I trust my name will stand on record when the money-makers will be forgot'.

1795 English and French émigrés Land at Quiberon Bay, Brittany, to assist the Chouans Royalists. They are defeated by Hoche in July when seven hundred are executed.

21st

22nd

23rd

24th

25th

26th

27th

THE UNITED STATES OF AMERICA

The most important part of the first British Empire, so painstakingly acquired during the previous century and a half by means of conquest, discovery and settlement, was lost during Nelson's early naval career. Its influence on him is less well understood than his assiduity to the French problem; nonetheless his interpretation of the Navigation Acts was unusual among his peer group, leaving much room for conjecture.

The thirteen Atlantic states in America, 'the tidewater colonies', evolved from settlements in Virginia by English travellers in 1607, and Massachusetts by the Pilgrim Fathers in 1620. By the middle of the eighteenth century settlement stretched from French Canada to Spanish Florida, north and south, and French Louisiana to the west.

In Europe, Britain and France opposed each other in the War of Austrian Succession 1741-48, a futile and bloody war which Walpole opposed but was forced to engage in following the Jenkins' Ear incident with Spain, a country which had secretly aligned herself to France through the Family Compact. The war had repercussions as far afield as India, Chile and Peru. Its result – stalemate; supremacy going to the British navy and French army, thus cancelling each other out. The Seven Years War 1756-63 began with the hallmarks of the previous conflict, the same protagonists fought over the same territories and for the same reasons. Britain fared rather badly to begin with but the exertions of Pitt eventually bore fruit, particularly in 1759, the year of victories.

During these wars, colonists in America supported the British against the French. As a result, Britain increased its possessions by the conquest of Canada and acquisition of the territory between the Alleghany Mountains and the Mississippi River. A huge financial burden accompanied these wars. In an effort to replenish the coffers various forms of taxation were proposed. All but the tax on tea were sub-

sequently discarded. Being forced to buy surplus tea from the British East India Company vexed the colonists in Boston who, as a reprisal, disguised themselves as Indians, boarded some tea ships and threw the tea into the harbour.

The British Parliament responded by passing the Coercive Acts that closed the port of Boston, redefined the government of Massachusetts and quartered British troops among the inhabitants. To counter these measures the first Continental Congress was assembled at Philadelphia on 5 September 1774. Battle lines were drawn between the Loyalists, who supported the mother country, and their opponents the Patriots. Hostilities, which were to last until 1783, broke out at Lexington and Concord.

On 1 June 1775, George Washington was appointed commander-in-chief of the Patriots' army and two days later the battle of Bunker Hill was fought. Although the Patriots were defeated, they took much comfort from the fact that among their numbers was a large volunteer element, who had all but matched the regular troops. In a fresh campaign in 1776, General Howe forced Washington to retreat. Washington was encumbered with having short-term conscripts who, on completion of their three month's period of service, returned to their homesteads, or, on the promise of pardon provided they took an oath of allegiance to the mother country, transferred to Howe's army. Many, in their hundreds, did.

A change in fortune began during the night of 25 December when Washington, with his exhausted troops, crossed the Delaware river during a blizzard. They surprised and captured a number of Hessian troops, hired by the British Government from a German prince, and a week later earned a brilliant victory over the British at Princeton. This victory enabled them to regroup at Morristown over the remainder of the winter and they were able to declare their independence on 4 July 1776.

The British launched a fresh campaign from Canada with a well-trained army under Burgoyne.

Portrait of Thomas Jefferson (see 28 June) from a contemporary engraving.

28th

⚓ *1803* ⚓ To the Right Honourable Henry Addington: 'I consider Malta as a most important outwork to India, that it will ever give us great influence in the Levant, and indeed all the southern parts of Italy. In this view I hope we shall never give it up'.

⚓ *1776* ⚓ *Thomas Jefferson presents a draft of the Declaration of Independence to separate the colonies from Britain, to the second Continental Congress. On 9 September, the United Colonies change their name to the United States.*

29th

⚓ *1799* ⚓ Carraciolo was tried by a court martial under Count Thurn. Before dinner Nelson, on the Sicilian frigate La Minerva, signs the death sentence and Carraciolo is hanged at five o'clock. Sir William Hamilton remarked: 'It was usual to give 24 hours for the care of the soul. Lord Nelson's manner of acting must be as his conscience and honour dictate, and I believe his determination will be found best at last'.

⚓ *1801* ⚓ *The results of Britain's first census giving the population of Great Britain as 16.1 million is published. A census is to be held every 10 years. A census in the United States on 1 August, 1790, gave a population of 4 million.*

⚓ *1797* ⚓ To the Reverend Dixon Hoste: 'Unless we can be united at home much good cannot be expected – let it be a War of the Nation, and what signify France, Holland, and Spain....We in the advance are night and day prepared for battle; our friends in England need not fear the event'.

30th

Richard Parker.

⚓ *1797* ⚓ *Richard Parker, ring leader at the Nore mutiny; which began on 23 May, is hanged on board Sandwich. A grandstand is erected on the coast for 'the better enjoyment of the edifying scene'.*

His first objective was the capture of New York but outnumbered and outmanoeuvred he was forced to surrender his whole army at Saratoga on 17 October. Meanwhile the later part of 1777 and early part of 1778 was difficult for Washington. His troops were camped at Valley Forge in impoverished conditions, trading only in the new and distrusted 'continental' paper money. Washington gained comfort from the news of the surrender of Burgoyne but better news broke after the same message had been carried to France by John Paul Jones. The French now openly declared for America. Up until this time the French had been secretly supplying arms and money to the Americans and indeed a number of their soldiers, of whom the most regarded was Lafayette, had joined the Patriot army. Under the terms of an open alliance France agreed to keep fighting until victory.

Spain, in a vain attempt to win back Gibraltar, sided with the Patriots, and Holland, for reasons of trade, also declared war on Britain. By now, a little local difficulty over tea taxes, had escalated into a conflict affecting the whole of the western world, British India and colonising efforts in the antipodes.

Britain still had hopes of a satisfactory outcome until they suffered a humiliating disaster at the hands of Admiral de Grasse. General Cornwallis, contained in Yorktown by Washington and the French fleet; which laid siege for twenty-one days, was forced to surrender on 19 October 1781 with 7000 troops. It was decisive and when the news reached London Lord North was said to have cried. A new ministry more favourable to the colonists took over but it was a further two years before the Treaty of Paris was signed on 3 September 1783. This Treaty recognised the independence of the thirteen colonies and granted them all the land to the east of the Mississippi except Florida which was returned to Spain to compensate for her failure to recover Gibraltar.

NEVER FEAR THE EVENT

THE INVASION THREAT AND THE GREAT BLOCKADE, 1800-1801

John Boxall

James Gillray's typically incisive depiction of the consequences of a successful French invasion – the English are taught to farm!

The war dragged on. Despite the dazzling victories of St Vincent and the Nile, the strategic situation remained more or less unchanged.

It was the battle of the elephant and the whale as the caricatures of the time pictured it. Napoleon's power ended where the waves lapped at the girths of his horse.

Neither England nor Republican France could really hurt each other. Despite the concentrated revolutionary fervour of the French army, their navy was pitifully weak. Not in ships: French ship design was the pattern for Europe. Most of the finest British warships were captures or based on French designs. The weakness lay in the officer class where sons of minor aristocracy had been purged and purged again in the cause of the Revolution. Revolutionary fervour was of more importance than seamanship. Every ship boasted a political officer and no commander might issue an order without having it criticised or discussed by the crew. Discipline thus was unattainable and only the most pliable officers remained.

To complicate matters even more, Napoleon, Dictator of France under the title of First Consul (soon to become Consul for Life), understood nothing of the sea. Used to marching large masses of men with relentless logistic planning from one end of Europe to the other, he had no notion of the upsets caused by wind or tide. All this from a man who in his youth considered becoming a sailor instead of a soldier.

Although brave, ships' crews were completely disaffected and undisciplined and were ignorant of how to fight as a cohesive unit. Treated very much as inferior to the army by the politicians in Paris, the navy lost out in supplies and equipment. Crews also had little experience as seamen because the French fleets remained harbour-bound.

Across the Channel, England had problems of her own. She lived constantly with the threat of inva-

sion. Twenty miles away 140,000 of Europe's best troops lay poised to invade; but reading the letters and diaries of the time, one would never know it.

The King and Queen Charlotte appeared to be oblivious to any apparent threat. Neither in 1799 nor 1800, did they hesitate to go sea bathing in Weymouth. Mary Frampton, a gossipy, well connected widow of a West Indian sugar planter accompanied them. Her diary entries are more full of her horror at having to give the King a cold collation when he visited her at short notice, and her worries as to the behaviour of Mary, her servant girl, than that the King might be in any physical danger. The only military duty he performed was to review the Dorset Yeomanry.

Jane Austen in Bath was more aware of the war. She had brothers in the navy, and met officers taking the waters for their health. But the conventions of the time would restrict the conversation in Pump Room or Assembly Room to genteel matters, not war and destruction. Her brothers' letters were family letters – service matters strictly excluded. Jane's own letters to her sister Cassandra dealt with people – their faults, foibles and intrigues – the stuff of novels, not military memoirs.

Yet the war was omnipresent. Pitt introduced many unpopular new taxes to ease the strain on the British Exchequer – income tax was most unpopular, savouring of revolutionary zeal almost! Taxes on servants, taxes on windows, on clocks and hair powder followed, all even more unprecedented.

The real truth that underlay all this was considerably starker. England was fighting alone. For her life. For her trade routes which were her life. Port after port of Continental Europe was closed to her by the seemingly uncheckable French armies. Nelson had saved for the present the trade route to India but the cost to the country of guarding thousands of miles of trade routes was crippling. Gold had to be poured in a continual stream to back up the only method Pitt saw to take the war to France by coalitions of the major European powers and each expensive, painstaking round of diplomacy was shattered by Napoleon's stunning victories.

After Marengo in 1800 and the Italian campaign, England's strategy was again brought to impotency. The British army was small, weak and unable to combat the military machine of France. No British general could hold a candle to Napoleon – indeed the soldier who would finally defeat him was a colonel fighting colonial battles for the expansion of the East India Company in India – Wellesley, later Duke of Wellington.

England's small standing army had been bundled out of the Low Countries at the commencement of the war. The only reputation the British Army had thus far gained was one of brutality and shocking violence against civilian rebels in Ireland – England's Achilles heel.

Constantly on the alert to the threat from Ireland as a base for a projected French invasion, England put down the sparks of an Irish rebellion, fuelled by the assistance of a rag-bag French invasion fleet, in 1798, with the kind of savagery only fear can engender.

The French force that supported the rebels was a hasty and ill-conceived mixture of French soldiers and Irish patriots. The whole project was defeated by the fierce gales of the Irish Sea before it even landed in Bantry Bay where the remnants were soon mopped up.

One odd off-shoot was the last attempted invasion of the English, or Welsh, mainlands. Hoche, commanding the French armies in the west, conceived of a diversionary attack in 1797 to draw attention from the Irish landing. Due to the length of time needed to get this invasion force together, Hoche was long distant by the time it sailed and probably oblivious to it in the heat of planning new continental strategies. The bedraggled group who landed in Pembroke Bay in 1797 under an Irish-American commander William Tate were a unit of ill-fame named the Black Legion. The whole farcical business was ended after a few skirmishes when they all surrendered to the Pembroke and Castle Martin Volunteers – all escape impossible.

Expeditions such as these were not confined to the French. In 1795 an equally ill-conceived strike was launched by the British at Quiberon. An ill-managed group of French émigré officers and mercenary troops landed and were summarily beaten off. Indeed, it was the grey uniforms taken by the French from these men that clothed the invaders of 1797 and led to their sobriquet of 'Le Legion Noire'.

These petty expeditions were like the commencing exploratory parries of two matched swordsmen – in themselves of little significance, neither being able to hurt the other materially. In England someone referred to them as 'breaking windows with guineas'.

As an Englishman is bound to, John Bull inevitably takes his pleasures with a frown. 'Ah, this cursed ministry!' he grumbles. 'They'll ruin us with their damned taxes! Why Zounds!' he adds, taking another slice of ye roast beef, 'they're making slaves of us all, and starving us to death.' A brilliant example of Gillray's use of irony.

The Martello Tower in Corsica. Similar defensive towers were erected along the southern coast of England against the expected invader.

All around the southern coasts of England defences were erected against the looming threat. Small round towers able to be held by a minimum garrison were built. These 'Martello' towers were named after the Corsican tower which had held off an attack by three English frigates in 1796 during the campaign in which Nelson lost his eye.

Lord St Vincent, Nelson's 'Dear Lord', was by now First Lord of the Admiralty. With remarkable speed, units of naval fencibles were raised to defend the coast, backed by local regiments of militia and volunteer cavalry. In Kent, a military canal was dug to hinder the inland advance of the French army.

But every Englishman knew that England's real defence lay in the power and command of her navy. Every major French invasion port – Boulogne, Toulon, Brest – was closely blockaded by a squadron of the British fleet. These fleets were constantly on station. Summer, winter, spring or autumn, it made no difference. These were the 'fleets in being' that rendered Napoleon impotent in his plans.

The foundation of this constant presence was discipline, a sense of duty, courage and professionalism of a high, almost consummate order. Fleet commanders, such as St Vincent himself, moulded his ships into formidable fighting units, not just individually, but as a whole, imbued with the same spirit and confidence in their ability to defeat any enemy of equal or superior force. This was done by an iron discipline. Attention to orders and strict respect for a superior were paramount.

St Vincent put down any disaffection in the fleet left over from the mutinies of Spithead and the Nore by draconian measures. But these would only have increased the mutinous behaviour if he had not instilled at the same time, a new sense of purpose and self-respect in all his crews. This he managed by encouraging skills in seamanship, ship-handling and above all, gunnery.

Gunnery was the key to victory – not just victory in battle but the moral victory of British seamen over French. British crews knew they were capable of firing three broadsides to the enemy's two – sometimes to their one – and that in the hell and noise and smoke of battle, keep to their stations, despite hideous sights and sounds and maintain the rate of fire regularly and accurately. Their officers told them, with unshakeable confidence, that if they could do this they were sure to triumph.

In seamanship, ship vied with ship in exercises. Topmasts were sent down and stowed and then set up again and re-rigged. Drills – watch against watch – run in clearing for action, lifting sails or hoisting away the boats. All and every drill in handling and fighting and sailing a ship of war was practised again and again until they became second nature to every man in the British fleet from the commander-in-chief to the lowest ship's boy.

The blockading fleets were usually organised into two squadrons. The inshore squadron standing off and on kept close watch on the enemy port, standing in at regular intervals to observe the state of preparedness of the blockaded ships for sea. Out of sight of prying telescopes, the main body waited, bearing up and down in regular exact station ready, if any enemy ships took advantage of a favourable wind and managed to evade the inshore squadron, to intercept and engage. Messages were passed between the squadrons by lines of 'repeating frigates' whose job it was to keep the lines of communication open and pass signals clearly.

Life on blockade was hard, boring and rigorous. The only hope for all was for the French to come out and engage. This would only be practicable when the weather was foul and the wind fair and off-shore; in such conditions Villeneuve broke out before Trafalgar. Small squadrons also sometimes ran from port to port for purposes of reinforcement or commerce trading.

The cost to the British fleet was enormous. The small ships – frigates and sloops – paid heavily for their close watch. The pages of the *Naval Chronicle* are filled with reports of ships and their crews lost to lee shores or squalls, sometimes embayed or hit by coastal batteries.

The ships of the line lost spars and sustained damage by collision or the sheer wearing force of the elements. The strain of exact station keeping in all weathers and constant alertness told. No ship was permitted to leave the squadron for any reason but re-fitting or detachment on service. Food and water were shipped out in victualling hoys and shore leave for all ranks was rare. The only occasional relief was the grant of an independent cruise in order to raid enemy commerce lines. These cruises only usually went to frigates.

For the average officer in a blockading squadron, dependent on distinguishing himself in some way in the interests of promotion, only two ways were open: a fleet action, for which all prayed; or the participation in a cutting-out expedition or raid on an enemy battery or telegraph station.

Boats from ships of the fleets, manned by armed sailors and commanded by lieutenants and midshipmen, would be sent to cut an enemy ship out from under the protection of shore batteries or ports. The dangers of such an attack were enormous.

The French would be prepared, with nettings rigged to ward off boarders, guns loaded with grape and canister to sweep the area around the ship and grenades, barricades and loaded muskets on deck ready at hand. To complicate things even more, ships' boats would have to co-ordinate their attack at night with only primitive night signalling available and exact timing difficult.

Yet these constant attacks had an effect. French communications were frequently disrupted. Coastal trade was so hazardous that supplying the invasion armies became haphazard. Large concentrations of invasion barges and chasse-marées were destroyed regularly, disrupting and delaying invasion plans, time after time. French morale suffered. Napoleon stormed at his naval commanders again and again,

oblivious to their inability to halt the inroads of a confident, audacious British navy.

By convention, command of these expeditions would be given to the senior lieutenants and commanders. Captains commanded the larger in scale. The conventions of the service gave these chances to those to whom mention in a gazette letter would give their step perhaps to post rank. Casualties could be high. But they were nothing compared to those sustained by the hard physical work of shiphandling in the age of sail. Hence the constant demand for men.

Fleet health generally improved the longer the fleet remained at sea. Nelson prided himself on the health of his crews. Away from the temptations of land and subject to a regular and monotonous diet, men grew hard and fit.

It was not all hard grind. Officers and men found ways of distracting themselves briefly from the day-to-day routine. Most good captains encouraged ship-to-ship visiting on Sundays and dancing contests. Officers amused themselves with amateur dramatics, glees and sometimes ship's choirs gave concerts. Captains dined frequently with each other and with the commander-in-chief in strict rota. These were the ways a good commander took the pulse of morale and kept in touch with the officers and men. The principal gain was the moral victory.

Cross section of a First Rate Ship of the eighteenth century showing the amount of space devoted to gunnery.

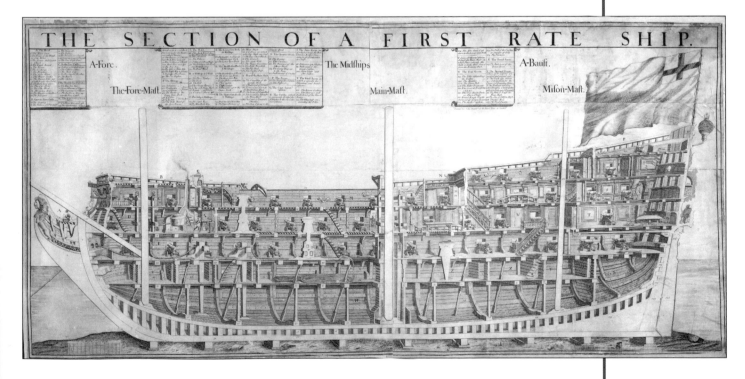

THE SECTION OF A FIRST RATE SHIP.

A-Fore.   The Midships   A-Bauft.

The-Fore-Maft.   Main-Maft.   Mifon-Maft.

French fleets remained shut up in harbour. No amount of dry drills could give the experience of seamanship in the open ocean in an age when it was reckoned that three months were needed to work up an efficient crew.

If Nelson was the most consummate wielder of naval power ever to emerge, the weapon he wielded, forged by such men as Sir William Cornwallis, George Keith, Lord Elphinstone and Sir Edward Pellew, was the finest instrument of war of its day. Only the skills and courage it contained could cause Lord St Vincent to stand up in Parliament and say of the invasion threat: 'I do not say they cannot come. I only say they cannot come by sea'.

After Copenhagen in 1801 the invasion scare was at its height. Napoleon had designed a peace at Lunéville with the Austrian Emperor and the full force of the Empire could be turned against England. On the south coast of England, people who could, moved inland and the defences were put on full alert. No one knew the plan for the invasion and speculation abounded. Some foresaw a two-pronged attack on the coast, splitting English defences. Some saw more wildly improbable means: balloons pulling invasion barges of vast size, powered by primitive paddle wheels or even tunnels driven under the Channel. Whatever the means the truth was that if the French fleet could control the Channel for twenty-four hours, the invasion threat would become a reality.

Nelson had arrived home from the Baltic in July of 1801. England's saviour by sea and the nation's hero, was at home to save the country from the French. The Admiralty gave him command of what it called 'a squadron on a particular service'. He was to command a flotilla of small craft and guard the coast between Orfordness and Beachy Head. He could be considered an odd choice for work of this nature. His reputation had been more in fleet actions, his experience of handling small craft was not extensive and his frigate days were long behind him. The name Nelson, however, carried the glow of invincibility in the public

ADMIRAL LORD NELSON.

eye. Privately, Nelson believed St Vincent and Troubridge, working at the Admiralty, were doing their best to separate him from Lady Hamilton.

The war, between Nelson and the Hamiltons on one side and Lady Nelson and her supporters on the other, was at its height, and occupied nearly as much of his thoughts as the prospective invasion. He was also at this time inactive, so any command was welcome to his ardent temperament. He had interviews with Prime Minister Addington and looked at all the intelligence available at the Admiralty. He then drew up his own memorandum on the subject. To him, the danger came principally from Flushing and the Low Countries. There it was reported was an army of 4000 men ready for a simultaneous double assault.

A first visit to the site of his command was not prepossessing. The sloops and gun-brigs were as he would hope, but the fencibles and militia were woefully inadequate, under strength and commanded by old and disabled officers. Also the administrative problems were enormous, leading to mountains of paperwork.

He was soon at sea though. On a brilliant sunny August day at Dover, people heard the sound of Nelson's bomb ketches bombarding the invasion barges at Boulogne. The news went around the town that 'Nelson was speaking to the French'.

Despite this, Nelson wrote to the Admiralty that he did not believe the invasion would come from Boulogne. He planned though, an attack in force by small boats: a giant cutting-out expedition to 'sink, burn, or destroy the enemy'. This attack on Boulogne was a rehearsal for a giant raid, more an invasion of Flushing with 5000 men, later.

Fifty-seven boats, armed and fully equipped, were manned, and picked officers appointed. At night they were to enter the harbour and create as much destruction as they could.

Nelson could only plan and fret on this occasion. An officer of his seniority could take no personal part in the attack. Strangely, he felt no certitude or confidence in this attempt. He was right. It was a disaster. The boats became separated. The co-ordination of the attack was all wrong and worst of all the French boats were all chained and hooked together in anticipation of such an attack.

Forty-four men were killed and 128 wounded. Among the dead was Edward Parker, a particular protégé of Nelson, who died from his wounds, in spite of Nelson's personal care. Nelson was devastated. For once his name was not the magic key to victory. The 'Nelson Touch' had faltered.

Nelson, in a letter to St Vincent, took full responsibility. 'No person can be blamed for sending them to the attack but myself.' The failure made no dent in his reputation. Nor should it have. He was a master at handling fleets in person. At Boulogne he could not have been on the spot and could have done nothing if he had. But perhaps he had been a little arrogant? Had he come to believe a little in his own myth? The failure was caused by a lack of reconnaissance, but could over-confidence in himself and the ability of his men to overcome all difficulties have been in some way to blame?

The Admiralty refused to bear the cost of burying Parker, so Nelson paid for an elaborate, almost heroic, funeral, attending in person with Emma. Was there an element of guilt in this? Was there a trace of public relations manipulation? Parker's death instead of being that of an officer in line of duty on service, became a heroic sacrifice, celebrated as one to confer something of the heroic on the whole abortive attack.

One thing is certain. Nelson's spirit was as determined and unshakeable as ever. His belief that England would never submit to invasion and that he and all his men would fight on at any sacrifice to thwart, was unshakeable. His plan for his command when he first took it up contained this phrase: 'Whatever plans may be adopted, the moment the enemy touch our coast be it where it may, they are to be attacked by every man afloat or on shore; this must be perfectly understood. Never fear the event.' Does this not echo a similar phrase uttered down the century in 1940 by another leader with complete and resolute faith in the people under his leadership?

Nelson finally paid his price in full – never doubting the price he had to pay, never hesitating. Those under his leadership paid too, in their thousands, equally gladly, equally without a doubt or hesitation.

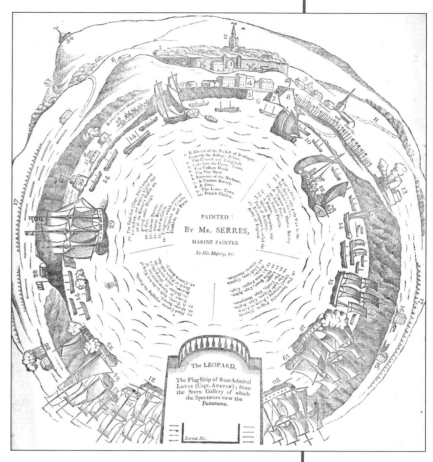

Yet, when the grief at Nelson's death had subsided, when the honours – the promotions, the swords and medals – had been presented, even then the threat was not over. Within a few years of Trafalgar, Napoleon's fleet was rebuilt. That fleet though, never challenged the Royal Navy again on any scale. The moral victory of Nelson lasted beyond the fall of Napoleon. It lasted for over a hundred years. That was Nelson's ultimate victory.

❧

John Boxall MA has an encylopaedic knowledge of the Nelsonian era. Indeed, he would readily admit to being far more intimately acquainted with the inhabitants of that period than he is with his modern-day contemporaries. He studied History at the University of Greenwich specialising in eighteenth-century social history and subsequently worked for and at the V&A, National Army Museum, and National Maritime Museum. His research contributed much to Flora Frazers' *The Unruly Queen*. He is presently employed as a freelance writer, guide and lecturer.

A panoramic depiction of the expedition against Boulogne made in mid August 1801, an attack that went badly, tragically wrong.

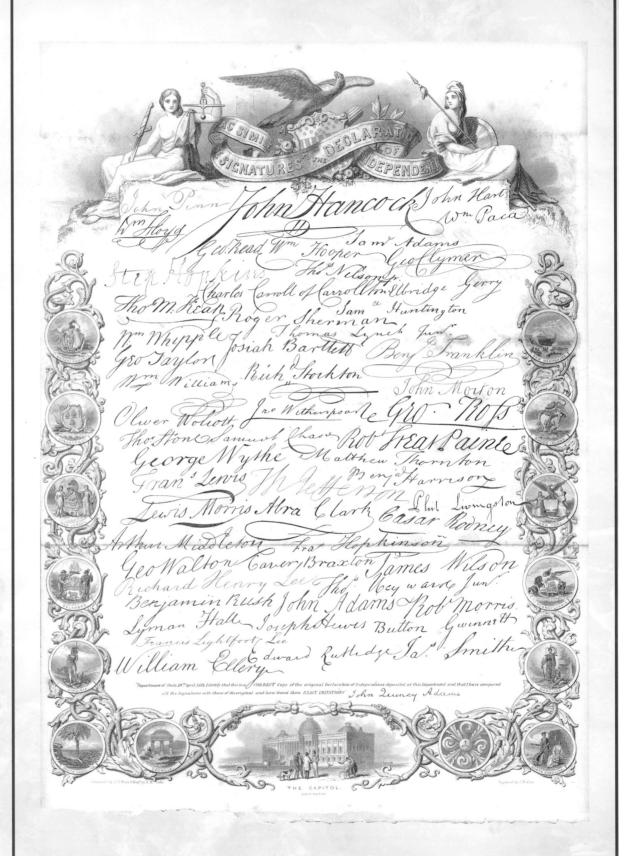

The signatories of the Declaration of Independence (see 4 July). Note John Hancock's bold hand at the top. 'I will sign my name so large,' he said, 'that King George will not need his spectacles to read it.'

1783 On team building: 'The disgust of the seamen to the Navy is all owing to the infernal plan of turning them over from ship to ship, so that men cannot be attached to their officers, or the officers care twopence about them'.

1781 The second Mysore War. Hyder Ali is defeated at Porto Novo in the Carnatic by the British.

1796 Nelson receives orders to prepare to blockade Leghorn and to prevent any attempt on Corsica by the French. To Sir Gilbert Elliot: '[I] have given orders to the Sardine and Vanneau to sail directly for Bastia...the way to Corsica, if our Fleet is at hand, is through Elba; for if they once set foot on that Island, it is not all our Fleet can stop their passage to Corsica'.

1757 Lord George Anson becomes First Lord of the Admiralty, the 29th holder of the post since James Duke of York, on 6 June 1666.

1797 To Jervis from Cadiz: 'We will begin this night by ten o'clock; and I beg that all the launches of the Fleet may be with me by eight, with their carronades, and plenty of ammunition.' Later, in the 'Sketch of my Life', he wrote: 'It was during this period that my personal courage was more conspicuous than at any other part of my life'.

1775 George Washington arrives at Cambridge, Massachusetts, to take command of the Patriot troops.

1787 Jervis writes to Nelson: 'Every service you are engaged in adds fresh lustre to the British arms, and to your character'.

1776 Jefferson's Declaration of Independence is officially adopted by the Congress at Philadelphia. According to some it was 'The day that all the gentlemen left America'.

DECLARATION OF INDEPENDENCE

Although dissatisfied with governorships, monopolistic families and religious differences few people were prepared openly to discuss their grievances until Thomas Paine, a former excise officer who emigrated to America in 1774, threw caution to the wind and published his *Common Sense*. Unencumbered by past history or local considerations he boldly declared that a new beginning through independence was the only way to begin a free and democratic government in America. The book's popularity confirmed that many covertly shared his view and soon the burgesses were hotly debating its content.

Thomas Jefferson who had long opposed a traditionally styled British government in America, and particularly disliked George III, began working on a new paper. It was propagandist, pro French, to whom he looked for military support and dispatched Silas Dean in February to negotiate aid, but bore the hallmarks of John Locke's theories of government which were written in England eighty-eight years before. It also drew on the works of the Swiss philosopher Emerich de Vattel.

The Continental Congress debated independence of the American colonies from Great Britain on 2 July 1776 and approved a statement, which had been drafted by Jefferson with assistance from Adams, Franklin, Sherman and Livingston to that effect, on the 4 July. Maryland, New Jersey and Pennsylvania were reluctant to declare for independence and New York abstained for eleven days. English ministers hoped that these differences would split American ranks. It was a major error of judgement; resentment of George III outweighed internal wrangles and formal signing by fifty-two congressmen began until 2 August, after two passages, one a libellous attack on the English people, the other a denunciation of the slave trade, had been removed.

Edmund Burke.
(See 9 July)

Sir Thomas Stamford Raffles (see 5 July) held a number of overseas clerkships including ports at Penang and Java. He established, without authority, a settlement at Singapore. On his return to England, he founded London Zoo. Courtesy of Antiques of the Orient.

EDMUND BURKE (1729-1797)

At a time when England was pursuing its unpopular policy towards the Americas, Burke was arguing, hotly and passionately, for justice and liberty. Challenged by the question, 'Should not America belong to this country?', he argued: 'If we have equity, wisdom and justice, it will belong to this country; if we have not, it will not belong to this country.'

Later, he opposed the French Revolution, expressing his views in a pamphlet *Reflections on the Revolution in France*. He believed that lawlessness and bloodshed in the name of democracy would bring no good. His views often ran counter to the main political parties and he found few friends in Parliament. He did, however, earn the respect of most and was offered a peerage by King George III.

🐚 **1797** 🐚 Nelson again attacks the Spanish gunboats at Cadiz with bomb vessels. To Jervis: 'Your encouragement for those Lieutenants who may conspicuously exert themselves, cannot fail to have its good effect in serving our country'.

🐚 *1826* 🐚 *Sir Thomas Stamford Raffles, founder of Singapore, who was born in 1781 on the West Indiaman Ann, off Jamaica, dies on the eve of his 46th birthday.*

🐚 **1796** 🐚 To Joseph Brame, HM Consul at Genoa as he begins a blockade of the port of Leghorn demanding the restoration of its legal government: 'It will be credited, if my character is known, that this blockade will be attended to with a degree of rigour unexampled in the present war'.

🐚 *1770* 🐚 *Battle of Chesmo. Orlov's Russian fleet defeats the Ottoman fleet off the Turkish coast. The fleets had engaged the previous day off Chios (ancient base for 100 Persian ships) without result.*

🐚 **1801** 🐚 Nelson, congratulating a Mr Nelson in Plymouth on the birth of a grandson says: 'I do not yet despair but that I may have fruit from my own loins'.

🐚 *1816* 🐚 *Richard Brinsley Sheridan, (b. 1751) politician, dramatist and drunkard dies. He is buried, through the generosity of friends, in Westminster Abbey.*

🐚 **1803** 🐚 To Emma: 'I am for assisting Europe to the utmost of our power, but no treaties, which England only keeps. I hope your next letter from Naples will give me news to alter my opinion of degenerate Europe; for I am sick at heart at the miserable cringing conduct of the great Powers'.

The Marquis de Montcalm.

🐚 *1758* 🐚 *A British force is defeated by the French under Marquis de Montcalm while trying to take Fort Ticonderoga.*

🐚 **1799** 🐚 A marine had struck and threatened to shoot an officer and was sentenced to death: 'Prepare everything for the execution of the Court Martial held on John Jolly; but when all the forms, except the last, are gone through, you will acquaint the prisoner, that, although there has been no circumstance to mitigate the severity of the law yet that I have reason to hope that the sparing of his life will have as beneficial an effect for the discipline of the service, as if he had suffered death. You will therefore respite the prisoner from the sentence of death'.

🐚 *1797* 🐚 *The politician, writer and would be financial reformer, Edmund Burke dies. He made a speech to the House of Commons on 22 March 1775, urging the adoption of a policy of reconciliation with America.*

🐚 **1796** 🐚 To Sir John Jervis, from Captain, off Porto Ferrajo, Elba, after a combined Army-Navy effort had taken possession of the forts and town: 'The harmony and good understanding between the Army and Navy employed on this occasion, will I trust be a further proof of what may be effected by the co-operation of the two services'.

🐚 *1777* 🐚 *Marie Joseph Marquis de Lafayette is appointed a major-general in the army of the United States of America.*

JAMES COOK (1728-79)

When accepted as a sea apprentice by John Walker in 1746, Cook began a career that was as fascinating as Nelson's was glorious. Rejecting the merchant navy, which he perceived as lacking the scope for his ambitions, Cook volunteered for the Royal Navy as an able-seaman. His natural aptitude for mathematics and navigation brought early advancement to boatswain of the *Eagle* (60). By the age of thirty he had achieved master of *Solebay* and *Pembroke*, and then saw action at Louisbourg and Quebec. These simple words belie the magnitude of achievement in a navy where transition from the lower deck to officer rank was very rare indeed. It was only the beginning. His charting of the St Lawrence River enabled unprecedented access by large ships and as a result Quebec was later taken.

Several years surveying off Newfoundland and his observations of an eclipse of the sun in 1766 received the favourable attention of the Royal Society. This resulted in his selection to command *Endeavour* on an expedition to observe the transit of Venus across the face of the sun, and a subsequent search for the southern continent.

Remarkable feats accompanied his diligence; following a six-month voyage not a man in his crew suffered from scurvy. His navigation was primarily lunar since Harrison had yet to perfect the chronometer. On his first voyage he proved that New Zealand is not connected to a southern continent, survived a grounding on the Great Barrier Reef and confirmed the separation of Australia from New Guinea. His luck failed on his return to England via Bolivia where malaria and dysentery took the lives of several of his crew. His only 'failure' was not being able to disprove the southern continent theory.

The Admiralty pressed for a second voyage. Commander Cook, *Resolution*, and Tobias Furneaux, *Adventure*, departed on 13 July 1772. This time they had a copy of Harrison's chronometer. Achievements on the second voyage of just over three years – prolonged on his choice because his ships and men were fit to continue – included the first ever crossing of the Antarctic Circle. He also proved that no southern continent existed at 60° latitude for about two thirds of the earth's circumference; re-discovered (from 170 years before) the Marquesas Islands; visited and accurately charted some of the Friendly Islands and discovered New Caledonia, the Isle of Pines and Norfolk Island.

He was promoted post-captain, elected Fellow of the Royal Society and awarded the Copley Gold Medal. Barely a year past before his third voyage began, again in *Resolution* which on this occasion had been poorly refitted. Cook's instructions were to go via Cape Town to the west coast of North America and search for the North West Passage. Eventually he reached 70° north after passing through the Bering Strait before being forced back by ice and fog. He returned to Hawaii for reparations and was greeted as a Polynesian God. The celebrations, however, seemed to have cost the islanders precious resources and strained their tolerance. Relations deteriorated to squabbles and on one occasion an affray began. Cook fired small shot at the natives who attacked him with clubs and knives, killing him before the marines could drive them away.

(The Hakluyt Society of Britain produced four volumes of the Journals of Captain Cook and his biography was written in 1939 by J R Murk.)

Captain James Cook, an engraving after the contemporary portrait by Nathaniel Dance, 1776.

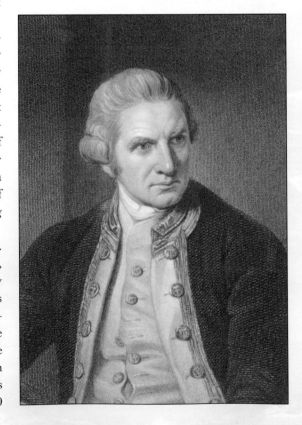

1799 Captain Foote to Dr Clarke on the capitulation of Naples: 'As I finally left Naples Bay on the 11th July, I was not a witness to the disgraceful scenes that passed, though I have been made acquainted with most of them by those who were. None of them suffered death on board the British ships, but Caracciolo was tried on board the Foudroyant, bearing Lord Nelson's Flag, by Neopolitan Officers'.

1776 Captain Cook, Resolution, accompanied by Discovery, sails from Plymouth on his third and fatal expedition. He is murdered by natives in Hawaii on 14 January 1779.

1794 To Fanny following the injury to his eye two days before: 'Reports we know, get about, and...it is best to say it myself – that I got a little hurt this morning: not much as you may judge by my writing'.

1799 An Act of Parliament is passed suppressing seditious societies; Freemasons are an exception.

1797 To Jervis from Theseus off Cadiz having spotted the red flag of mutiny: 'When I saw the Red flag hoisted on board an Admiral's Ship in harbour two days past, I had no doubt in my own mind but a meeting was commencing. By night four red flags were up, and yesterday they amounted to seven. My officer asked [Mazzaredo] if their fleet was à la Nore. He said, "yes; that they would be paid their wages"....In Spain it will never end but in revolution'.'

1793 Jean Paul Marat, one of the prime movers of the French Revolution is assassinated whilst at work in his bath by Charlotte Corday. The murderess is executed four days later.

Jean Paul Marat.

1797 From Jervis: 'You are to proceed with the utmost expedition off the island of Tenerife, and there make your disposition for taking possession of the town of Santa Cruz by a sudden and vigorous assault'.

1789 The fall of the Bastille. The King exclaims 'Why, this is a revolt!' 'No, sire.' comes the reply, 'It is a revolution.'

1799 Miss Knight, writing from Palermo says: 'A cutter arrived this morning from Lord Nelson, with the Rebel Standards, which were dragged through the streets, and afterwards burned by the hangman before the Castle. The Queen went to Church yesterday, to return thanks for deliverance of Naples'.

1815 Napoleon surrenders to Captain Frederick Maitland, Bellerophon, in Basque Roads. He died in exile in St Helena on 5 May 1821.

1800 Miss Knight writes to Lord Minto on moving the Italian royal family to safety: 'It is, at length, decided that we go by land; and I feel all the dangers and difficulties to which we shall be exposed. Lord Nelson is going on an expedition he disapproves and against his own convictions, because he has promised the Queen. I pity the Queen'.

1795 Start of the Admiralty telegraph system to Chatham. Electricity was proposed as a means of communication as early as 1753, but was not used until Chappe introduced it in France in 1792.

11th

12th

13th

14th

15th

16th

Napoleon leads his troops to victory at the Battle of the Pyramids. (See 21 July.)

1797 In a memorandum on preparations for the attack on Santa Cruz: 'The Culloden and Zealous to each make a platform for one eighteen-pounder. The Theseus to make a slay for dragging cannon. Each Ship to make as many iron ram-rods as possible, it being found that the wooden ones are very liable to break when used in a hurry'.

1790 The philosopher and economist Adam Smith who produced 'An Inquiry into the Nature and Causes of the Wealth of Nations', dies aged 67.

17th

1796 To Sir John Jervis during the blockade off Leghorn: 'I have only now to beg, that whenever you think the enemy will face you on water, you will send for me; for my heart would break to be absent at such a glorious time'.

1789 The French revolutionary and journalist, Camille Desmoulins, publishes 'La France Libre', the first manifesto of the French Republic.

18th

1799 Nelson had been ordered to Minorca by Lord Keith, but feeling it unwise to abandon Naples, stays put. 'I am fully aware of the act I have committed; but, sensible of my loyal intentions, I am prepared for my fate which may await my disobedience....I have done what I thought right; others may think differently; but it will be my consolation that I have gained a kingdom, seated a faithful ally of His Majesty firmly on his throne, and restored happiness to millions'.

1799 A stone engraved with parallel inscriptions of Egyptian ancient writing, demotic characters and Greek is discovered near Rosetta on the Nile. Archaeologists believe the 'Rosetta Stone' will enable them to decipher hieroglyphics.

19th

1805 Nelson notes in his journal: 'I went on shore for the first time since 16th June 1803; and from having my foot out of the Victory, two years wanting ten days'.

1795 The Royalist émigrés, who, with Pitt's assistance, made a descent at Quiberon Bay, are routed by Hoche.

20th

1795 Captain Cockburn (under Nelson's command), brought in the Nostra Signora di Belvidere. To Hotham: 'I have no doubt that her cargo is French property; the gold, silver, and jewels, which were found in the cabin, are on board Agamemnon, but things of much more consequence, I understand, are in the hold'.

1798 The Battle of the Pyramids. Napoleon easily defeats the 60,000 strong but ill-equipped Mameluke army and gains possession of Lower Egypt. The battle lasts about 2 hours and is remembered as being one of Napoleon's most decisive victories with a loss of less than 200 Frenchmen.

21st

1797 Nelson advises the Earl of Cork as to the training of his son, as a midshipman: 'In the first place, my lord, it is necessary that he should be made complete in his navigation; and if the peace continues French is absolutely necessary. Dancing is an accomplishment that probably a sea officer may require. You will see almost the necessity of it, when employed in foreign countries'.

1798 Napoleon enters Cairo. It is recaptured with the help of the British on 27 June 1801.

22nd

1805 To Lord Barham, lamenting erroneous information received from St Lucia: 'The Fleet is complete, and the first Easterly Wind, I shall pass the Straits: it has almost broke my heart. But the name of General Brereton will never be forgot by this generation; but for him our Battle would have been fought on June 6th'.

1803 The rising in Dublin by Irish patriots under Robert Emmet (who had obtained Napoleon's promise of aid when he visited France in 1802) is suppressed

23rd

Josiah was in the boat with Nelson at Santa Cruz when he was wounded and subsequently lost his arm (see 27 July). Nelson's gratitude on this occasion turned sour at Josiah's later behaviour which led to their final estrangement.

Josiah Nisbet (1780-1830)

Josiah took the name from his father, an Edinburgh doctor who had his family home in Nevis and St Kitts. His mother, Francis, was the daughter of the local judge. In 1772 Dr Josiah Nisbet became seriously ill, returned to England and died near Salisbury. Nelson became Josiah's stepfather when he married the young widowed Francis in 1787.

The family returned to England at the resumption of peace, taking up residence with Nelson's father at Burnham Thorpe. Fanny taught Josiah to speak French while Nelson found occupation raising the boy during the long and frustrating period on half pay.

Eventually Nelson took command of *Agamemnon*, giving Josiah a midshipman's berth. Together they saw action off Toulon and Naples in 1793, Josiah earning much praise from Nelson for his seamanship skills. The attack of Calvi in 1794 brought a shift in emphasis; Nelson continued to lavish praise in his letters but began complaining that the young man was headstrong and wanted his own way too much. This independence (or initiative?) was later to save Nelson following his abortive attack on Santa Cruz.

After the Battle of the Nile, Josiah (and his stepfather) became infatuated with Lady Hamilton. Josiah was tormented by Nelson's apparent rejection of his mother in favour of another man's wife. He was also extremely jealous. Encouraged by drink he began berating Nelson in public. Emma had broken the bond between the two men.

The slowness of communications to and from the Admiralty tended to compound the problem, but eventually praise from Nelson earned Josiah command of HMS *Dolphin*. He soon gained a better ship, *Thalia*, but at the age of twenty, probably as a result of the change in tone of his stepfather's letters, was put on half pay never to return to sea. He lived with his mother until he was thirty-nine; then on 31 March 1819 he married Frances Evans. Following the Napoleonic Wars Josiah, making use of the French taught to him by his mother, joined the Paris Bourse. He lived in Paris then at Quay d'Orsay where he maintained a small yacht. Just before his fiftieth birthday, Josiah died suddenly from pleurisy. He is buried near his mother at St Margaret's Church, Littleham.

Maxmilien de Robespierre (1758-1794)

Born in Arras and educated in Paris Robespierre became one of the great leaders of the French Revolution. He was a shy, austere man who renounced a judgeship, but went on to become a chief figure in the Jacobin Club and leader of the people of Paris. He was instrumental in bringing Louis XVI to trial declaring: 'He must die that the country may live.' He was a student of Rousseau and based his belief in a superior being on Rousseau's teaching. Robespierre, a radical, made many enemies. He sent Danton, who proclaimed 'Robespierre will follow me; he is dragged down by me', to the guillotine. On 27 July 1794 he was arrested, being shot in the jaw in the attempt, and guillotined the next day.

La Dernière Charette, 9 Thermidor (27 July) 1794. The tumbril trundles Robespierre and his condemned cohort to the guillotine, victims of their own regime.

❧ **1797** ❧ To St Vincent, prior to Santa Cruz: 'Tomorrow my head will probably be covered with laurel or cyprus.' He loses his arm and having demanded a rope should be thrown to him on his return to Theseus exclaimed: 'Let me alone, I have yet my legs left, and one arm. Tell the surgeon to make haste and get his instruments. I know I must lose my right arm, so the sooner off the better'.

❧ *1802* ❧ *Alexandre Dumas (d. 1870), who wrote 'The Count of Monte Cristo' and 'The Three Musketeers', is born at Villers-Cotterets, 50 miles from Paris.*

24th

❧ **1801** ❧ England is gripped by fear of an invasion from France. To Marsden on the defence of the Thames: 'Whatever plans may be adopted, the moment the enemy touch our coast, be it where it may, they are to be attacked by every man afloat and on shore: this must be perfectly understood. Never fear the event'.

❧ *1799* ❧ *The Battle of Aboukir. Napoleon and Joachim Murat, his cavalry commander, defeat an Ottoman-British force on their return from Syria.*

25th

❧ **1803** ❧ To Hugh Elliot on hearing a rumour that Algiers has engaged in the war, but more concerned that the French will join the Spanish because his fleet is already split on two fronts: 'I may have two fleets to fight, but if I have the ships' the more the better'.

❧ *1758* ❧ *Fort Louisbourg, a fort on the St Lawrence held by the French, falls to the British under Amherst and Wolfe.*

26th

❧ **1797** ❧ Nelson writes his first letter with his left hand to Jervis praising Josiah Nisbet for bringing him to Theseus: 'I am become a burthen to my friends, and useless to my country....When I leave your command, I become dead to the world; I go hence, and am no more seen. I hope you will be able to give me a frigate, to convey the remains of my carcass to England'.

❧ *1794* ❧ *Conspiracy of Moderates leads to the arrest of Maximilien de Robespierre.*

27th

❧ **1801** ❧ To St Vincent on the fear of invasion: 'Everything, my dear Lord must have a beginning, and we are literally at the foundation of our fabric of defence. Should the Enemy approach our Coast near the Thames, our Dock-yards can man Flat-boats if they are kept in readiness; and this yard [Sheerness] has 100 men, who can man two Flats which are ordered to be fitted out'.

❧ *1794* ❧ *Maximilien de Robespierre, French leader of the Jacobins during the Revolution, is executed with nineteen other revolutionaries.*

28th

❧ **1795** ❧ On Hotham being appointed commander-in-chief, in the Mediterranean, to vice Hood: 'Hotham has no head for such enterprise, perfectly satisfied that each month passes without any losses on our side. I almost, I assure you, wish myself an admiral, with the command of a fleet. Probably when I grow older, I shall not feel all that alacrity and anxiety for the service which I do at present'.

❧ *1777* ❧ *An American garrison leaves Fort Edward to the British.*

29th

❧ **1794** ❧ Nelson records in his journal, on Calvi following an attempt to seek a truce: 'By dusk, 3 or 4 of their guns were totally disabled. During the night the enemy only fired three or four guns: we fired a gun every three minutes'.

❧ *1793* ❧ *Toronto, known as York until 1834, is founded by General John Simcoe.*

30th

❧ **1798** ❧ On the eve of the Battle of the Nile: 'Before this time tomorrow, I shall have gained a peerage, or Westminster Abbey'.

❧ *1803* ❧ *John Ericsson (d. 1889), the Swedish engineer is born in Vermland. His steam engine was narrowly beaten by Stephenson's Rocket in 1829.*

31st

HONOR EST A NILO

NELSON AND THE NILE

Stephen Howarth

The Battle of the Nile (1-2 August 1798) was one of the most complete naval conquests there had ever been, setting in Britain a new high level of expectation of, and dependence upon, the efforts of the Royal Navy. It was also Nelson's first battle as an independent fleet commander.

Nineteen years earlier, he had appeared to be, in the words of Prince William Henry (later King William IV), 'the merest boy of a captain'. When he led his fleet into battle at the Nile, he was a rear-

admiral, a Knight of the Bath, and still astonishingly young – all of thirty-nine years and ten months old. Flag rank had come in 1797, with the then automatic promotion into dead men's shoes, and by happy coincidence his knighthood (in England's second oldest Order) was conferred just a few weeks later, as a reward for his outstanding initiative and courage at the Battle of Cape St Vincent (14 February 1797), when he captured two Spanish warships, boarding one from the deck of the other. But the boyish appearance had long gone. In 1794, his right eye had been virtually blinded when a chance shot at the siege of Calvi threw gravel into his face; in the summer of 1797 he lost his right arm in the failed assault on Tenerife. He had learned to wear, in exceptionally bright weather, a protective green shade above his good left eye, and he now looked much as most people easily remember him – 'the little one-eyed, one-armed admiral'. No one could doubt his personal bravery, and none who met him remained untouched by his unique blend of thoughtfulness, kindness and professionalism. But until the summer of 1798, no one could be certain how well that blend would work when he was given command of a fleet.

The French Revolutionary Wars had reached a critical point. The strategic summary was as follows. Begun in 1792 when France declared war against Austria, Hungary and Bohemia, the conflict spread rapidly until Prussia, Sardinia, the Netherlands, Britain and Spain were all included in the coalition

A portrait of Nelson by Arthur Devis, clearly showing the shade, which formed part of his cocked hat, that he wore to protect his good left eye from strong sunlight.

against France. However, in 1796 Spain changed sides; one by one the other combatants fell away; and very early in 1797 the coalition collapsed, leaving Britain to fight alone. The possibility of a cross-Channel invasion seemed frighteningly real, and, faced with Spain's opposition and no further support from Sardinia, the Royal Navy was obliged to withdraw from the Mediterranean.

Outside the Straits of Gibraltar, the fleet commanded by Admiral Lord St Vincent (John Jervis, ennobled for his leadership at the Battle of Cape St Vincent) began a long tiresome blockade of Cadiz, keeping the Spanish navy in harbour – and wishing all the time they would come out and fight. Nelson's ill-starred summer raid on Tenerife was an attempt to provoke them into some active retaliation. When it went wrong, St Vincent was generous: remarking that mortals could not command success, he did not blame Nelson for the failure. Nor did anyone in Britain, as Nelson found when he returned home to convalesce through the autumn and winter of 1797. On the contrary: the adventure confirmed his courage, and as one newspaper said, with such men to protect Britain 'we may defy the malignant threats of our enemies, and look with contempt upon the wild project of an invasion'.

Coincidentally, Napoleon Bonaparte also thought that an invasion of Britain would be a wild project. He was even younger than Nelson: at the start of 1798 he was still only twenty-eight years and three months old, but he was already a brigadier general and France's pre-eminent soldier. Though determined to defeat Britain, he judged the cross-Channel route as too risky, and instead evolved an indirect but far more flexible plan. With the Mediterranean empty of British warships, he could lead an invasion of Egypt. When achieved, this would offer him and his army a choice: they could either proceed northwards, to bring the Holy Land and the Turkish Ottoman Empire under French rule before rolling up the rest of continental Europe from the east; or they could go further east from Egypt – even to India, the heart of the British Empire. There was nothing petty about Napoleon's planning, and the Battle of the Nile was a crucial one in the history not only of Britain, but of Europe, the Near East and beyond.

Despite every precaution, the preparation of Napoleon's vast enterprise could not be kept completely secret. As the winter of 1797-98 turned to spring, even the blockaders off Cadiz were aware that a huge French fleet was assembling at Toulon. If rumour was to be believed (and in this case it was), the warships and troop transports together numbered somewhere between three and four hundred. But in two vital respects French secrecy had been maintained absolutely: no one else knew where this monstrous fleet would go, or when. It could be destined for Sicily, or Naples, or even for rebellious Ireland. That would have been a difficult target, not least because of the need to defend some hundreds of transports filled with seasick soldiers in a 2000-mile voyage. Off Cadiz, Nelson's friend Cuthbert Collingwood said, 'If those people should attempt to pass the straits, we shall certainly make a fine uproar amongst them.' But Ireland had to be considered, for its people would probably welcome the French, and a secure base there would mean that in practical terms France had encircled Britain. If, on the other hand, the fleet was aimed against Naples, Sicily or any part of the Mediterranean further east, it was clear that that would be almost as bad. It made no difference: wherever its destination, the French fleet had to be found and brought to battle.

Earl Spencer, First Lord of the Admiralty, had no doubt about whom to choose as leader. The stump of Nelson's arm was healed, and in March 1798 Spencer wrote to St Vincent: 'I am happy to send you Sir Horatio Nelson again...I believe I cannot send you a more zealous, active and approved officer...'. St Vincent's response was immediate and delighted. He had been on blockading duty for a year, and replied: 'I do assure your Lordship that the arrival of Admiral Nelson has given me a new lease of life, you could not have gratified me more in sending him...his presence in the Mediterranean is very essential.'

At the end of April, Nelson reached Cadiz in *Vanguard* (Captain Edward Berry), a 74-gun ship of the line – that is, a major warship capable of standing in the line of battle. St Vincent at once dispatched him into the Mediterranean with a squadron of two additional 74s (*Orion*, Captain Sir James Saumarez, and *Alexander*, Captain Edward Ball) and three scouting frigates. His task was reconnaissance – to find out where the French fleet was bound, so that preparations could be made accordingly. If he managed to capture anything, that would be all to the good. St

Vincent thought he would: 'The odds are that my gallant and enterprising rear admiral will lay hold of something.' and Nelson was equally optimistic, telling his commander-in-chief, 'I will present you at least with some frigates, and I hope something better.'

Soon after Nelson had gone, St Vincent received instructions from Lord Spencer that when reinforcements from Britain arrived off Cadiz, the squadron of reconnaissance should be made into a full striking force with at least ten sail of the line. Nelson should have the power not only to seek, but also if possible to destroy. This chimed so well with St Vincent's view that he decided not to wait for the reinforcements: though it weakened his own fleet considerably, he immediately sent ten 74s and one 50-gun ship to join Nelson. All told, he judged that the united force would 'consist of the ships which are really and truly the élite of the fleet under my command'.

This was a huge privilege, for the two lords had chosen Nelson to lead the hunt in preference to many other more senior (and very offended) admirals. One, Vice-Admiral Sir John Orde, was so furious that he challenged his commander-in-chief to a duel. Spencer and St Vincent selected Nelson because they recognised they had at their command a rare asset: a much admired and still youthful natural leader who was totally devoted to his nation's service and who inspired a similar personal devotion in his own subordinates. Yet before many days had passed, they nearly lost him altogether.

Before the extra ships reached Nelson's squadron of reconnaissance, it captured a French corvette, whose captain confirmed that Bonaparte himself was at Toulon, with thousands of soldiers embarked in the transports, and fifteen sail of the line under Admiral François Brueys, all ready for sea. However, since the corvette captain did not know the fleet's goal, Nelson turned towards Toulon, and on the night of 20-21 May, in a tremendous gale, *Vanguard* was blown hard towards southern Sardinia, dismasted and almost driven onto the rocks.

Both Nelson and St Vincent saw the hand of God in this. Writing frankly to his wife of his pride and conceit at the role he had been given, Nelson, much chastened, added: 'I ought not to call what happened to the *Vanguard* by the cold name of accident; I believe firmly that it was the Almighty's goodness, to check my consummate vanity.' St

Vincent for his part decided that divine intervention had saved Nelson's life, for on the 20th the enormous French fleet had emerged, and, on the wings of the same gale, had swept past Nelson's squadron. Neither set of ships even sighted the other, yet in fairer weather Nelson's would almost certainly have been found, fought and beaten.

The gale had two further consequences. Firstly, Nelson's three fast scouts, the frigates, went back to report events to the main fleet, met his reinforcing ships on the way, and told them where to find him. Secondly, the frigate captains believed *Vanguard* was too badly damaged to contemplate offensive action soon, so having reached Cadiz they did not return to Nelson at once. Yet by extreme effort *Vanguard* was fully repaired in a few days, and, with his first battle-fleet assembled and knowing the enemy was out, Nelson felt he could not wait: the frigates, which he called 'the eyes of the fleet', must catch up. But they never did. Without them the fleet sailed blind under the brilliant Mediterranean summer sun, guided only by logic, deduction and sailorly instinct.

On 8 July, seven weeks after the gale, an entry in the log of Admiral Brueys' flagship – the giant 120-gun *L'Orient*, one of the largest and most powerful warships in the world - gave a concise account of intervening events:

> 'The English fleet has played with ill luck on its side. First it missed us on the coast of Sardinia; next, it missed a convoy of 57 sail coming from Civitavecchia, with 7000 troops of the Army of Italy on board. It did not arrive at Malta until five days after we left there; and it arrived in Alexandria two days too soon to meet us. ...We shall certainly meet it at last; but we are now moored in such a manner as to bid defiance to a force more than double our own.'

With the rest of her fleet, *L'Orient* was riding at single anchor in Aboukir Bay, roughly equidistant between Alexandria (15 miles to the west) and Rosetta, at the mouth of the Nile. The voyage from Toulon had been safely accomplished; on the way, Malta had been ransacked, and the treasures of the Knights Hospitallers were stowed in *L'Orient's* hold. Now the army's transports were moored in Alexandria harbour, and led by General Bonaparte, the army itself was marching towards Cairo. Seeing the narrow harbour entrance at Alexandria, Admiral Brueys decided against keeping his warships there, and declined Bonaparte's suggestion that they should go to Corfu. He felt perfectly safe where he was.

Nelson at the same time was in an agony of uncertainty. He knew how junior an admiral he was; he knew the importance of his mission; but he could not find the French. He had decided early on that they would not have gone westward; the winds were too difficult. This was confirmed when he learned about their treatment of Malta. Of all destinations further east, his preferred choice was Egypt, for precisely the reasons that Bonaparte himself laid out. So from Malta he had hurried his fleet on to Alexandria, but found nothing. Then he had turned back and tried Turkey; then Crete; then Sicily. As the hunt mounted into thousands of miles, he repeatedly cursed his lack of scouting frigates, and wrote an impassioned self-defensive letter to St Vincent. Summarising the reasons for his moves, he concluded: 'The only objection I can fancy to be started is, you should not have gone such a long voyage without more certain information of the enemy's destination. My answer' – and he underlined it – 'is ready: *Where was I to get it from?* His second-in-command, Saumarez, wrote privately, 'We are proceeding on the merest conjecture only', then added thoughtfully, 'Should the chief responsibility rest with me, I fear it would be more than my too irritable nerves could bear.' But the French *had* to be somewhere to the east. Cyprus? From Sicily, that would be another 1200 miles – probably ten more sailing days, during which time the French could be doing anything.

Once again, weary and frustrated, the British fleet weighed anchor; and as they were passing Greece, they captured a French brig. No doubt its cargo of wine was welcome, but much more welcome was the information gained from it and sources on shore: the French armada's destination was indeed Egypt, just as Nelson had supposed – and it always had been. Suddenly the confusion became clear. When both fleets had been headed for Alexandria, the British had outsailed the French, reached the port first, found it empty and gone away; and then, while they cast about, here, there and almost everywhere, the French had arrived.

Alexandria! Throughout the hunt Nelson had sailed his fleet at between 5 and 6 knots, nearly their best possible speed. More than 500 miles remained, which they covered in three days, at speeds which ships of the line scarcely ever achieved. But when they reached Alexandria at ten o'clock in the morning of 1 August 1798 they were too late: there were no warships in the harbour, merely the mocking masts of empty transports.

Sick at heart, he turned eastward from the port again. After ten weeks of hunting, it appeared he had failed everyone – himself, his first fleet, his king and country. 'I do not recollect', wrote Saumarez, 'ever to have felt so utterly hopeless as when we sat down to dinner. Judge then what a change took place as, when the cloth was being removed, the Officer of the Watch came running in saying "Sir, a signal is just now made that the enemy is in Aboukir Bay and moored in a line of battle." All sprang from their seats and, only staying to drink a bumper to our success, we were in a moment on deck.'

During the long search, Nelson had not wasted his unwelcome abundance of time. Before his fleet was completely assembled he knew five of his reinforcing captains personally, and the others by reputation. After their rendezvous he had begun at once to work, upon all of them, the wonder of his command. At every opportunity he had summoned them to the flagship and, in a series of completely informal open conversations, discussed all possible shapes of battle, including the dread prospect that if the French fleet were safe in some harbour, there might be no battle at all, but merely another interminable blockade. His captains came to know his thoughts as closely as he knew theirs, and all became intimate friends. As he said of them: 'I had the happiness to command a band of brothers.' And by the end of summer, they were a group of unequalled heroes.

The French fleet could have been virtually impregnable. Its ships were protected by shore batteries and unmarked shoals and, moored in a slightly convex line ahead, they formed in effect a very long shore battery themselves. Moreover, the British possessed only one out-of-date chart of the bay, while the French had new and reliable ones. As Captain Berry in *Vanguard* remarked, they had 'the most decided advantages, as they had nothing to attend to but their artillery'. In addition they appeared to have time on their side. They had not been sighted until 2pm. The sun would set at 6, and by the time the British were in

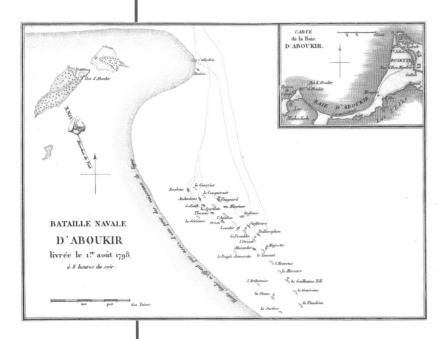

BATAILLE NAVALE
D'ABOUKIR
livrée le 1ᵉʳ août 1798,
à 8 heures du soir.

Plan of the battle showing the relative position of the British and French fleets with (inset) a map of Aboukir Bay.

officers in other ships overheard snatches of sailors' talk. It was optimistic, and he added happily: 'I knew what stuff I had under me, so I went into the attack.'

The British fleet sailed into battle cheering and laughing – 'three such cheers as are only to be heard in a British man-of-war', a sailor wrote. 'This intimidates the enemy...It shows them all is right, and the men, in true spirit, baying to be at them.' The French tried to do the same, 'but they made such a lamentable mess of it', said a midshipman, 'that the laughter in our ships was distinctly heard in theirs.'

Nelson's key (essentially the same as at Trafalgar) was 'to throw what force I had on a few ships'. Rather than the traditional duel between two more or less equal parallel lines, a concentration of fire power on one or two sections of the line would reduce even a stronger enemy fleet to manageable numbers. His captains understood perfectly: so much so that in their approach *Vanguard* needed to make only four signals. Given the direction of the wind – straight into the bay – Nelson's first signal, at 3pm, was to prepare for battle and anchoring by the stern. Had his ships anchored by the bow as usual, the wind would have swung them around, and while swinging they would have been vulnerable to enemy fire. His other signals were equally simple: at 5pm, 'I mean to attack the enemy's van and centre', since (as his captains understood straightaway) the contrary wind would prevent the French rear from moving; at 5.30, 'Form line of battle as convenient'; and at 5.40, the last one, for close action.

Captain Thomas Foley, the man with the out-of-date chart, led the way in *Goliath*. It was only on entering the bay that he could see that the French ships, 500 feet apart, were moored by the bows alone. This meant that if the wind changed direction they would swing, possibly towards the shore, a few hundred yards distant; *ergo*, between them and the shore there must be sufficient depth of water for other 74s to sail in. And so, eagerly followed by *Zealous* (Samuel Hood), *Orion* (Sir James Saumarez), *Audacious* (David Gould) and *Theseus* (Ralph Miller), Foley did. No one had told him to, but it was just the kind of intelligent initiative that Nelson practised and encouraged. It meant the French would be engaged from both sides at once – something which Brueys had so little expected that on the landward side, his ships' ports were shut, and the great guns were covered with fur-

a position to approach, it was already twilight; so if an assault were launched that evening, it would have to be carried out in the dark. Even Nelson said later that if his fleet had been fresh out of England, 'I would sooner have thought of flying, than of attacking.'

But against the French were three significant disadvantages. Firstly, although Admiral Brueys considered sailing out in order to challenge the British at sea in the morning, the wind was blowing directly into the bay, which would have made the manoeuvre difficult and slow. Secondly, the prolonged absence of the British had brought a degree of relaxation to his fleet. Ships were being painted, and were not in proper condition for battle; working parties were on shore digging wells, and being protected by others from the local Bedouin tribesmen. With insufficient men on board, Brueys could either sail or fight, but not both, so naturally and sensibly he chose to stay put for the time being: the prospect of a night action seemed unlikely. But his third disadvantage (as Berry noted) was that more than two months earlier, Nelson had worked out and thoroughly explained how he planned to fight an anchored fleet, by day or night.

From the moment the French mastheads were sighted, every one of the British captains and sailors knew precisely what to do. Nelson declared that by dinner time next day he would have gained either a peerage 'or Westminster Abbey', the burial place for heroes. As they sailed towards the enemy, he and niture, barrels and pots of paint. It also meant the leading French 74, *Guerrier*, could be raked with a broadside as her bow was rounded. While *Goliath* and *Orion* swiftly sank a foolhardy frigate, *Zealous* shot down *Guerrier*'s foremast 'in about seven minutes'. *Theseus* joined in, and 'a second breath could not be drawn before her main and mizzen were gone also.' *Goliath* then anchored inshore of the second French 74 and opened fire; *Theseus* moved inshore of the third, anchoring and opening fire on her 'precisely at sunset', and at the same moment *Vanguard* did the same from the seaward side.

Thus battle was joined, and when it was fully dark, the head and centre of the French line were brought under concentrated fire at very short range from both sides, while the wind prevented their rearward ships from coming to their aid. But by no means the battle went the British way. In her eagerness to engage, *Culloden* (Captain Thomas Troubridge) fell foul of one of the natural hazards, an unmarked shoal, and to the mortification of all on board she remained stuck fast, harassed by a small shore battery and able to support her colleagues only as an unwilling marker buoy. Her absence from the fight was an important, but fortunately not crucial, diminution of the British fleet's power, and afterwards Nelson made sure that her officers and men received the same awards as those who had been directly involved in the mêlée. *Bellerophon*, or 'Billy Ruffian', suffered more severely: her captain, Henry Darby, discovered too late that his chosen adversary was *L'Orient*. In the general confusion, *Bellerophon* remained unsupported and for over an hour fought her colossal opponent alone, until, dismasted and carrying about 200 dead or wounded, the British ship drifted out of line.

Her casualties were only a fraction of the whole. The entire battle was fought in an area barely a mile long and 200 yards wide. Under the night sky of Egypt, more than a thousand guns were firing within that tiny tract of sea, and when the night was over the combined fleets counted about 5450 men dead and several thousand more wounded. Of the dead, about 5230 were French.

When the battered *Bellerophon* drifted out of line, other British ships took her place against *L'Orient*, and one of the French killed was her flag-captain, the Count of Casabianca, who refused to save himself when, with his ship terminally ablaze, his son was trapped below. In the same vessel, another desperately wounded and dying man was the fleet's admiral, François Brueys, who displayed almost unbelievable endurance and bravery. Not just one but both of his legs had been shot off. When the stumps had been bound with tourniquets, he ordered his men to seat him in a chair on deck, from which he continued to direct the fighting until another cannon shot cut him in half.

These were men who in their reportedly total stoicism gave an example of which any navy could be proud – and perhaps especially the navy of France during the revolutionary years. In comparison, Nelson's own wound was nasty, but superficial: after two hours' close action, he was hit above his good eye by a fragment of shot. It tore open his forehead, exposed an inch of his skull and covered his eye with the fallen flap of skin; and being a head-wound, of course it bled profusely – all of which convinced him he had been completely blinded and was about to die. Falling down, he gasped, 'I am killed – remember me to my wife...'. People remembered this and wrote about it, not because of the sentiment but because he would not let the surgeon give him precedence for treatment ('No, I will take my turn with my brave fellows'). When he learned he was not dying after all, he called for his secretary and then his chaplain to take dictation. Both were too shellshocked to help, so while he lay recovering he himself began drafting a report of the battle, to be sent to St Vincent. Its text became famous all over Europe. 'My lord,' it began, 'Almighty God has blessed His Majesty's arms in the late battle...'. Though the cannonading and slaughter had not ceased, he was already sure that victory would be won; the only question was its extent, and he wrote modestly: 'I was wounded in the head, and obliged to be carried off the deck, but the service suffered no loss by the event: Captain Berry was fully equal to the important service then going on, and to him I must beg leave to refer for every information relative to the victory.'

In the course of the battle Nelson, wounded above his good eye by a splinter, was forced to retire below. This contemporary engraving shows him passing command to his trusted deputy Captain Edward Berry of HMS Vanguard.

The climax of the battle was marked by the explosion of Bruey's flagship L'Orient. *From an engraving published shortly after news arrived in England in October 1798 by Edward Thompson.*

Even as he was writing this, information came from Berry on deck. Fuelled by fresh paint and tar, the blaze in *L'Orient* had become absolutely uncontrollable. Nelson struggled up to witness the terrible spectacle. The heat was so intense that the pitch in other ships' seams was melting. Illuminating both fleets, the dazzling glare could be seen both in Rosetta and Alexandria, 15 miles in either direction; and when it came, the inevitable shattering explosion was heard clearly in both towns as well. 'At 10,' wrote a shocked British lieutenant, '*L'Orient* blew into the air!!!'

Abruptly, all firing ceased. The impact of the detonation was so powerful that in many ships, people believed that somewhere very close to them, their own vessel must have been hit; and in the sudden enveloping darkness the fighting stopped completely for several minutes, as fragments of corpses and burning scraps of wood and canvas came tumbling out of the sky.

The destruction of *L'Orient* was not the end of the battle, which continued until dawn, but it was the climax. If Nelson had been killed, his achievement that night would still have earned him contemporary Britain's gratitude and admiration and, probably, a place in naval history not far short of what it is now. Viewing the scene in the morning, he said, 'Victory is not a name strong enough', and he was right: the enemy's fleet had been almost annihilated, with a disproportionately small loss in the British ships.

Even so, it could be said that the victory was less complete than it might have been. Seven more years would pass before the culminating Battle of Trafalgar and Nelson's final overthrow of France's naval pretensions, and ten years beyond that were needed to defeat the French on land as well; because in 1798 Napoleon Bonaparte, though temporarily trapped in Egypt, was safe on shore. But that was the luck, good or bad, that attends every campaign and every action

in war. No one can say what might have happened if the fleets had met earlier in the open sea, before the band of brothers had gained their absolute mutual understanding. It could be entertaining to speculate, but profitless; and it would be crass to criticise, for hardly anyone in contemporary Europe did, apart from the Revolutionary French, who considered their dreams of further conquest had been destroyed.

When news of the victory reached Britain, it prompted unrestrained rejoicing everywhere. The first Lord of the Admiralty fainted with relief, and some bright individual invented a popular anagram: 'Horatio Nelson' could be re-written as *Honor est a Nilo*, 'Honour is at the Nile'. So it was, for he was now Lord Nelson, Baron Nelson of the Nile. There were celebrations too in every continental country which had not come under French rule, and today one outstanding work still brings over the ecstatic spirit of the time. As messengers rode north through Italy, Franz Joseph Haydn was in Vienna, completing a new mass in honour of the birthday of one of the Austrian princesses. Though it was sacred music, he intended it as a triumphant piece, full of energy and exuberance. 'When I think of God,' he said once, 'my heart is so full of joy that notes flow like a fountain; and since God has given me a joyous heart, He will pardon me for having served Him joyfully.' The new mass had reached the point of rehearsal when the thrilling report of the victory arrived, and at once the music acquired a new name: the Nelson Mass. It rang out with a sense of liberty and release which few had imagined possible.

Stephen Howarth is the author of several notable books of naval and maritime history, including *Morning Glory: A History of the Imperial Japanese Navy 1895-1945*, *To Shining Sea: A History of the United States Navy 1775-1991* and *The Story of Shell's British Tanker Fleets 1892-1992*. With his late father David Howarth he co-wrote *The Story of P&O: The Peninsular and Orient Steam Navigation Company 1837-1987* and *Nelson: The Immortal Memory*. He was contributing editor of *Men of War: Great Naval Leaders of World War II* and co-editor, with Derek Law, of *The Battle of the Atlantic 1939-1945: The 50th Anniversary International Naval Conference*. He has just finished a major work tracing the centenary history of the Shell Transport and Trading Company. He is a Fellow of both the Royal Historical Society and the Royal Geographical Society, Chairman of The 1805 Club, and a retired officer of the Royal Naval Reserve. He lives with his wife and two sons in Nottinghamshire.

Medals issued following the British victory at the Battle of the Nile (not to scale). (See 1 August.)

An air of conviviality pervades the scene as these Greenwich Pensioners, who with the help of a few clay pipe stems, dispute the finer details of the Battle of the Nile.

❦ 1798 ❦ The Battle of the Nile

Battle honours and medals are issued. From his narrative: 'The action commenced at sun-set which was at thirty-one minutes past six P.M., with an ardour and vigour which it is impossible to describe'.

❦ 1779 ❦ *Francis Scott Key (d. 1843), the American poet who wrote the 'Star-Spangled Banner', which became the official anthem of the United States in 1931, is born in Corrall County, Maryland.*

❦ 1796 ❦ To Fanny: 'I will relate an anecdote, all vanity to myself, but you will partake of it: A person sent me a letter, and directed as follows, "Horatio Nelson, Genoa". On being asked how he could direct in such a manner, his answer, in a large party, was, "Sir, there is but one Horatio Nelson in the world." The letter certainly came immediately....I am known throughout Italy; not a kingdom or a state where my name will be forgotten. This is my Gazette'.

❦ 1802 ❦ *Napoleon is created Consul for Life, with the right to appoint his own successor. Three and a half million Frenchmen voted in favour, with 8000 against.*

❦ 1798 ❦ Writing in his journal on the Battle of the Nile: 'The enemy was moored in a strong line of battle for defending the Bay, flanked by numerous gunboats, four frigates, and a battery of guns and mortars on an island in their van; but nothing could withstand the squadron your Lordship did me the honour to place under my command'.

❦ 1778 ❦ *La Scala opera house opens in Milan.*

❦ 1794 ❦ On hearing of Lord Howe's action in the Bay of Biscay: 'Laurels grow in the Bay of Biscay – I hope a bed of them may be found in the Mediterranean'.

❦ 1791 ❦ *Austria and the Ottoman Empire sign the Peace of Sistoua. Belgrade is returned to the Ottomans.*

❦ 1799 ❦ Nelson in Foudroyant conveys the Sicilian royal family from Naples to Palermo. To Nepean: 'As I am proceeding with his Sicilian Majesty on board for Palermo, for the good of His Majesty's service, that the Command of this Squadron should be left with an Officer above the rank of captain, especially as the Russian and Turkish squadrons are expected in this Bay, I have, therefore, thought it right to give Captain Troubridge an order to wear a broad Pendant'.

❦ 1796 ❦ *Bonaparte defeats the Austrians at Castiglione in Italy.*

❦ 1794 ❦ Following the siege of Calvi: 'We have lost many men from the season, very few from the enemy. I am here the reed amongst the oaks; all the prevailing disorders have attacked me, but I have not strength for them to fasten upon; I bow before the storm, whilst the sturdy oak is laid low. One plan I pursue, never to employ a doctor; nature does all for me, and Providence protects me'.

❦ 1775 ❦ *The Irish nationalist leader and agitator of Ireland, Daniel O'Connell (d. 1847), who replaced the elder Keogh as leader of the Catholic Committee in 1808, is born.*

❦ 1804 ❦ To the commissioners of the Transport Board: 'It having been represented to me by the Captains of the Squadron, that the coals supplied their respective Ships from the Harmony Transport at the Madalena Islands in May last, were nearly one-eighth short in their measure. I therefore desire a severe example being made of this man for such dishonest practice'.

❦ 1815 ❦ *Napoleon sails from Plymouth in Northumberland to exile in St Helena.*

1st

2nd

3rd

4th

5th

6th

7th

CALVI

Hood, having succeeded in taking the towns of San Fiorenzo and Bastia had new orders for Nelson – the siege of Calvi. This was likely to be the most difficult of the Corsican trilogy since its fortification comprised high cliffs and massive walls, in all some 200 feet of escarpment and only one apparent landing area under the protection of shore batteries.

Nelson, thorough as ever and accompanied by General Stuart, conducted a reconnaissance of the immediate area on 17 June and found one tiny inlet where a boat, at its peril, could be rowed to an inshore beach. The risks to life and limb were outweighed by the lack of options and on the next morning, before sunrise and mercifully in fine weather, Nelson set about transporting 250 men, plus tackle and cannon to the beach. Within a day they had completed the landing and began preparations for the march to a high ground position about a mile short of Calvi's un-alerted rear where they would prepare battery positions to attack the town and its forts.

It was not until early July that preparations were sufficiently advanced to begin an assault. When it began the temperature – climatic and ferocity of battle – increased. Nelson had a narrow escape on 8 July when an enemy shot destroyed a battery close by; then on the 12th, while he was observing the battle an enemy shot struck a rock and scattered shards. Stones and debris hit Nelson in the face. He later wrote to Hood: 'I got a little hurt this morning...'; to Suckling: 'My right eye is entirely cut down...'; and to Fanny: '...a very slight scratch towards my right eye...'. In reality he had all but lost sight in his right eye where his vision was limited to distinguishing between dark and light.

Nelson had suffered but so too had many of the assault party. Many had been exposed to malaria at Bastia and were now feeling the effects while others were simply exhausted by toil and sun. Perhaps half of his available troops were rendered useless.

On 18 July Colonel Moore led an attack on Fort Mozzello where an apparent breach in its walls had been made. It was successful and enabled General Stuart to begin an assault on the city, but first he offered the French an opportunity to surrender. General Casabianca ignored it, but about a week later, taking cognisance of his diminishing victuals and ammunition, he offered to negotiate a surrender in the event that he had not been re-supplied. He was clearly not aware that the British forces were so depleted as to be considering lifting the siege. The French managed to break the blockade but only landed food. On 1 August Casabianca sent word that he would surrender in ten days if no more supplies were received. This was indeed the outcome and fifty-one days after beginning the campaign British troops entered and took Calvi.

The lion lies dying; a carving done to commemorate the decimation of the Swiss Guard in the Tuileries (see 10 August). Their lives were sacrificed in defence of the French royal family; with them perished any chance of a constitutional monarchy. Courtesy of Mr Maurice Johnson of the Swiss Cheese Union.

1804 At sea, to his brother: 'I have been expecting Monsieur La Touche to give me the meeting every day this year past, and only hope he will come out before I go hence....You will have seen Monsieur La Touche's letter of how he chased me and how I ran. Keep it; and by God, if I take him, he shall eat it'.

1786 *Mont Blanc is conquered by Dr M Paccard and his guide Jacques Balmat.*

1783 To Hercules Ross (a leading planter and businessman) after the American War: 'I have closed the war without a fortune; but I trust, and from the attention that has been paid to me, believe that there is not a speck in my character. True honour, I hope, predominates in my mind far above riches'.

1801 *Austria joins the Anglo-Russian alliance against Napoleon. Later Russia will coerce Prussia into joining.*

1794 Siege of Calvi ends in capitulation to Lieutenant-General Stuart and Captain Nelson. To Sir Gilbert Elliot: 'The Garrison will lay down their arms at the water side, and before night I hope to have them all embarked. The business is certainly done, and high time it is. We are all sick, the Enemy are said to have lost eighty killed or wounded, – the Town and Works much damaged'.

1792 *The Girondins fail to control the Paris mob who attack the Tuileries and massacre the Swiss Guards.*

1801 To Captain Hamilton at Margate: 'Four River-Barges I have directed to be sent to Whitstable Flats, and as they will only have the Master and two men, I fancy, on board them, it is necessary that they should be laid in a place of safety – It is expected that the Fencibles of Whitstable will frequently go on board, and exercise the cannon'.

1770 *King George III, by letters patent, elected the province of Nova Scotia in British America into a Bishop's See and appointed Dr Charles Inglis to be bishop.*

1804 To Marsden: 'The Diligent Transport has brought out frocks and trowsers but instead of their being made of good Russian duck those sent out are made of course wrapper-stuff, and the price increased. I therefore think it necessary to send you one of each in order that their Lordships may judge of the quality and price'.

1774 *Robert Southey (d.1843), poet laureate and author of 'The Life of Nelson' (published 1813), is born at Bristol.*

1801 In the Downs, supporting the strategy of fighting the enemy in his own arena: 'To crush the enemy at home was the favourite plan of Lord Chatham, and I am sure you think it the wisest measure to carry the war from our own doors'.

1788 *A triple alliance between Britain, Prussia and the Netherlands is agreed as a counterbalance to the coalition of France, the Holy Roman Empire and Russia.*

1782 A year after first getting under way in Albermarle her log records: 'At 3 P.M. five sail in sight coming from Boston – gave chase. At 4 discovered the above vessels to be four Line-of-Battle Ships and one Frigate. Half past, one of the Line-of-Battle Ships made a signal with a gun, upon which the three Ships made sail after us. We wore and made sail from them, knowing them to be part of the French squadron which got into Boston last Friday'.

1782 *David Tyrit, a navy office spy, is executed on Southsea Common.*

1801 Some notes on the attacks on the Boulogne flotilla: 'Two boats from each division to be particularly allotted and prepared for the purpose of cutting the Enemy's cable and sternfast. When any Boats have taken one Vessel, the business is not to be considered as finished, but a sufficient number being left to guard the Prize, the others are immediately to pursue the object, by proceeding to the next, and so on'.

1769 *Napoleon Bonaparte is born in Ajaccio, capitol of the island of Corsica. His father was a lawyer.*

Alexander Davison (1750-1829)

Alexander Davison was Nelson's prize agent and, for a good many years, his friend and confidant. They first met in 1782 when Davison was on the legislative council in Quebec.

For the right officer, being prize agent was a lucrative business. Davison was also generous, contributing a large sum of money for Nile medals to be struck and awarded to officers and ratings present at the battle. He also assisted Nelson in his acquisition of Merton Place.

Although a shipping agent, Davison had aspirations to enter politics which came to an abrupt end when he was sent to prison for wholesale bribery of the electorate in his prospective constituency of Ilchester. He served another prison sentence in 1805. His family home was Kirknewton where he is buried in the family vault.

Joseph Priestley (1733-1804)

The preacher and chemist was born at Fieldhead, Yorkshire on 13 March 1733. He held several posts in the ministry where he was non conformist and revolutionary, but turned to chemistry and in 1766 gained a fellowship in the Royal Society. His work concentrated on the examination of gases and he independently (of Scheller) defined the properties of oxygen. In 1794 Priestley emigrated to America and lived there until his death on 6 February 1804.

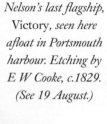

Nelson's last flagship, Victory, *seen here afloat in Portsmouth harbour. Etching by E W Cooke, c.1829. (See 19 August.)*

1797 To Sir John Jervis after his failure at Santa Cruz and the loss of his arm: 'A left handed admiral will never again be considered as useful, therefore the sooner I get to a very humble cottage the better, and make room for a better man to serve the State'.

1780 *General Lord Cornwallis leads the British to a victory over the Patriots in a battle at Camden. He was appointed governor-general in India in 1786.*

1801 Following an unsuccessful attack on La Touche-Tréville's ships in Boulogne. Nelson directed but did not lead the attack: 'I own I shall never bring myself again to allow any attack to go forward, where I am not personally concerned; my mind suffers much more than if I had a leg shot off in this late business'.

1794 *Joseph Priestley, Presbyterian minister and scientist, discovers that plants give off a gas called oxygen.*

1805 Ever mindful of the health of his people Nelson writes to Marsden from Victory at Spithead: 'The companies of the Victory and Superb are in most perfect health, and only require some vegetables and other refreshments to remove the scurvy'.

1792 *Earl (Lord John) Russell (d. 1878), British statesman, is born. He was one of the four statesmen entrusted with framing the Reform Bill of 1832.*

1805 Nelson strikes his flag in Victory and returns immediately to Merton, arriving early the following morning. From Victory's log: 'At 9 P.M., hauled down Lord Nelson's flag'.

1796 *A treaty of peace, offensive and defensive, between France and Spain, is signed at Ildephonso. On 11 October Spain declares war on England.*

1797 Nelson shifts his flag from Theseus to Seahorse after Tenerife and returns to England. From the Admiralty: 'Whereas we think fit that you shall strike your Flag, and come on shore. You are hereby required and directed to strike your Flag and come on shore accordingly. Given under our hands, the 2nd September, 1797'.

1765 *John Harrison presents his fourth chronometer to the Board of Longitude and finally qualifies for the £20,000 prize.*

1786 To Fanny: 'Have you not often heard, that salt water and absence always wash away love? Now, I am such a heretic as not to believe that Faith; for behold, every morning since my arrival, I have had six pails of salt water at daylight poured upon my head, and instead of finding what the Seamen say is true I perceive the contrary effect'.

1793 *In France a levy of the whole male population capable of bearing arms is ordered. Fourteen armies are put into the field.*

1804 To Alexander Davison: 'I dare say Monsieur La Touche will have a different letter to write, If I can once get a shake at him. Whether the world thinks I ran away or no, is a matter of great indifference. If my character is not fixed by this time, it is useless for me to try to fix it at my time of life'.

1788 *The settlement Sierra Leone is founded on the west coast of Africa, to be used as a home for freed slaves from England.*

1796 In a letter to Fanny saying he intends to visit the Pope: 'I do not think he will oppose the thunder of the Vatican against my thunder; and you will, I dare say, hear that I am at Rome in my barge. If I succeed, I am determined to row up the Tiber, and into Rome'.

1775 *King George III rejects the American colonies' offer of peace known as the 'Olive Branch Petition'.*

WILLIAM WILBERFORCE (1759-1833)

*Rear-Admiral
Richard Kempenfelt
flew his flag in* Royal
George, *shown here
in the background.*

William Wilberforce, 'the man who freed the slaves' was born on 24 August 1759. His great passions were the abolition of the slave trade and reformation of manners and the moral order. An evangelical Christian who wished to take holy orders, he was persuaded instead to remain in Parliament where he was a supporter of Pitt the Younger.

The slave trade, as conducted by Europeans, was started by the Portuguese in 1481. They began exploiting their human assets from Angola and the Congo, but the sphere quickly expanded to a tract covering virtually all the tropics. Men and women were bred for sale to Christian nations and for fighting. Sir John Hawkins was the first Briton to trade in slaves, procuring negroes from the coast of Africa in 1562 and selling them in the West Indies. By 1776 England employed 130 ships on the trade and carried off 42,000, or about half of the total world figure for that year. It was estimated by Abbé Raynal in 1777, that three and a half million slaves had been exported by that date.

As a parliamentarian, Wilberforce formed the Society for the Suppression of the Slave Trade but lost a motion on its abolition in 1789. Lord Grenville re-introduced the issue in 1806 and on 25 March 1807 the act for the abolition of the slave trade was passed. Wilberforce continued to fight against slavery until 1833 when it was finally abolished throughout Britain's colonies.

THE LOSS OF THE ROYAL GEORGE

The *Royal George* was laid down in 1756. There had already been two other ships to bear the same name. They, like the new ship, were First Rates of 100 guns. This *Royal George* was to have been called *Royal Ann*, but was re-named prior to her launch. She was flagship to Admiral Sir Edward Hawke at Quiberon Bay in 1759. Later she flew the flag of Rear-Admiral Richard Kempenfelt, an innovative officer of Swedish descent. He introduced many improvements to the navy such as a divisional system of welfare for his people, changes to the signal code and tactical use of types of ship.

Royal George was laying at Spithead on 29 August 1782. Almost the entire crew were already on board together with many women and children, and she was being prepared for the fitting of a sea cock below the water line. The technique to expose the hull was known as a parliamentary heel, an inferior method to the more traditional careening or docking but with the advantage of keeping the ship in a better state of preparedness for sea. Its limitation was the maximum heel that could be introduced before the lowest gunports reached the waterline and was achieved by rolling the guns away from the side of intended for working.

Suddenly she took on water, filled and sank so quickly that some nine hundred souls, together with the Admiral, perished. The cause was never established. One theory is that the hull was so rotten that it gave way while being worked on; another was that the carpenter had introduced too much heel bringing her gunports below the water. Evidence given at the court martial held on 9 September 1782 supported both arguments but failed to rule out one or the other. It was said that the officers became alarmed at the heel and sent for the carpenter to reduce it, but it was also said that a rotted frame gave way. It is certain from letters that the ship's hull was in a sorry state and either theory or a combination of the two could be true.

The tragedy inspired William Cowper to write the lament 'Toll for the Brave'. More lamentable was the attitude of Parliament who never introduced a proper memorial to the lives lost.

1805 From Victory, responding to Marsden's letter regarding prize money, having left a prize crew on board: 'I have been honoured with your letter, inclosing Mr Gosling's report upon Maria Theresa, taken by the Ambuscade, when she was Prize to the Victory...the vessels manned by Officers and Men belonging to His Majesty's Ships taking Prizes, they have in every instance been condemned as Prizes taken by the Ship, to which such Officers and Men belonged'.

1759 William Wilberforce, philanthropist and campaigner against slavery, is born at Hull.

24th

1793 Nelson, in Agamemnon, quits the Toulon blockade for Naples and Leghorn. He writes: 'The perseverance of our Fleet has been great, and to that only can be attributed to our unexampled success. Not even a boat could get into Marseilles or Toulon, or on the coast, with provisions and the old saying, "that hunger will tame a Lion" was never more strongly exemplified'.

1770 The Bristol poet Thomas Chatterton, famous for his Rowley poems, commits suicide aged 18.

25th

1803 Of General Dumourier: 'Advise him not to make enemies, by showing he knows more than some of us. Envy knows no bounds to its persecution'.

1743 Antoine Laurent Lavoisier (d.1794), son of a French lawyer, father of modern chemistry is born. He was sent to the guillotine as 'The Republic has no need of scientists.'

26th

1801 On the purchase of Merton, and against the advice of his solicitor: 'I wish very much to have the place at Merton and agree that £9,000 with the furniture should be given for it'.

1789 In France 'The Declaration of the Rights of Man' (Droits de l'Homme) is published.

27th

1804 To Captain Parker, Amazon: 'I hope you are making haste to join me, for the day of Battle cannot be far off, when I shall want every Frigate; for the French have nearly one for every Ship, and we may as well have a Battle Royal – Line of Battle Ship opposed to Ships of the Line, and Frigates to Frigates'.

1791 Pandora, sent to recover the Bounty mutineers, is wrecked on the Great Barrier Reef.

28th

1787 To Philip Stephen, at the Admiralty, defending the appointment of a boatswain: '[Joseph King] was quite fit for the employment. I know not of remonstrations – I never allow inferiors to dictate. As to his being insane, and in consequence thereof, deprived of his employment as Boatswain, I beg to acquaint the Board that as he was squaring the yards he was struck with the sun, which, renders a man for some length of time wholly unfit for employment'.

1782 Royal George sinks off Spithead with all lives lost.

29th

1780 To Sir Peter Parker: 'Having been in a very bad state of health for these several months past, so bad as to be unable to attend my duty on board the Janus, and the faculty having informed me that I cannot recover in this climate; I am therefore to request that you will be pleased to permit me to go to England for the re-establishment of my health'.

1801 French troops under General Menou begin their withdrawal from Alexandria following defeat at the hands of the British.

30th

1805 On approaching Lord Barham on Berry's behalf: 'I will certainly, with much pleasure, mention you for a Ship, But Lord Barham is an almost entire stranger to me. However I can speak of you, as one of who's abilities I am well acquainted'. (Berry later takes command of Agamemnon).

1787 Pitt orders the withdrawal from the Corsican entanglement.

Portrait of Captain Berry.

31st

THE PROPERTY OF THE KING OF NAPLES

THE STRATEGIC POSITION OF MALTA

Fiona Fraser Thomson

The overthrow of French domination on Malta by the British was due to two correlating incidents: without the one, the other would not have been successful. In other words, an almost perfect example of cause and effect.

Primarily, the 'cause' was a conspiracy hatched within that hitherto most respected, exalted, admired and feared great fighting arm of the Christian church, The Sovereign Military and Hospitaller Order of the Knights of St John of Jerusalem, of Rhodes and Malta. Without the guiding light of Holy Wars to sustain them, the Knights had become degenerate, greedy, overbearing and lax, their vows of obedience, poverty and chastity forgotten. Nonetheless, it may be wondered why the greatest fighting force in Christendom should have opened the doors of Malta to Napoleon Bonaparte virtually without a fight. However, the wholesale confiscation of their extensive lands and properties in France and Spain following the French Revolution sheds a somewhat clearer light on the despair felt by many of the Knights as their spiritual and financial support crumbled away.

Thus the conspiracy, hatched by a handful of renegade Knights led by Bosredon de Ransijit who, by betraying the Order in secretly corresponding with Bonaparte, largely set in motion the unstoppable forces that were to contribute to the downfall

of Malta's Golden Age. Widespread disaffection was felt also by many of the Knights for the ineffectual government of their current Grand Master, von Hompesch and allied to this, a growing antipathy by the Maltese, which manifested itself in the seeds of civil disturbance.

Simultaneously, correspondence was being nurtured between the Order and the Russian Tsar Paul I, who sought to exploit the situation by offering to become the Order's protector. In return, Russia would thereby own the most strategic naval base in the Mediterranean!

Throughout her colourful and turbulent history, Malta's geographical position at the exact centre of the 'Middle Sea' has made her extremely attractive to the eyes of conquering and acquisitive nations. So it was that the correspondence with Russia, allied to the traitorous correspondence received in France from conspirators within the Order, focused Bonaparte's attention on Malta as a suitable base for his expansionist policies. In effect, Malta was set to become another pawn on Bonaparte's chessboard.

Writing to his foreign minister Talleyrand on 13 September 1797, Bonaparte asked: 'Why should we not take possession of Malta? [with this] we shall be masters of the Mediterranean.' The French Directoire, fearing that Austria, too, secretly nursed the idea of

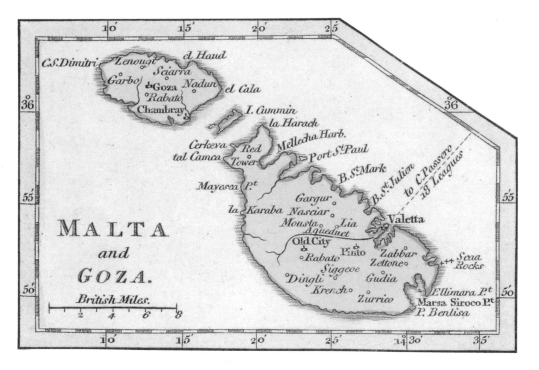

Map labels: C.S.Dimitri, Zenougl, el Haud, Sciarra, Garbo, Goza, Nadur, el Cala, Rabato, Chambray, I. Gummin, la Harach, Mellecha Harb., Cerkeva tal Camca, Red Tower, Port St Paul, B.St Mark, B.St Julien, to C.Passero 18 Leagues, Mayesca Pt, Gargur, Nasciar, la Karaba, Mousta, Lia, Valetta, Aqueduct, Old City, Pinto, Rabato, Zabbar, Siggeoe, Zettone, Dingli, Gudia, Krerch, Zurrico, Scra Rocks, E.llimara Pt, Marsa Siroco Pt, P. Benlisa

MALTA and GOZA.

British Miles.
2   4   6   8

Malta's geographical position at the centre of the 'Middle Sea' made the island extremely attractive to Bonaparte as a base for his expansionist policies.

acquiring Malta as a naval base, instructed Bonaparte to take all necessary steps to acquire the island. Later, it would be seen that the capture of Malta was the first step in Bonaparte's ambitions to overthrow British power in Europe and the East. Furthermore, the breakup of European alliance and Spain's declaration of war against Britain in 1796, had led to the evacuation of the British fleet from the Mediterranean and so left the way open for Bonaparte.

The French fleet arrived off Malta on 9 June 1798, with Bonaparte on *L'Orient*. To preserve the illusion that he was merely en route to Egypt, he asked the Order for permission to enter the harbour 'for water'. The Knights had long operated a defensive policy of no more than three ships at any one time being granted access to the harbour; Bonaparte's large number of ships challenged this, posing a menacing presence, and the Knights denied him access, so providing Bonaparte with an excuse to attack. Shortly thereafter, with barely a salvo fired, the Order capitulated. Bonaparte's task was unexpectedly made easier by the subsequent civil uprising because the hatred felt by the Maltese people for the Knights' degeneration and mistreatment of the local population had overcome any initial distrust of the French.

Local enthusiasm did not, ultimately, last for long. Remote from the tides of European power poli-

cies, the Maltese had little conception that they had exchanged bad for worse. One of the most devoutly Roman Catholic countries in the world ever since St Paul was shipwrecked there in AD 60 when, as a colony under the yoke of Rome the islanders, to a man, converted to Christianity, Malta's countless churches are viewed by her people with immense pride; extravagantly decorated as perhaps nowhere else in the world. It is easy to imagine the national shock, therefore, when one of the first acts committed by the French was the stripping of the wealth of the churches of Valetta and the pillaging of the Exchequer in the Citta Vecchia to augment the Napoleonic war chest; the plundered silver being given to the French officers as a 'gratification d'embarquement'. Worse was to follow, with the systematic ransacking and suppression of the monasteries and the subsequent sale of all monastic possessions. The harshness of French rule and the desecration of all that the Maltese most revered was insupportable, and the taper of revolt was lit. Malta, once again, looked outward for succour appealing first to Naples.

It may be useful to mention the background to this connection which dates back to the twelfth century when the islands were a fiefdom of the Kingdom of Naples and Sicily. The Normans lost Naples and Sicily to Spain in 1504. Upon the death of Ferdinand

Portrait of Sir
Alexander Ball,
whose efforts to free
the Maltese from the
French earned him a
permanent monument
on the island.

of Spain (in 1516) his grandson, the Emperor Charles of Austria, ceded Malta and Tripoli to the Knights of St John in 1530 for the feu of a falcon to give the illustrious Order a home following their expulsion from Rhodes by the Turks.

The islanders' petition to Naples failed to bring any immediate help, King Ferdinand being rather more taken up with his own pressing problems of the imminent overthrow of his Bourbon dynasty by the French. Subsequently, the Maltese Deputies sent a letter to Lord Nelson dated 12 September 1798, requesting British aid and stating that the French 'since the 10th of the past June, have exercised the most tyrannical government on the islands.' At this time, Britain had no particular ambition towards Malta as, indeed, a letter from Lord Grenville to Sir William Hamilton dated 3 October 1798, states: 'His Majesty does not entertain any idea of acquiring the sovereignty of Malta.'

Nonetheless, on 4 October 1798, Captain Alexander Ball was ordered by Nelson to proceed from Naples in *Alexander*, taking the *Terpsichore*, *Bonne Citoyenne* and *Incendiary* with him, with orders to co-operate in a blockade of Malta. That this directive had come by way of general orders for Nelson to defend Naples and which included, almost as an afterthought, the order to 'assist in the blocking up of Malta', says much for British disinterest in the situation at this time.

At first, the blockade was established by a Portuguese squadron assisted by Ball's four ships. Nelson, preparing to join Ball, wrote to the Earl of St Vincent on 13 October 1798, saying:

'We shall sail on Monday morning. When at sea, I shall detach *Audacious* and *Goliath* to join my dear friend Ball off Malta, to whom I shall entrust the blockade. The Government here are very sanguine about Malta, expecting to get hold of it in a short time. I am not so sanguine. The French have bread and water. I shall send to the French commanders a proper letter offering my mediation with the injured and plundered Maltese, but should the French ships escape, in that case I shall not trouble myself either with the capitulation or in obtaining mercy for the deluded people who have joined them...the island is certainly the property of the King of Naples...'.

With the addition of the *Minotaur* and the *Mutine*, Nelson arrived off Malta on 24 October 1798.

The first Maltese petition to the King of Naples eliciting no immediate response, a second was sent and a copy handed to Nelson on 25 October 1798 who, meanwhile, had summoned the French commanders Vaubois and Villeneuve to surrender; a command, not unnaturally, repulsed. Nelson, therefore, wasted no more time and set sail for Naples on 31 October 1798, leaving Alexander Ball once again in command. In the ensuing months, Ball so endeared himself to the Maltese by his enthusiasm and sympathy that they wrote to Nelson on 31 January 1799 pleading for Ball to be given a command on shore, such was their high opinion of him.

One of the inevitable results of any lengthy siege is boredom on the part of the besiegers. Thus it was that at about this time there came into being the legend of the Promotion Hook. This was originally an instrument of pillory in the form of a monstrous metal hook, devised by the Inquisitor of the Order for the summary punishment of anyone heard blaspheming. With time on their hands, the punishment hook was used from the earliest days of the siege to test young midshipmen in the belief that if they were able to squeeze through the hook, they could look forward to rapid advancement in their career – hence the name, Promotion Hook! Sited in St John's Square, it is still in evidence today.

Within three months, the effects of the blockade were beginning to be felt. That the Maltese were amongst the first to suffer was clearly revealed in another letter from the Maltese Deputies to Nelson: 'Our desolation is complete and the urgency is inexpressible.' Nelson urged Naples to send money and corn to the beleaguered islanders if the Maltese were not to be reduced to destitution and starvation, yet still little practical aid was forthcoming.

In February 1799, a letter to Alexander Ball from Vincenzo Borg, one of the Maltese leaders, contained the first suggestion that the island should be put under British protection: 'La plus part de nous en très-grand nombre se proteste ouvertement qu'il ne desire rien autant que de ne voir l'Isle dominée que par les Anglais et Malteais, et gouvernée par le Commandant Ball.' In Ball's letter to Nelson of 4 February 1799, he states that whenever Vaubois should capitulate, he would immediately grant passage to the Maltese Deputies who desired to consult with Lord Nelson regarding British protection. Nelson, however, felt that Malta should be ceded to the King of Naples and urged Ball to do everything to protect these rights.

Ball remained convinced otherwise and, only a few days later on 9 February 1799, he wrote again to Nelson stating that public opinion on Malta was swelling towards the island belonging to Great Britain. This was formally expressed in a further petition of 31 March 1799, signed again by Vincenzo Borg and the other Maltese Deputies. Still Nelson's opinion remained unaltered and in his letter of 6 April 1799 to the First Lord of the Admiralty, Earl Spencer, he stated the view that 'the possession of Malta by England would be a useless and enormous expense'. British assistance, meanwhile, continued to be given to Malta, notably when 800 regular soldiers and 400 marines under the command of Brigadier-General Sir Thomas Graham were sent to fortify the blockade. Graham's initial reaction, that he believed the defences of Valetta to be so strong as to render any assault impracticable, was duly reported. Meanwhile, disease added to the misery of starvation being endured by the Maltese, and Nelson, justly distressed, ordered the capture of any passing vessel containing corn to alleviate the islanders; this being, without

doubt, in the best traditions of British privateering!

During the close of 1799 and early 1800, as the siege intensified, the desperation of the islanders was so tellingly described in Graham's reports to his superiors General Fox in Minorca, and to Sir William Hamilton in Palermo that, as a result, at the end of February 1800, Lord Keith ordered Nelson to take command and by any and all necessary measures bring the blockade to an immediate and satisfactory conclusion.

Nelson duly set sail in his flagship, the *Foudroyant*, together with the *Northumberland, Culloden, Lion, Success, Alexander, Bonne Citoyenne, Stromboli, Minorca, Penelope* and *Vincenjo*. He stayed with the British squadron off Malta from mid February until the first week in March 1800 when, disobeying Lord Keith's explicit orders to remain on hand to see the blockade through and citing ill-health as an excuse, he returned to Palermo (and Lady Hamilton). Not for the first time was the infatuation of Nelson for Emma Hamilton to cloud his judgement with, at best, direct insubordination; at worst, possibly disastrous results.

However, Nelson did return to Malta on 24 April 1800, with Sir William and Lady Hamilton on board as passengers. He dropped anchor in St Paul's Bay on 4 May 1800, where they stayed for sixteen days until, still disobeying orders, he withdrew in early June 1800 to offer his services as a personal envoy to the Queen of Naples. The outcome of this disregard for duty on Nelson's part was undoubtedly to prolong the siege conditions being endured on the island. After this, Nelson never again returned to Malta.

The surrender of the French on 4 September 1800 was brought about unequivocally because of the privations suffered equally now by the French garrisons as by the Maltese. What perhaps neither Bonaparte nor General Vaubois had quite so readily assimilated was the unique situation of the island, which depended to an almost total degree on other countries for the plupart of its food supplies. The availability or withholding of such supplies was controlled entirely by whomsoever held sway in the Mediterranean. Thus, the fate of Malta and all on her depended not on her hereditary protectors, the Knights of St John nor, indeed, on the power and ambition of Bonaparte, but on the greater force at sea at that time – the British.

The surrender of
Malta to the British
after a two-year siege,
4 September 1800.

Heroic though the Maltese were, the fall of the French in Malta was unarguably due to the successful blockade by the British fleet, and it is a little known but extraordinary fact, amongst the listings of other extraordinary battle facts (Agincourt, Flodden, Quatre Bras), that given the length of the siege (two years), coupled with the widespread deprivation and disease suffered, only 300 Maltese lost their lives, and not one British soldier lost his. Valetta remained largely intact despite prolonged bombardment; a testament, surely to the extraordinary building skills of the island's previous protectors.

In what seems an occasion of *déjà vu*, the Maltese were yet again to be treated with contempt, this time by the British Government who refused the Maltese battalions a share in the prize money. This, despite the most vociferous testimony by Ball and Graham, who unstintingly praised the Maltese people's courage and steadfastness. It is little wonder Alexander Ball was so dearly loved! It speaks for itself that, today, where no trace of Nelson remains on the island, Alexander Ball is forever commemorated by a superb monument on the promontory overlooking Fort St Elmo, where it may fancifully be supposed that the spirit of Alexander Ball still watches over and guards the Maltese people whose love and admiration he so justly earned.

For those interested in what happened next in Malta's chequered history, the outcome of this two year naval siege was thus. The capitulation by the French did not automatically bestow upon Malta the status of a British colony. Long after the surrender, the 'Malta Question' remained a tilting ground for international power politics played out by the main protagonists of Britain, Russia and – unbelievable though it may seem – France. By September 1801, Malta's future was being bandied about by the British Foreign Office like so much market barter – even to the quite astonishing act of re-offering it back to France!

By 1802, the preliminaries to the Treaty of Amiens recorded that Malta should be given back to the Order and defended by Russia 'or some other power'; this, to a people who had formally recorded their hatred and distrust of the Knights and who had formally sought to be placed under the protection of Great Britain! Given too, the rumours circulating through Europe at this time that Bonaparte meant to re-acquire Malta as a base for his re-conquest of Egypt, this could be viewed less like succour than disaster. Malta seemed to be poised to be sacrificed, yet again, on the wider altar of political expediency.

Fortunately, the galling thought of Bonaparte's megalomaniac ambitions brought a measure of sanity back to the British Government and others, who now began to perceive the strategic importance of Malta. Nelson, revising his original dismissive opinion, decided to take the offensive rather than compensate the British with Malta, and with the Russian Tsar Alexander interfering in British politics, the British Government now suddenly converted to a determination 'to preserve the rock'.

Though Britain might have acquired Malta outright with the almost universal approval of the islanders, it was not until the signing of the Treaty of Paris in 1814 that the 'Malta Question' was finally resolved. Thus are the fates of whole populations, countries and lives decided.

Fiona Fraser-Thomson was born in 1945 in India. She was educated privately, attended two finishing schools and went to study history and archaeology at the University of Lausanne. Other academic achievements include a Diplome Distinguée in French from the Institute of Linguistics, and bronze, silver and gold medals from the Poetry Speaking Society. Fiona is a skilled historian and has created several historical interpretations for visitor attractions throughout the country and abroad; her particular field of expertise lies in antiquities. She is also a gifted poet, having received several certificates as an award winning finalist in many prestigious poetry competitions. She is about to be published in hardback for the first time in no less than three forthcoming anthologies. As well as her literary calling, Fiona has pursued a career in public relations for the past twenty-six years. She speaks several languages, and her creative flair extends to her love of cooking and gardening.

Gillray's representation of the barbarities of the West Indian slave trade. A slave, through ill health is unable to work, and is punished for his perceived indolence by being steeped in a vat of boiling sugar juice. Slavery was abolised in the British Empire in 1807 and throughout her colonies in 1833. But it was not until after the civil war in America that slaves in the South were finally emancipated. (See 1 September.)

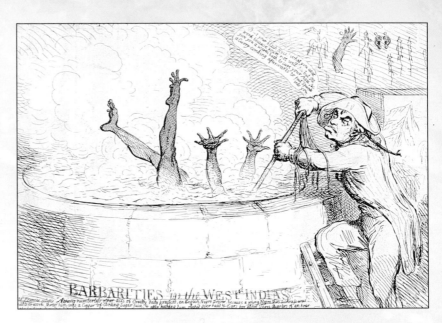

THE TREATIES OF PARIS

Paris was the venue for two important treaties during Nelson's life. The first marked the conclusion of the Seven Years' War. It was signed by Britain, France and Spain on 10 February 1763.

The Treaty of Paris of 3 September 1783, marked the end of the American Revolution. Britain's world-wide influence, so assisted by the first treaty, now suffered its first colonial reversal by recognising the United States of America.

Admiral Lord Keith.
(See 2 September.)

1787 To Philip Stephen on the unusual event of desertion from his ship, Boreas: 'A seaman deserted yesterday morning from duty. I have therefore thought proper to send you a description, that their Lordships may, if they think fit, take such measures as may be necessary for apprehending him. I have no doubt of his having gone for London'.

1773 *Phillis Wheatley, a 20-year old former slave from Boston, publishes her 'Poems on Various Subjects, Religious and Moral'.*

1st

1805 To Blackwood who had called at Merton: 'I am sure you bring me news of the French and Spanish Fleets, and I think I shall yet have to beat them'.

1801 *Alexandria capitulates to forces under Admiral Lord Keith, Foudroyant. The French Justice and five others are taken.*

2nd

1799 From the Samuel and Jane transport to Captain Cockburn: 'You are hereby required and directed to proceed to Gibraltar, and put yourself under the command of Rear-Admiral Duckworth, or the senior Officer of that place. But should it happen that you are the senior officer at that place, you will use your endeavours to succour the Garrison, and yield them every assistance in your power to procure supplies and keep the Ports on the Coast of Barbary open'.

1783 *The Treaty of Paris recognises the independence of the 13 colonies of America, declared two years before.*

3rd

1805 Emma writes to Lady Bolton: 'My dear friend I am again broken-hearted, as our dear Nelson is immediately going. It seems as though I have had a fortnight's dream, and am awoke to all the misery of this cruel separation'.

1804 *The Royal College of Surgeons in Dublin appoints Abraham Colles as professor of anatomy, physiology and surgery.*

4th

1799 To Rear-Admiral Duckworth: 'Should the force sent down to Gibraltar be more than is necessary for guarding Cadiz, you will send me the Northumberland; or such Ship as may be able to keep the sea during winter for the Russian Admiral has already told me his Ships cannot. In short, for active operations, none but the English Ships are of use'.

1774 *The first Continental Congress assembles at Philadelphia; shortly afterwards armed conflict begins at Lexington and lasts until 1783.*

5th

1803 To William Hazlewood, his solicitor for his will and prize money, relating to the disposal of Merton: 'I send you a Codicil to my Will, which you will not communicate to any person breathing; as I would wish you to open, read it, and if not drawn up properly, send me a copy, and I will execute it. It is possible that my personal estate after the disposal of the furniture at Merton, may not amount to £4,000; and sooner than this legacy, or any other, should go unpaid, I would saddle Bronté, or any other estate with legacies'.

1776 *Sergeant Ezra Lee, commanding America's first submarine, Turtle, built by David Bushnell in 1775, attacks Howe's flagship Eagle in New York harbour, but he fails to attach his explosive charge.*

6th

1798 To Sir William Hamilton on the extraordinary measures needed to keep ships at sea: 'The Culloden sails so heavy, by having a sail under her bottom in order to stop her leak, that it has coursed me to be a much longer time than I can at present spare to make passages'.

1757 *Marie Joseph Paul Yves Roch Gilbert du Motier, Marquis de Lafayette (d. 1834), French statesman and Captain of the dragoons is born. The Continental Congress votes to accept his services as a general on 31 July 1777.*

7th

GEORGE III

An engraving showing the palace of George III at Kew in Surrey.

King George III was born on 4 June 1738 and succeeded his grandfather George II who died on 25 October 1760. His father, Frederick, Prince of Wales had died in 1751 during a game of cricket.

George III was the first of the Hanovarians to actually be born and educated in Britain, and he reigned through many challenges in foreign affairs; the wars in Europe, conflict in India and the emergence of independent America. More obstinate than able, he wished to see a strong Britain but inflicted great damage on the country through his mishandling of the thirteen colonies. Lecky wrote:

'[He] inflicted more profound and enduring injuries upon his country than any other modern English King...obstinately resisting measures which are now almost universally admitted to have been good, and in supporting measures which are as universally admitted to have been bad.'

George built up a parliamentary following, 'the King's friends', through bribes and titles and was able to manipulate Lord North as a figurehead minister. This arrangement finished abruptly when the colonists triumphed at Yorktown. He succumbed to attacks of insanity, brought on, it is believed today, by the disease porphyria, but towards the end of his reign his popularity increased again, earning him the sobriquet 'Farmer George'. He died on 20 January 1820.

The death of General Wolfe on the Heights of Abraham (see 13 September), by the American artist, Benjamin West. Wolfe, perhaps because of the manner of his death, became a national hero. It was the kind of death Nelson approved of, so much so that he persuaded West to paint a similar portrayal of his own demise when it should arise.

☙1802☙ Writing from Merton to the Lord Mayor of London about Copenhagen: 'Never, till the City of London think justly of the merits of my brave companions of the second of April, can I, their commander, receive any attention from the City of London'.

☙1761☙ George III marries Charlotte, daughter of Charles Duke of Mecklenburg-Strelitz in Westminster. They meet for the first time on their wedding day.

8th

☙1787☙ To the Admiralty: 'William Pope, a seaman under my command was arrested for a debt of £21 at the suit of John Rowe, a Landlord at Gosport; other publicans, as well as this man, having declared they have taken out writs against several of the men, have a right to take them out of the Ship. I beg their Lordships' orders whether I am to give up these men, or in what manner I am to act'.

☙1790☙ Battle of Tendra, west of the Crimea. Ushakov again attacks the Turks, captures two ships but one blows up with the captors on board.

9th

☙1789☙ On half pay, Nelson asks Locker: 'Is there any idea of our being drawn into a quarrel by these commotions on the continent? I will take care to make my application in time'.

☙1801☙ Egypt and Syria are evacuated by the French. Syria is next invaded by Mehamet Ali in 1831.

10th

☙1785☙ To Frances Nisbet: 'My greatest wish is to be united with you; and the foundation of all conjugal happiness, real love and esteem, is, I trust, what you believe I possess in the strongest degree towards you'.

☙1777☙ The patriot troops led by George Washington are defeated at Brandywine Creek. Philadelphia falls to the British. General Howe hesitates, allowing Washington to withdraw his troops.

11th

☙1804☙ Nelson informs the Admiralty he has appointed Mr Edward Flin of Victory to Niger. The night before he had jumped overboard to save James Archibald: 'I must observe that Mr Flin's conduct very justly merits my approbation. I therefore hope their Lordships' will approve of my having placed him in this invaliding vacancy'.

☙1792☙ The first heads roll from the French guillotine.

12th

☙1805☙ In his private diary: 'At half-past ten drove from dear dear Merton, where I left all which I hold dear in this world, to go to sea to serve my King and Country. May the Great God whom I adore enable me to fulfil the expectations of my Country; and if it is His good pleasure that I should return, my thanks will never cease being offered up to the throne of His Mercy'.

☙1759☙ Wolfe and Montcalm receive fatal wounds on the plains of Abraham in the hour of victory. Quebec capitulates, deciding the fate of Canada for two hundred years.

13th

☙1805☙ On arrival at Portsmouth: 'At six o'clock arrived at Portsmouth, and having arranged all my business, embarked at the Bathing Machines with Mr Rose and Mr Canning at two; got on board the Victory at St Helens, who dined with me; preparing for sea'.

☙1759☙ The first English board game, 'A Journey through Europe', goes on sale, priced eight shillings.

14th

☙1805☙ Victory proceeds in company with Euryalus, leaving Royal Sovereign, Agamemnon and Defiance to join when ready. To Captain Lechmere, Thunderer: 'Off Cape St Vincent where a Frigate will be stationed to give information where I am to be found. In the event of not meeting said Frigate, the Ship in search of me must call off Cape St Mary's and Cadiz, approaching them with the utmost caution'.

☙1784☙ Vincenzo Lunardi rises in a hydrogen filled balloon from the Artillery Ground, London, accompanied by a pigeon, a dog and a cat. By 16 September 1803, Gay Lussac had extended the altitude record to 22,942 feet.

15th

*'Hoorah, me boys for freedom.' A highly romanticised image of
Robert Emmet, the patriot and would be rebel leader who lived
and died for a united Ireland. But support for the uprising he
sought to foment in 1803 proved to be as elusive, and its
execution as unsuccessful, as it had been in 1798.
(See 20 September.)*

⚓1803⚓ To Major General Villettes: 'She [Spain] must go to war either with France or us; and all the blame is laid at our door because we will not bow to France'.

⚓1795⚓ *The British, under Admiral Elphinstone and General Clarke, take Capetown. It is restored under the Treaty of Amiens but retaken on 9 January 1806, by Baird and Popham.*

16th

⚓1805⚓ Off the Eddystone, to Emma: 'I entreat my dear Emma, that you will cheer up; and we will look forward to many happy years, and be surrounded by our children's children. God Almighty can, when he pleases, remove the impediment [his marriage]'.

⚓1771⚓ *Tobias George Smollett (b. 1721), the Scottish novelist best known for his picturesque adventure novels, dies at Livorno, Italy.*

17th

⚓1796⚓ Nelson takes the island of Capraja. To the Governor, enclosing capitulation terms: 'Had your answer [to a letter of 11 September] been a refusal to treat, our attack by Land and Sea would have commenced, and the lives and property of innocent inhabitants would have been sacrificed by your fruitless attempt against the superior forces attacking you'.

⚓1777⚓ *In advance of the British Army's occupation, the Liberty Bell is moved from Pennsylvania, where it was hidden in a church. It was moved back on 27 June 1778.*

18th

⚓1794⚓ Nelson arrives at Genoa flying the union flag at the fore topgallant masthead. To Fanny: 'We were in the Mole before they saw us from the Signal house. None of us having been here, I had the Signal up for a Pilot, which, by the Consul's account they took for a Flag of a Vice-Admiral; and although it was struck a full quarter of an hour before they saluted, which they did with fifteen guns, and I returned in equal number'.

⚓1792⚓ *Thomas Paine flees to France to seek refuge following charges of high treason in Britain for his book 'The Rights of Man'.*

Gillray depicts the author of 'The Rights of Man' and 'Common Sense' as a fugitive from justice enjoying only a troubled sleep.

19th

⚓1796⚓ To Don Juan de Sannova, La Vengeance, illustrating the difficulty in obtaining news: 'It is not possible to desire a Spanish Officer to do what would be considered in the smallest degree dishonourable, I am in doubt, Sir, whether it is War or Peace between the two courts. You, Sir, say you are sure that all is Peace, and that the most perfect good understanding subsists between the two courts'.

⚓1803⚓ *Robert Emmet, Irish nationalist, convicted of treason, is hanged.*

20th

⚓1796⚓ Nelson explains to Jervis that because of Spain's neutrality he would not take the Spanish vessel La Vengeance, 'Although I own my fingers itched for it'.

⚓1795⚓ *The Battle of Diamond in Armagh is fought. To commemorate this conflict between 'Peep-o-day Boys' and 'Defenders' the first Orange Lodge was formed.*

21st

⚓1801⚓ On the mortally wounded Captain Edward Parker, to Dr Baird: 'Although Parker has had a bad night, yet with your nursing I have great hopes; and, let what will happen, great consolation from your abilities and affectionate disposition'.

⚓1792⚓ *In France the Convention, having declared a republic two days earlier, begins its new calender. This day becomes the first day of Year One.*

22nd

JOHN PAUL JONES (1742-1790)

Born as John Jones at Kirkbean, Galloway in 1742, he joined the British merchant marine in 1761, and until 1773 operated predominantly from the Solway Firth, London and Africa to the West Indies and Virginia. He soon became a master but when he killed a man in Tobago in self defence he fled to Virginia.

When England and the thirteen colonies engaged in combat John Paul Jones obtained a commission as a first lieutenant, then command of the sloop *Ranger* in October 1707. On 2 December 1777 he visited Paris where Benjamin Franklin, the American colonies' commissioner in France, befriended him. Jones received orders to 'distress' the enemy (Britain) and embarked upon a series of short raids, notably at Whitehall and including an attempt to take as hostage the Earl of Selkirk from St Mares Isle for American sailors. The following day on 24 April 1778 he defeated the *Drake* after an hour's fierce fighting and towed her to Brest. *Drake's* people were later exchanged for American prisoners. He was next appointed to command a squadron on *Bonhomme Richard*, a converted East Indiaman, with USS *Alliance*, the French frigate *Pallas*, and some smaller vessels, all under the American flag.

Their first cruise departed Lorient on 14 August 1779 but was dogged with difficulties. A cutter immediately became lost off the Skelligs and never rejoined the squadron. Later, durng the encounter at Flamborough Head, Landias, *Alliance*, acted independently throughout, except during *Bonhomme Richard's* action against *HMS Serapis* when he fired into both ships, causing more damage to the former than the latter. (He was eventually court martialled and dismissed.)

On 23 September 1779, Paul Jones' squadron intercepted a battle convoy of forty-seven sail escorted by HMS *Serapis* (Captain Richard Pearson) and HMS *Countess of Scarborough*, and a bitter encounter – the Battle of Flamborough Head – ensued. Pearson saw to the safety of the convoy then engaged *Bonhomme Richard* while *Countess of Scarborough* engaged the larger *Pallas*. After fighting muzzle to muzzle for two hours *Serapis* knocked out all but two of *Bonhomme Richard's* guns but at the point of boarding fire broke out in *Serapis* and Pearson was forced

to surrender. Having suffered more, *Bonhomme Richard* sank two days later; both crew and captives were transferred back to the *Serapis* where, with the assistance of the remainder of his squadron, Jones was able to limp back into Texel on 3 October.

There he remained blockaded by the British until 27 December, but then sailed in *Alliance* for Lorient, reaching port on 19 February 1780 where he was well received by the French. With his reputation growing he went to America in the sloop *Ariel* where Congress rewarded him with command of the half-built *America*, the only 74 under construction. In a change of heart Congress refused to support a peace-time navy and presented her instead to France. Jones returned to France to seek a commission without success but finally achieved one with the Imperial Russian Navy. Although he obtained flag rank, he was never 'accepted' and returned once again to France where he died on 18 July 1790.

Jones was a great innovator and tactician – qualities lost to his own generation but recovered from his many letters and manuscripts. In 1905 his body was exhumed and carried to Annapolis. He was finally laid to rest in the crypt of the Naval Academy chapel. Possibly one of the finest strategists the US Navy never had!

THE MAGIC FLUTE

Mozart's penultimate and perhaps best know opera – *The Magic Flute* (*Die Zauberflaute*) was based ostensibly on the fairy story 'Lulu' as published in a collection of Wieland's *Oriental Fairy Tales* of 1786. But equally, much has been made of its covert, or perhaps overt, allusion to Freemasonry, which was at that time a much discussed subject. Its practice in Austria had been forbidden by Maria Theresa and armed forces had been employed by break-up lodges.

The Magic Flute, was, some have argued, a chance or convenient vehicle to perform these forbidden rites on stage. The scene is, after all, set in Egypt where the Craft is believed to have originated. Likewise, the ordeals undergone and the tasks performed by Prince Tamino, the hero, in his quest for the love of Pamina, daughter of the Queen of the Night, have a certain resonance in the rituals of the ancient Craft.

⚓ **1803** ⚓   Nelson complains to His Highness the Bey of Tunis about privateering against vessels of nations at peace (British) and asks for an enquiry: 'Reports have reached me that some Vessels who call themselves French Privateers but who I can consider in no other light than as Pirates, lie under the island of Zimbra. I understand they have, passing for a cruizer belonging to your highness, taken possession of an English Ship'.

⚓ *1779* ⚓   *John Paul Jones captures Serapis but loses his own ship Bonhomme Richard off Flamborough Head.*

23rd

⚓ *1793* ⚓   Off Leghorn: 'An express came that a French man-of-war, and three sail under her convoy, had anchored under Sardinia....Unfit as my ship was, I had nothing left for the honour of our country but to sail, which I did two hours afterwards....It was necessary to show them what an English man-of-war would do'.

⚓ *1776* ⚓   *The St Ledger is run for the first time, at Doncaster. Its founder, Colonel Barry St Ledger leaves afterwards to join General Burgoyne in Hudson Valley.*

24th

⚓ *1805* ⚓   Nelson off Cape St Vincent, sends Thunderer and Euryalus ahead to announce his approach. To Collingwood: 'If you are in sight of Cadiz not only no salute may take place, but also that no Colours may be hoisted, for it is well not to proclaim to the Enemy every Ship which may join the Fleet'.

⚓ *1807* ⚓   *George Coyley publishes a paper on hot air engines and the use of internal combustion engines for flight.*

25th

⚓ *1799* ⚓   To Spencer, assuming the French will augment Malta: 'I have certain information from Toulon, on 15th September, that five Vessels are loading salt provisions for Malta; also that two old Venetian ships were loading stores for the above destination'.

⚓ *1799* ⚓   *Massena, who began the battle the previous day, routs a new Russo-Austrian army at Zurich and Suvorov evacuates Switzerland.*

26th

⚓ *1801* ⚓   Captain Edward Parker, wounded during the attack of the French Flotilla moored before Boulogne, on the night of 15 August, dies. Nelson said, 'He suffered much and can suffer no more'.

⚓ *1802* ⚓   *Fire destroys much of Store Street, off Tottenham Court Road. The extent of the property destroyed is described as immense.*

27th

⚓ *1805* ⚓   Concerned at alerting the enemy of his arrival at Cadiz, Nelson writes a general memorandum: 'It is my particular directions that no junior Flag Officer salutes on joining the Fleet under my Command'.

⚓ *1770* ⚓   *Bender, which offered asylum to Charles XII of Sweden after his defeat by Peter the Great, is taken by storm by the Russians.*

28th

HORATIO NELSON'S DATE OF BIRTH

⚓ *1804* ⚓   To Emma: 'This day, my dearest Emma, which gave me my birth, I consider as more fortunate than common days, as, by my coming into this world, it has brought me so intimately acquainted with you, who my soul holds dear. I well know that you will keep it, and have my dear Horatia to drink my health'.

⚓ *1801* ⚓   *The Treaty of Madrid ends the War of the Oranges between Spain and Portugal. Portugal agrees to bar English naval vessels from her ports.*

29th

⚓ *1805* ⚓   To Sir Alexander Ball in Malta: 'I got fairly into the fleet yesterday, and under all circumstances I find them as perfect as could be expected. The Force is at present not so large as might be wished, but I will do my best with it; they will give me more when they can, and I am not come forth to find difficulties, but to remove them'.

⚓ *1791* ⚓   *The first performance of Mozart's 'The Magic Flute' takes place in Vienna. Mozart died of typhus in Vienna on 5 December 1791, and is buried in the common ground of St Mark's churchyard.*

30th

A Good Day's Work

THE BATTLE OF TRAFALGAR

David Harris

A plan of the British attack on the combined fleet off Trafalgar that shows how events unfolded during the battle.

The Battle of Trafalgar is at once complex and simple. Complex because a lingering reluctance by the Admiralty to understand and embrace evolution blighted technical and tactical progress; continuous chronic European dynastic wars and perfidious diplomacy among the protagonists encumbered those who fought the battles; and there was a bewildering array of measures to censure the commanders at sea should they fail to fulfil the aspirations of their masters.

Simple because it was not in Nelson's persona to countenance anything else.

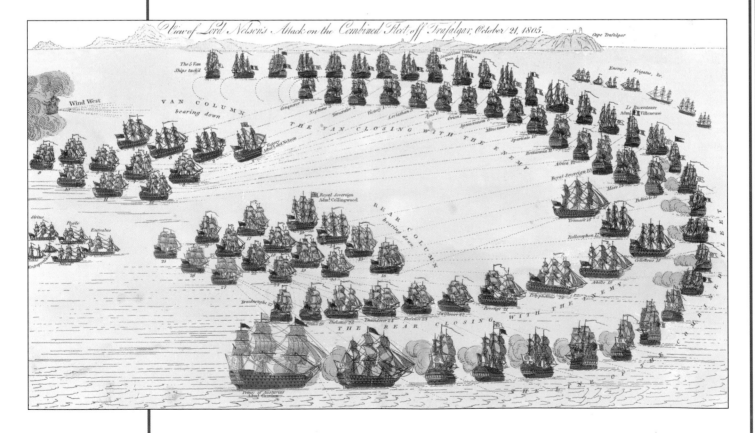

View of Lord Nelson's Attack on the Combined Fleet off Trafalgar, October 21, 1805.

Trafalgar had a galvanising effect on public esteem for the navy; which it has largely retained to the present day, although its effect on Britain and Europe may still be unresolved. That it established British supremacy over waterborne commerce; an objective of the earlier Navigation Acts, is without question. Arguably it secured Britain against invasion although Napoleon, disenchanted with his navy, had already begun his withdrawal from Boulogne on 27 August 1805, from which time the French have proclaimed a sea battle irrelevant. The immediate legacy to France and Spain was simple; their fleets, neither equipped, motivated, or even capable of doing serious battle, were destroyed. To the British it instilled an indelible confidence in their navy, a confidence which had faltered under James II, re-emerged in 1759, but waned again during the American campaigns. Tragically, the cost was the life of our foremost naval hero, and there is some poignancy in the contemporary observation that to the British fleet the loss of its commander was more important than the victory!

It would be imprecise to choose a point at which a naval action, off Cape Trafalgar or elsewhere, became inevitable, although the breakdown of the Treaty of Amiens on 16 May 1803, which had been brokered on 12 October the previous year might legitimately be considered pivotal.

During the peaceful interlude, Nelson, frustrated and on half pay, was reduced to the role of an observer, while Napoleon, with commendable industry, supplemented his arsenal (which included surplus British war stores), re-built his fleet, set about building a flotilla of small craft, and generally prepared his multi-faceted plan for Europe, one dimension of which was an invasion of southern England. Ultimately he denounced Britain for failing to withdraw from Malta. Britain, its parliament in disarray, army poorly equipped and navy worn out, had no choice but to resume hostilities. Meanwhile, Spain in a measure calculated to re-secure her West Indian trade while severing British' interest there, pledged thirty ships of the line to France, although it is said the Spanish navy detested the French only marginally less than the British and were never wholeheartedly behind the campaign.

Recalled to duty and stationed off Toulon from May 1803 to August 1805, Nelson blockaded first La Touche Treville (who died according to the French newspapers from his daily walk to the signal post upon Sept to observe the British fleet, but according to Nelson's diary it was colic), and then Villeneuve who had escaped destruction at Aboukir. Once, during a lull in the tempestuous weather and with the co-operation of the Spanish, Villeneuve slipped out of port, but his ships scattered before the gale and limped back to Toulon. 'These gentlemen', said Nelson, 'are not accustomed to a Gulf of Lyons gale.'

On 4 August *Phoebe* signalled that the French admiral was again at sea. Information reached Nelson - they had cleared the straits of Gibraltar, passed Madeira, and in June had reached Barbados. The Great Chase followed. Unable to strike a blow against British West Indies trade, running short of supplies and in deteriorating health, the French fleet headed home, followed just as assiduously by Nelson who returned via St Vincent to Gibraltar to re-victual, going ashore for the first time in two years save ten days. He remained for just two; barely long enough to replenish stores before resuming the chase – up and down the Bay of Biscay, to Ireland, back to Ushant, but never an encounter. Finally he returned to Portsmouth and Merton, sick at heart and more shattered than his ships.

But on 2 August Captain Blackwood called at Merton. Nelson greeted him with: 'I am sure you bring me news of the French and Spanish fleets'.

It was so – the French had re-fitted at Vigo and were now in Cadiz.

'Offer your services', implored Blackwood.

So too did Emma: 'However we may lament your absence offer your services – they will be accepted and you will gain a quiet heart by it; you will have a glorious victory and then you may return here to be happy'.

His services were accepted.

'Choose your officers', said Lord Barham on handing him the Navy List.

'Choose yourself, my lord', was Nelson's reply. 'The same spirit stirs the whole profession – you cannot choose wrong.'

In France things were not as tranquil as they were at Merton, as can be seen from the following paper.

Secret Project for the Emperor and King.

Paris, Fructidor 22nd Year XIII (September 11th, 1805)

Fred Roe's late nineteenth-century visualisation of events as Nelson waves to the crowd as he leaves the shore to board Victory *on 14 September 1805.*

'England believes herself to be freed from the fear of an invasion, at least for the time being. This is precisely the moment to strike a blow at her'.

At 8.30pm on Friday, 13 September he kissed Emma and Horatia for the last time and departed from 'dear, dear Merton': on 14 September he embarked at Portsmouth surrounded by the city's population swollen by adoring mobs who impeded his short journey to the steps. Men followed him into the water just to touch his hand for they saw in Nelson the only man who could defeat Napoleon. They loved him truly and as fervently as he loved England.

Victory, joined by *Euryalus*, *Ajax* and *Thunderer* made fair passage to Cadiz where Nelson immediately withdrew the main body, in battle formation, to a position hull down and out of sight. He had ensured no cannon would be fired to signal his arrival and left his 'eyes', the advance squadron, led by *Mars*, under Duff, to watch the harbour.

Meanwhile, the following paper was sent to Villeneuve:

The 3rd complementary day of Year XVIII. (September 20th).

'M. Le Vice-Amiral, His Majesty the Emperor and King has just appointed Vice-Amiral Rosily to the command of the naval forces assembled at Cadiz and has given orders that you are to proceed to Paris in order to give an account of the campaign on which you have recently been employed'.

Nelson's plan of attack was based on Napoleon's favourite strategy of smashing the enemy at its centre and turning quickly on the two broken halves. He modified it to concentrate downwind of the breach where he would bring one fourth greater fire power to bear than the enemy could muster and, naturally, make best use of the wind. It was to become known as the 'Nelson Touch'. Later, it was extolled by post battle commentators conveniently sweeping aside the inefficiencies, blunders and obsessive conservatism that bedevilled the era, and used it to laud the glory of all things naval thereafter – a blinkerd wisdom confusing, rather than clarifying, our understanding of Nelson. Closer inspection of his memorandum, which he despatched to Collingwood on 9 October, reveals his ability to collect and exploit to his advantage practical events from the past. This was the real Nelson Touch.

The Nelson Touch, although ostensibly a secret paper, had been rehearsed with Keats. *Prima facie* it was seriously flawed. Against an equal enemy it must surely fail but Nelson's force, depleted by the release of six ships to re-provision Rear-Admiral Louis, was by no means even equal. He wrote to Emma: 'When I came to explain to them "The Nelson Touch" it was like an electric shock...'.

Blackwood recalled, 'It was new – it was singular – it was simple.'

It was new.

Very little was fundamentally new. Drake, like most of the Admiralty was an advocate of the blockade: 'The best way to protect England is to pin the enemy in their own harbours'.

Nelson was competent at this form of warfare but had little patience for it, preferring to lure the enemy to sea where he could get at them.

Howard held council at sea immediately prior to the Armada; Collingwood did not but this practice was very quickly re-introduced by Nelson at Cadiz.

The signal book was introduced by Howe and Kempenfelt in 1782 and revised by Home Popham in 1800. Nelson exploited its advantages but was careful to ensure a contingency plan in the event of unforeseen circumstances. 'In case signals can neither be seen or perfectly understood, no captain can do wrong if he places his Ship alongside that of the enemy.' Borrowed from Lord Hawke, Locker had said much the same to a young Horatio Nelson.

The line of battle was broken by Rodney at the Saintes and in the same action Hood turned out of line to find his own gap in the enemy line after which it became an acceptable manoeuvre. Howe 'instructed' his captains to break the line on the Glorious First of June. Even then breaking the line was not new; elaborate plans had been drawn up by the Admiralty in the early 1600's showing in graphic detail how to break the enemy line in various wind conditions. And even at Nelson's most glorious victory, Aboukir, it can be argued, his action was based on a plan used by Ushkakov.

The Nelson Touch was then the scene of action commander's fighting instructions – Fighting Instructions were first introduced by James II when he was Lord High Admiral. It was an orchestration of proven independently successful ideas. It was not new, though Nelson's style of leadership and the way he exploited prevailing circumstances was, and that was one of his marks of brilliance.

It was singular.

Nelson had sought an opportunity to implement his passionate wish to destroy the French navy, perhaps his last chance if he guessed wrong and Villeneuve escaped, by attacking the instant he found them and with the conviction that God was for England, which he firmly believed. Clearly not a plan to survive scrutiny but one delivered with such conviction that complexities of wind, lee shore and shoals were relegated to afterthought. He even admitted that 'Something must be left to chance...'.

It was indeed singular in intent.

It was simple.

Apparently so. It might also be described as reckless. The lead ships in each column were seriously endangered, outnumbered on every count: ships, guns, grenades, and muskets in the fighting tops (which Nelson never cared for). It could have been a catastrophic failure.

Few of the combined fleet of France and Spain could boast cap squares, their rate of fire and accuracy would be inferior to the British gunners, they would use chain and bar shot against rigging, unlike Nelson who fired round shot at hulls. Furthermore they had no carronades, lethal to men on an exposed deck at pistol shot range, and they had practised little. Nor was their seamanship in practice. Their problems were compounded by lack of a substantial signal book or a common language. There was discord among the admirals and lack of confidence in Villeneuve by Napoleon, as well as Gravina and a good many other commanders in the fleet. Nelson understood a great deal about these factors. He also understood that his officers were second to none, whereas the French had lost many of their best ones to the guillotine.

In summary, his plan was to command the weather line while Collingwood in *Royal Sovereign* commanded the lee. Collingwood was to cut through at about the twelfth ship from the rear; Nelson would strike the centre while the advance squadron would lop off the van. The plan would be adapted so that at each break point the English would be one fourth superior to those they cut off – a large proportion would remain untouched at the beginning but it would be some hours before they could turn and provide assistance. Close for a decisive action. The object was simple.

Coincidental with Nelson's arrival on station, the

French Emperor had previously ordered Villeneuve to sea even though Admiral Rosily, his successor was on his way and already in Madrid. Much has been made of Villeneuve's conduct but few reports credit him for his undoubtable courage. His character was blackened in the eyes of Napoleon, unjustly, by General Lauriston, his accomplice in *Bucentaure*. Villeneuve (who was unaware of this treachery) had never openly been criticised, and assumed that he would remain as Rosily's second-in-command. 'I shall be happy to yield the first place to Rosily, if I am allowed to have the second; but it would be hard to give up all hope of being vouchsafed the opportunity of proving that I am worthy of a better fate.' He was also unaware that Rosily had the discretion to avoid engagement with a superior force. His own orders were emphatic and explicit. To sail!

Rosily was held up in Madrid, conditions were favourable overnight of 18 October and at dawn Villeneuve made the signal to sail. The light north-easterly abated and during fits and starts seven ships of the line and two frigates under Admiral Magon were able to work out of harbour by nightfall. Their presence was duly reported to Nelson. Clearly battle could still be averted but Villeneuve persisted and at dawn on 20 October the remainder of the fleet got underway. Villeneuve, aware of the geographical dangers and the limitations of his crews had not attempted to get underway overnight. A measure which frustrated Nelson who was bereft of information. Fate now played its hand. The weather became squally and the wind had backed to the west. The incompetent crews were unable to form up and Villeneuve now had a foul wind for the strait. He could not go west towards the British and had to tack along the coast, each tack making leeway towards the rocky shores; worse, each tack would render formation into line of battle more difficult. Nor had they left harbour in proper order and when news of the proximity of the British fleet reached Villeneuve at about 8.30pm, his order to form single line of battle (from their column formation) was virtually impossible to expedite without skilled crews and a comprehensive signalling system.

Relentlessly, albeit at snail pace, the combined fleet struggled to make good a course of south southeast, Nelson maintaining a similar course some 15 miles ahead until 4.30 the following morning when he wore round to a course of north northeast. The die had been cast.

Dawn for Villeneuve confirmed his worst fears – disarray in his line, an uncomfortably close lee shore, and a British fleet bearing down on him under a full spread of canvas intent upon his destruction. He hoisted the signal to form line of battle in normal sequence. It wasted precious time, created further confusion and virtually stopped his fleet in the water. Confusion was compounded when Villeneuve, decided his only chance to salve something from the day would be to wear together and return to Cadiz. In retrospect it emerges that his van was probably just in a position to escape to the Mediterranean.

Nepomuceno was vehement in his attack on Villeneuve for wearing. Villeneuve argued his motive was to protect his rearguard. In the event, and with the benefit of analyses, it was unlikely that his fleet could ever have cleared the shoals and we must therefore give him some credit for courage and naval pride in that he accepted a course which would guarantee a battle. The following exchange between Blackwood and Nelson would seem to endorse this view:

'What would you consider a victory?'

'Considering their apparent determination for a fair trial of strength...' (meaning that they had elected a course which was bound to bring about an engagement).

The ships prepared for battle, after a final meal the galley fires were extinguished, loose timbers and other impediments were stowed below, placed in the ships' boats or cast over the side. Shot was de-scaled, measured and placed in the racks, fuses and match buckets were placed at the guns, while water to douse the sponges and sand to throw quickly on spilled blood or fires were made ready. Finally the powder monkeys began to bring up the powder from the magazines.

Then, as the range closed Nelson turned to Pascoe and said, 'I should like to give the fleet something by way of a fillip, suppose we telegraph that England confides that every man will do his duty.'

Pascoe advised the admiral that 'confides' was not in the signal book and would have to be spelt out, he suggested that 'expects' should be substituted.

'Very well but make it quickly, I have one more signal to send.'

As the bunting spread from the halyards cheers

went up along the British line as each ship in succession interpreted the code. Collingwood was less enamoured: 'I wish Nelson would leave off sending signals, we know what we are about.'

Inexorably the gap closed. In *Victory* the musicians played 'England Strikes Home' while across the sea the French sang the 'Marseilles'. Apart from the music and half hourly bell from the belfry there were few other sounds. Tension prevented chatter.

Blackwood was still on board having delivered the news that the French were at sea. He tried to persuade Nelson to shift his flag to *Euryalus*. 'It would be safer and you can better control the battle from a faster ship.' Nelson would not hear of it. 'It would be a bad example'.

Around noon, puffs of smoke were observed from the French line, spouts of water appeared beside *Royal Sovereign* and then the dull booms of the reports carried across the calm sea.

The great battle ensigns were unfurled and at *Victory's* masthead the cross of St George. Signal 16 was broken out:, 'Engage the enemy more closely'. It was superfluous since the British fleet were bearing down on the combined fleet with as big a press of sail as could be carried, even the stud sails were set but under the clear mid morning sun and in such light airs the gap was closing at an agonisingly slow pace.

At eight minutes past noon *Santa Anna* concentrated her fire on *Royal Sovereign*; several minutes later, already severely damaged, the *Royal Sovereign* passed under the stern of *Santa Anna* and as she did so fired each cannon in succession along her decks. Nearly 400 French mariners perished.

In *Victory*, every glass was trained on the enemy line seeking Villeneuve's flag, but it was not spotted. Nelson gave the order to steer for the largest ship, the *Santissima Trinidad*, a four-decker with 140 cannon, wearing the flag of Rear-Admiral Cisneros. As the weather line closed *Victory* attracted the attention of ranging shot until at about 12.25 a ball passed through the fore topgallant. The enemy had the range, there was a brief pause, an exchange of signals, then, in a concerted effort, six or seven of them fired a broadside at *Victory*, the biggest ever fired at a single ship. In the next moments twenty of *Victory's* company were cut down. Secretary Scott was cut in half by a cannon ball, his body quickly cast over the side before his blood rendered the deck slippery. The wheel was shot away and six marines on the poop were killed. 'This is too warm work to last long', said Nelson to Hardy as they paced the quarterdeck.

With still no sign of Villeneuve's flag and unable to bring her guns to bear, *Victory* gradually closed the

'It is too late now to be shifting a coat...'. Nelson on the quarterdeck of Victory *in the heat of the battle.*

Scene at the Battle of Trafalgar at 2.30pm, a chromolithograph after the painting by W L Wyllie, published in 1905. Victory is shown in the centre of the painting with the Santissima Trinidad featured in the right foreground.

gap while taking terrible punishment.

The enemy realised Nelson's intent to attack *Santissima Trinidad. Bucentaure* closed up, forcing the barely manoeuvrable *Victory* under her stern and bringing upon herself tragic results. At two minutes past one *Victory's* port carronade, loaded with a 68-pounder ball and 500 musket shot fired into her stern window. Then as *Victory* slowly passed under her stern every available cannon on the port side fired along her decks killing about 300 of her company, but strangely none of her masts came down. However, the damage was done and she took no further part in the battle.

Redoubtable drew alongside *Victory*, fired one broadside then closed her gunports to prevent the British from boarding her. Lucas, her captain had used his time in harbour well and had trained grenade throwers and marksmen who now packed the fighting tops. Each time the smoke of battle drifted away they rained fire on *Victory's* decks. On one such occasion a French marksman was to cause more damage to the British than the entire combined fleet: suddenly, one pace short of his normal turning point, Nelson fell to one knee. Hardy sprang to his side.

'They have done for me at last'.

'I hope not My Lord'.

'Yes, my backbone is shot through'.

Sergeant Sekker of the marines and two seamen carried him to the cockpit four decks below where Nelson was made as comfortable as possible. Forty injured seamen were already there awaiting the surgeon's knife.

Suddenly *Redoubtable* launched a boarding party, a fierce but short skirmish ensued in which a further eighteen marines and twenty sailors fell but *Temeraire* drew alongside sandwiching the *Redoubtable* as she had done *Victory*. Fire broke out on *Redoubtable* and for a moment the fighting stopped as the common enemy was tackled. *Redoubtable* struck, but not until her gallant captain had fought to a standstill losing some 300 dead and 222 injured from a crew of 640.

Events were similar, perhaps even fiercer in the lee line where *Royal Sovereign*, bearing the brunt of the enemy's withering fire, fought to a near stand-still in one of the most ferocious actions ever undertaken by a ship of the line. The horrific punishment inflicted on the lead British ships brought mercifully few casualties, while carnage and destruction visited the combined fleet. No ship, however gallant its captain and crew, could have survived such attention for long. *Royal Sovereign's* salvation was a fortunate breeze which speeded Collingwood's rearmost ships into action. In moving up the line they quickly overwhelmed each ship they came upon through superior sailing and gunnery skills.

Some of the British fleet were reduced to little more than hulks, *Belleisle* for example was totally dismasted, her ensign nailed to the stump of the mizzen. The enemy, particularly Gravina, *Principe de*

Asturia, and Lucas, *Redoubtable* fought with great courage and tenacity amid the slaughter. No English captain surrendered his colours but periodically an enemy ship was taken. Nelson, mortally wounded, was said to have derived much satisfaction each time he heard the cheers from his own sailors as an enemy's colours were struck. Had he not said he wanted twenty prizes, and had one of his sailors not remarked how fine they would all look in Spithead?

Although the life was draining from Nelson's body his contribution to the proceedings was not quite over. In the sure knowledge that a storm was brewing, he exhorted Hardy to anchor.

'Shall we make the signal, Sir?' said Hardy clearly believing Collingwood had assumed command.

'Yes, for if I live, I'll anchor.'

Neither were to be.

As dusk approached it was apparent to anyone in possession of an eye glass that as few as eight British ships were severely damaged. What relief! But what sorrow came with the setting of the sun. No lanthorns were lit in the commander-in-chief's cabin.

Of the enemy, eleven limped towards Cadiz, seventeen were taken, and the hapless *Achille*, a burning hulk, later exploded. And what the British gunners didn't achieve on the day a storm took care of soon after. It was a route. The historic result was denial of the sea lanes to Napoleon, glory for the British seamen and immortal memory for Nelson. After so much heartache, misery and toil, it is recorded in naval annals as: 'a good days work.'

David Harris MBE is a retired naval officer who began his career as a shipwright but after one commission in HMS *Bulwark* was promoted and trained as a seaman officer at Britannia Royal Naval College, Dartmouth. After brief spells in both minesweepers and frigates he began a career in submarines, serving in six *Oberon* class, two on exchange to the Canadian Armed Forces. He worked for a number of years in the Sonar and Action Information Systems research division at the Admiralty Underwater Weapons establishment, Portland, was first lieutenant of the Fleet Air Arm training school, HMS *Daedalus* and his last appointment was in command of HMS *Victory* at Portsmouth. He is now deputy director, HMS *Belfast*, the museum ship of the Imperial War Museum, moored in London. He is editor of the *Trafalgar Chronicle*.

PITT THE ELDER
(1708-1778)

Born on 15 November 1708, William Pitt had reached the pinnacle of his career when Nelson was in his infancy. A series of victories during the Seven Years' War culminating in Vice-Admiral Charles Saunders' and Major-General James Wolfe's success in Quebec, 1759, marked him as a leading British politician. His early political life was engaged in opposition to Walpole then Pelham. He enjoyed first favour then opposition from the common people but fell out with successive Kings, George II and George III.

Pitt resigned in 1761, but returned to office in 1766. It was a short-lived return because he suffered a temporary mental collapse and resigned again in 1768. He continued to canvas for a peaceful settlement in America, and was much respected for his military grasp and political aptitude. He was also widely regarded as the Great Commoner. William Pitt died on 11 May 1778.

The death of the Great Commoner, Pitt the Elder.

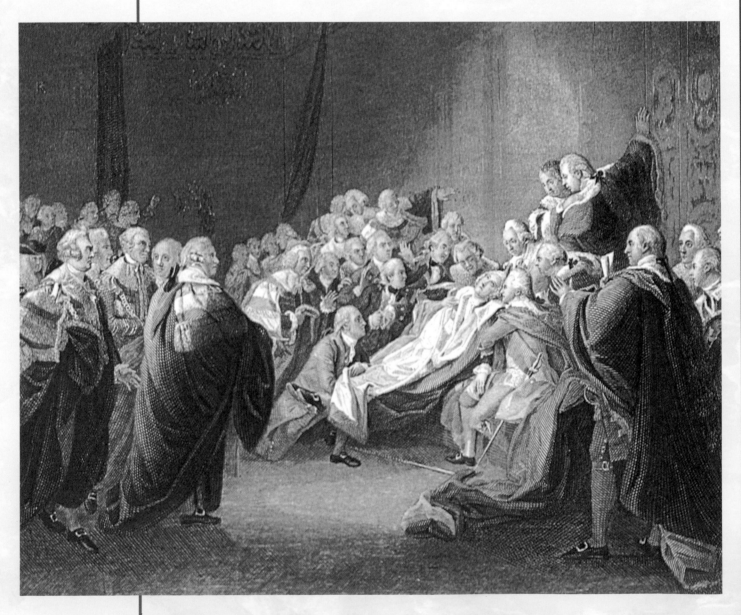

1805 To Castlereagh advocating the use of Congreaves rockets against Cadiz: 'The far greater part of the Combined Fleets is in harbour, and indeed none can be called in the Bay of Cadiz; they lie in such position abreast of the town, and many entirely open, over a narrow strip of land, that Congreave's rockets, if they will go one mile and a half, must do execution'.

1801 The preliminary articles of the peace between Britain, France, Holland and Spain are signed in London.

1st

1805 Captains Brown and Lechemere are recalled to England to attend at court martial, and Admirals Louis and Austen are sent to Gibraltar. Louis says: 'You are sending us away my Lord – the Enemy will come out, and we shall have no share in the battle.' Nelson replies: 'I have no other way of keeping my Fleet complete in provisions and water, but by sending them in detachments to Gibraltar.'

1780 Americans hang Major John André as a British spy. He had been captured in possession of papers revealing a plot by Benedict Arnold to surrender West Point to Sir Henry Clinton.

2nd

1805 To an unknown addressee: 'The reception I met with on joining the Fleet caused the sweetest sensation of my life. The Officers who came on board to welcome my return, forgot my rank as Commander-in-Chief in the enthusiasm with which they greeted me. I laid before them the Plan I had previously arranged for attacking the enemy; and it was not only my pleasure to find it generally approved, but clearly perceived and understood'.

1776 Congress is forced to borrow $5 million to prop up depreciation of the hated paper money, printed to finance the revolution.

3rd

1805 Nelson orders the frigates to their observation positions, to Captain Duff, Mars: 'As the Enemy's Fleets may be hourly expected to put to sea from Cadiz, I have to desire that you will keep, with the Mars, Defence and Colossus, from three to four leagues between the Fleet and Cadiz, in order that I may get the information from the Frigates stationed off that Port, as expeditiously as possible'.

1777 George Washington is defeated when he attacks General Howe's army at Germanstown.

4th

1805 To Barham with the news the French and Spanish have embarked troops: 'The French and Spanish Ships have taken troops on board, which had been landed on their arrival, and it is said they mean to sail the first fresh Levant wind'.

1761 William Pitt the Elder resigns as prime minister in disgust when George III refuses to declare war on Spain. He is awarded a pension of £3000 and a peerage for his wife.

5th

1805 To the Right Honourable Secretary of the Treasury, George Rose: 'It is, as Mr Pitt knows, annihilation that the Country wants, and not merely a splendid victory of twenty-three to thirty-six, – honourable to the parties concerned, but absolutely useless in the extended scale to bring Buonaparte to his marrow-bones'.

1789 Lafayette rescues the French royal family, moving them to Paris.

6th

1804 To Hugh Elliott. A party from Bittern had attempted to search a French brig for four deserters. The commander refused, not having express permission from the French Ambassador, Chevalier Micheroux, of whom Nelson advises: 'Implicit confidence must be placed in him...the greatest distrust must prevail'.

1769 Captain Cook, Endeavour, reaches New Zealand.

7th

1783 To Philip Stephens at the Admiralty: 'I am to request that you will be pleased to move their Lordships to grant me six months' leave of absence to go to Lisle, in France, on my private occasions'.

1774 London's Lord Mayor, John Wilkes, is arrested for criticising George III. Wilkes claimed immunity as a Member of Parliament but was expelled.

8th

The stout-hearted Adam Duncan it was who blockaded the Dutch coast with a fleet of only two ships, the rest being in a state of mutiny at the Nore. Britannia here crowns the escutcheon granted to Duncan by His Majesty in honour of his victory. (See 11 October.)

His Majesty's Dockyard at Woolwich, as it appeared in the late eighteenth century. (See 14 October.)

The printed word had a great deal of influence in the eighteenth century; the arbiter of taste, and therefore an influencial figure had been Pope (1688-1744). Both Blake and Burns began a Romantic Revival but leading literary contemporaries of Nelson were Johnson and Gibbon.

Dr Samuel Johnson (1709-1784 was born to a struggling Lichfield bookseller. He attended Pembroke College, Oxford, and went into journalism specialising in parliamentary debates. Later, at the age of forty he began the dictionary that was to bring him fortune and fame. As well as literature, Johnson was renowned for his wit and the extent of his encyclopaedic knowledge.

Edward Gibbon (1737-1794), perhaps England's greatest historian, was born at Putney. At fifteen he went up to Magdalen College where he describes his fourteen months as: 'the most idle and unprofitable of my whole life', although he studied Greek, Latin, French and English scholars. It took great industry to write *The Decline and Fall of the Roman Empire* published in 1776 – a work that covers the age of the Antinines to the fall of Constatinople.

1801 To Davison: 'I am trying to get rid of my command, but I am to be forced to hold it, to keep the Merchants easy till hostilities cease in the Channel'.

1799 Lutine is wrecked off Holland and goes down with a cargo of £1 million in gold and silver. Her bell was later recovered and is now at Lloyds. On the same day Napoleon, having returned from Egypt, lands at Saint Raphael having avoided a British fleet.

9th

1801 The Western Approaches were the key to the Channel in the days of sail. To St Vincent: 'Every attention is paid to cover our channel, and I do not think the French can with impunity send anything into the channel'.

1780 A hurricane sweeps Barbados killing 40,000. On 31 October of the same year another hurricane sweeps away half of all the houses in the Bahamas.

10th

1797 Nelson starts a letter to Locker which Fanny is obliged to finish: 'I sincerely wish my arm....Thus far my husband has begun his letter to you, but an appointment with a friend of his prevents his concluding'.

1797 Admiral Adam Duncan defeats Jan Willem de Winter at Camperdown.

11th

1793 To Fanny, regarding an accolade to Hood: 'All the Foreigners at Toulon absolutely worship him; were any accident to happen to him, I am sure no person in our Fleet could supply his place'.

1782 Spain sends 10 ships of the line converted into 'Battering' ships to Gibraltar to assist in the Great Siege.

12th

1804 To Emma: 'The dreadful effects of the yellow fever, at Gibraltar, and many parts of Spain, will naturally give you much uneasiness, till you hear that, thank God, we are entirely free from it, and in the most perfect health, not one man being ill in the Fleet. The cold weather will, I hope, cure the disorder. Whilst I am writing this letter, a Cutter is arrived from England with strong indications of a Spanish war'.

1792 The cornerstone of the White House, official residence of the US president, is laid by George Washington. It took a further seven years to build and won its architect, James Hoban, a £500 award for its design.

13th

1881 On completion of fitting out at Woolwich, from Albermarle's log: 'Sunday 14th October – Going down the River to the Nore'.

1791 Theodore Wolfe Tone sets up the Belfast Society of United Irishmen, calling for the emancipation of Catholics. He spent his life working for the Irish cause, first in Ireland and later as part of the French invasion 'expeditions', but was finally captured and taken to Dublin where he was sentenced to death and hanged on 19 November 1798.

14th

1805 To Ball: 'I send you our last newspapers. The combined Fleets are all at the Harbour's Mouth, and must either move up again or move off, before the winter sets in. I trust we shall be able to get hold of them'.

1764 Gibbon, musing among the ruins of Rome, is inspired to write 'The Decline and Fall of the Roman Empire'.

15th

1805 Dr Beatty, the surgeon on Victory, noted: 'All the forenoon employed in forming the Fleet into the Order of Sailing' while Nelson notes in his private diary: 'Fine weather, wind Easterly; combined fleets cannot have finer weather to put to sea'.

1793 Queen Marie Antionette, fourth daughter of Maria Theresa and wife of Louis XVI, goes to the guillotine.

16th

'The Surrender at Ulm' by Gillray. Boney and Mack come to a sensible understanding – one that involves substantial sums of money and the minimum amount of bloodshed. 'What signifies fighting,' says the prostrate General Mack, his eye on the bags of gold, 'when we can settle it in a safer way.' The disaster at Ulm was tempered to some degree by news of the victory at Trafalgar. (See 17 October.)

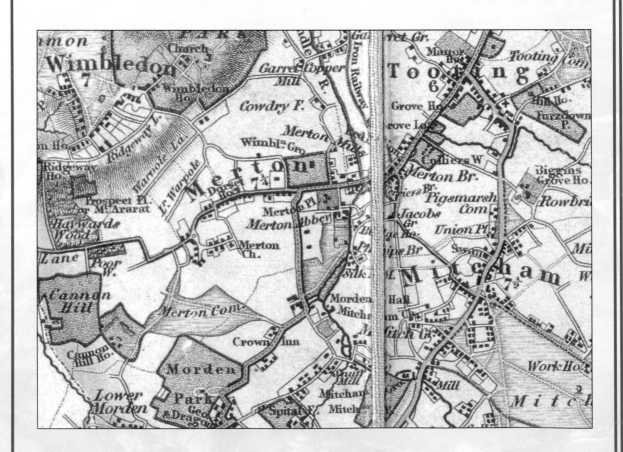

Dear, dear Merton. Detail of a contemporary Map of the Environs of London showing Merton Place in Surrey. (See 23 October.)

1801 In a letter to Emma, Nelson writes: 'The cold has settled my bowels. I wish the Admiralty had my complaint; but, they have no bowels – at least, for me'.

1805 *General Mack surrenders an army of 28,000 (Napoleon said 33,000) Austrians to the French at Ulm. Napoleon wrote: 'I have from 60,000 to 70,000 prisoners; more than 90 flags; and 70 peces of cannon. Never has there been such a catastrophe in military annals.'*

1805 To his brother: 'For two days last week I was in a fever. A frigate spoke a Spanish Vessel in the night, who said that he had seen a Fleet of twelve sail of Men-of-War off Minorca, steering to the Westward, It was thick for two days and our Frigates could not look into Toulon; however, I was relieved, for the first time in my life, by being informed the French were still in Port'.

1797 *Austria and the French Republic sign the Treaty of Campo Formio effectively isolating Great Britain from the rest of Europe.*

1805 To Emma: 'May the God of battles crown my endeavours with success! At all events I will take care that my name shall ever be most dear to you and Horatia, both of whom I love as much as my own life. And as my last writing before the battle will be to you, so I hope in God that I shall live to finish my letter after the battle'.

1781 *General Cornwallis surrenders with 7000 troops at Yorktown, Virginia, ending the American War of Independence.*

1805 Nelson is told that Admiral Collingwood and Captain Rotherham are not on good terms with each other: 'Terms! Good terms with each other!' He sends for them and says: 'Look, yonder are the enemy!' He then makes them shake hands.

1793 *The French royalists of La Vendée are defeated at Cholet, marking the turning point in the struggle against republicanism.*

1805 THE BATTLE OF TRAFALGAR AND THE DEATH OF LORD NELSON

'Thank God I have done my duty.'

1779 *The tricolor is chosen as the national flag of France.*

1805 Collingwood, from Euryalus: 'The ever-to-be-lamented death of Vice-Admiral Lord Viscount Nelson, Duke of Bronté, the Commander-in-Chief, who, fell in the action of the 21st, in the arms of Victory, Covered with Glory, whose memory will be ever dear to the British Navy...leaves me to return my thanks [to the officers and men of the Fleet]'.

1797 *The first recorded parachute jump is made by André-Jaques Garnerin from a balloon above the Parc Monceau, Paris.*

1801 Nelson arrives at Merton for the first time. The previous day he had written to Nepean, Secretary of the Admiralty Board: 'It is my intention to set off this evening for Merton, agreeably to the leave of absence their Lordships have been pleased to grant me'.

1753 *The Royal Naval Hospital Haslar, near Gosport, admits its first patients.*

Horatia (1800-1881)

Few relationships can be more difficult to audit than that between Horatio and Horatia. Most primary information is contained in Nelson's letters to Emma, written in farcical circumstances and kept by her against his implicit instructions to destroy them, as he did hers. They were published anonymously in 1814 by Harrison, acquired by Crocker in 1817 and resold on his death. Finally they were published by Alfred Morrison in 1894. The story is disproportionately virtuous in two respects: Nelson was as besotted by Horatia as any other living thing and history has not, as is so often the case, burdened the child with the sins of the father. Nelson takes much credit for that and did everything he could to provide for her and shield her from the circumstances of her birth.

Horatia was born under Sir William Hamilton's roof in early February 1800 while Nelson was at sea. The infant, no more than a few days old, was taken to Mrs Gibson in Little Titchfield Street – a woman who had been provided to take charge of the baby, by Emma, purporting to be acting charitably on behalf of the child's *real* mother, Mrs Thomson (or was it Thompson?). The twin sister, Emma, was committed to the foundlings but the story which eventually reached Nelson was that the child had been born dead. She was rarely referred to again. Nelson was consumed by Horatia, who he first saw on 24 February. She was christened on 13 May 1803 at St Marylebone Church. No parents were mentioned and she was given a date of birth of 29 October 1800.

While Sir William was alive Nelson was obliged to disown the child; nevertheless she influenced him in an overriding and practical way. He wished to find a home for her and entrusted the task of finding one to Lady Hamilton. 'I am very anxious to have a home...I wish you could find me a comfortable house.'

Merton Place, referred to as the farm by Nelson, was acquired by him and settled on Emma in the event of his death 'as a safe home for Horatia...'. It was not until Sir William's death on 6 April 1803 that Horatia could be brought to Merton but Emma resisted. It was a difficult time for her, captured by Gillray in his cartoon 'Dido in Dispair'. She was pregnant again, her suitor was at sea, her daughter

thought to be suffering from smallpox – Nelson had tried to insist the child be vaccinated but she had not carried out this instruction – and she was accumulating debts. She had also become accustomed to taking summer vacations at the seaside and was in Southend when Nelson returned suddenly to Spithead in August 1805.

Emma hurried to Merton and had just twenty-four hours to demonstrate an established family, and only that long because Nelson was detained over quarantine regulations. For a few moments Nelson shared his daughter, establishing her as part of the family; she joined his pew at church and was given her own silver cup and cutlery set. She could hardly have known him but she was forever in his mind as can be seen from his last codicil: 'I also leave to the beneficence of my country my adopted daughter, Horatia Nelson Thompson; and I desire she will use in future, the name of Nelson only...'.

VERSES

SPOKEN BY

MISS HORATIA NELSON,

TO

ABRAHAM GOLDSMID, Esq.

THE INTIMATE FRIEND OF HER GLORIOUS AND IMMORTAL FATHER.

At ABRAHAM GOLDSMID's patriarchal name,
My bosom seems to feel a sacred flame;
Such as when, in the Book of Heav'n, I read
Of the first ABR'HAM, and his righteous seed!
Whate'er he undertakes, assur'd success
Is found his virtuous energies to bless:
On him, and his, prosperity attends;
Riches, and health, and happiness, and friends!
While a whole people, injur'd much and long,
His merits shield from suff'ring farther wrong.
Nor is the tenor of his noble mind
To his own race, or family, confin'd:
For worth oppress'd, wherever it appears,
The potent standard of his pow'r he rears;
And, in whatever cause that's seen display'd,
Approving Heav'n is surely found to aid.

How my great Father lov'd thee, well is known:
Alas! with him, how many friends are flown!
But thy bless'd friendship even seems improv'd,
By acts of kindness shewn to all he lov'd.
Oh! gen'rous GOLDSMID, with my weakness bear,
Nor doubt I feel for all thy tender care;
What words can but imperfectly express,
Take from these lips, and never love me less!

Printed by MACDONALD and SON, 46, Cloth Fair, London

Verses spoken by the infant Horatia to Nelson's erstwhile intimate friend and neighbour at Merton, Abraham Goldsmid. He remained a loyal and generous friend to Emma after Nelson's death.

🔱 1799 🔱 On hearing that Napoleon had abandoned Egypt: 'No Crusader ever returned with more humility'.

🔱 1795 🔱 *Stanistlaus II of Poland abdicates, resulting in partition among Austria, Russia and Prussia.*

🔱 1796 🔱 To HRH The Duke of Clarence (the future William IV) from Captain: 'I am happy to say that not only Bastia, but every other place in the Island [of Corsica] is completely evacuated'.

🔱 1760 🔱 *George II dies, aged 77, and is succeeded by his grandson George III.*

🔱 1798 🔱 Preface to a very long letter to John Spencer Smith Esq., Constantinople, from Vanguard off Malta: 'Having only one hand, I must trust to your forgiveness for my making letters wrote by me as brief as possible'.

🔱 1797 🔱 *The Executive Directory decrees: 'There shall be an assembly without delay, on the coast of the ocean, an army which shall be called the Armée d'Angleterre.'*

🔱 1795 🔱 To Sir William Suckling Esq. from Agamemnon off Marseilles: 'To me, I own, all Frenchmen are alike; I despise them all...even Louis XVIII receives our money, and will not follow our advice'.

The Duke of Clarence as a young midshipman.

🔱 1778 🔱 *Lord North fails to prevent a Franco-American alliance in America and his commission returns to England.*

🔱 1799 🔱 To Captain Ball at Malta: 'My Dear Ball, The King of Naples sends 4000 ounces to assist the poor Islanders who bear arms; this will do for the present; the large sum required must come from the three Allied Courts'.

🔱 1776 🔱 *General Howe defeats Washington at the Battle of White Plains.*

🔱 1787 🔱 London, to his brother, the Reverend Mr William Nelson: 'As to news, the Papers are all Peace; but, in my opinion, nothing can prevent a War. In the Naval line, every exertion is made use of to man the Fleet'.

🔱 1800 🔱 *Horatia Nelson Thompson is born (according to the register of baptism).*

🔱 1799 🔱 To His Excellency, J Spencer Smith, British Minister at Constantinople from Palermo: 'I cannot want to crop any man's laurels: the world has been over bountiful to me'.

🔱 1791 🔱 *Pandora and Resolution sight each other for the first time in four months.*

🔱 1801 🔱 To Captain Sutton, Amazon, off Deal, from Merton: 'You will see my Maiden Speech – bad enough, but well meant. I may be a coward, and good for nothing, but never ungrateful for favours done me'.

🔱 1765 🔱 *Two hundred New York merchants join a non-importation movement pledging not to buy British goods until the Stamp and Sugar Acts are repealed.*

24th

25th

26th

27th

28th

29th

30th

31st

THE POSTMAN IN THE PICKLE

THE DELIVERY AND IMPACT OF THE NEWS

Anthony Cross

Collingwood assumed command of the fleet at the end of Trafalgar and chose the Pickle *to carry his dispatch to the Admiralty.*

The banner believed to have been commissioned by Cornish fishermen.

In a Cornish church, lichen-spattered granite without, a placid and orderly archive of nearly seven centuries within, there is a banner. A well kept secret perhaps, but you may borrow the key as easily as whispering a request to a librarian and see for yourself. By the north door it hangs, framed and glazed, perhaps 3 feet square. Black paint, dextrously applied, but by a signwriter rather than an artist, to a canvas the colour and texture of an old cheese rind; and under a canopy of palm fronds reminiscent of the Nile, his chief claim to fame and emblematic of his fearsome reputation, these words:

> 'Mourn for the Brave
> the Immortal NELSON'S gone
> His last Sea fight is fought
> his work of Glory done'

Besides a neat epitaph, the banner also proclaims – and commemorates – in quiet, self confident Cornish: 'We were the first ashore to get the news. Even before the King had styled it Trafalgar.'

About four hours after the guns ceased firing on that memorable day, 21 October 1805, First Lieutenant W Pryce Cumby of the *Bellerophon* noticed there were no admiral's lights on board the *Victory*: 'from which we were left to draw the melancholy inference that our gallant, our beloved chief, the incomparable Nelson, had fallen.' The penny had dropped and its ripples spread.

The all important news of victory over the combined fleet of France and Spain and the death of Admiral Lord Nelson was contained in Collingwood's dispatch to William Marsden, Secretary to the Board of Admiralty. Collingwood had begun its composition on board *Euryalus* in the immediate stormy aftermath of the battle, but it did not actually begin its journey to London – and into history – until the morning of Saturday, 26 October. The great storm which began on the evening of the 21st and which showed no sign of abatement preoccupied Collingwood just as it affected every shattered man and ship. Nonetheless, sandwiched between the proper Royal Naval rhetoric, but moving with what Callender describes as 'the dignity of an anthem', the dispatch was a succinct account of about 1200 words. He gave the glory to

AN ACCOUNT OF THE VICTORY OVER THE
Combined Fleets
OF FRANCE AND SPAIN;
AND THE
DEATH of LORD NELSON.

Plymouth, Nov. 5, 1805.

Messrs. T. and W. EARLE and Co.
Gentlemen,

THE Pickle arrived here this morning—Captain Sykes of the Nautilas, went off express for London. On the 21st of October, the fleet under the command of LORD NELSON, consisting of 27 sail of the line, engaged the combined fleets off Cadiz, consisting of 33 sail of the line, *nineteen Line of Battle ships of the enemy, of the number of four flags, taken, one sunk, and one blown up.*

Villeneuve is board the Royal Sovereign: Gravina with 9 sail got back to Cadiz.

A gale of wind came on soon after the action, right on shore, and 'tis said that two sail which had struck, got back to Cadiz, that the large four-decker, Santissimo Trinidad, was in tow, but sunk; the Royal Sovereign, Victory, Revenge, Bellisle, Temeraire, Bellerophon, and Mars, suffered most. The Temeraire engaged two ships and took them, as did the Neptune two three-deckers, which struck to her. The Royal Sovereign, it is said, had 400 men killed.

Great as this victory has been, the country has to mourn the loss of LORD NELSON, who was killed by a Musket Ball in the breast from the tops of a three-decker, Santissima Trinidad, with whom the Victory was engaged, and actually lashed together. His Lordship was, at the moment he received his wound, expressing his delight at the conduct of his Second in Command Admiral Collingwood. Before he died, he made the signal, *that England expected every man would do his duty.* This, I understand, he was enabled to do, by having brought his telegraph signals to such perfection. We have also to lament the loss of Capts. Duff and Cook, and Lord Nelson's Secretary. Capt. Tyler wounded but not dangerously.

No other particulars of the loss have reached us. On the 24th, the Pickle and Donegal were at anchor off Cadiz, in charge of the captured ships. Six sail are said to have sunk.

I write in great haste,
And am yours, &c.

P. S. 'Tis said by some of the crew of the Pickle that they saw 14 sail in tow; the Nautilus is also arrived with duplicate dispatches.

Tasker, Printer.

A broadsheet printed and published in Plymouth on 5 November 1805. Despite the rush with which it was no doubt composed, the news it contains is remarkably accurate – Lapenotière only having disembarked at Falmouth the day before.

Lieutenant John Richards Lapenotière, of the Pickle.

God, not to man, and was modest enough not to mention himself.

The messenger was chosen – not Blackwood, Nelson's watchdog, but the obscure Lieutenant Lapenotière of HMS *Pickle*. It is suggested that Collingwood might have selected him in order to repay an outstanding service, and also that it was intended, before *Victory*'s crew strenuously protested, that *Euryalus*, would carry Lord Nelson's body home; but perhaps more prosaically the topsail schooner was, amongst other things, a good dispatch vessel and most likely to make a fast passage. In any case, it was a singular honour. John Richards Lapenotière (1770-1834) was a Devon man born at Ilfracombe, the great, great grandson of a French nobleman – a Huguenot refugee perhaps – whose family had connections with the court of William of Orange, and with whom they arrived in England. He first went to sea with his father at the age of ten, and for thirteen years had 'fought the wind and stemm'd the wave' engaged in commercial adventure. In March 1794, however, he joined Sir John Jervis' flagship the *Boyne*. His scrupulous attention to duty was rewarded by commendation and eventually by promotion. In Spring 1802, he gained command of the schooner *Pickle*. Originally called *Sting*, and apparently Bermuda-built, she had been bought into the Royal Navy about 1800 and renamed. She was one of the new-fangled schooner rig, described in one contemporary account as 'a clever fast schooner – coppered – and in every respect suited to the service'. As one of the fleet's auxiliaries, albeit the second to smallest, she was therefore ideal.

In retrospect, *Pickle* is the perfect name for a vessel that was to contain and preserve for a while the gist and flavour of such a momentous event, but it was really only one of the many parts she played. In the weeks before the battle she had joined the fleet screening and observing the combined fleet in Cadiz. She had performed the important duty of capturing a Portuguese settee out of Tangier laden with a cargo of bullocks – fresh meat for the fleet, made more sweet by its denial to the French and Spanish blockaded in Cadiz. *Pickle* it was identified, counted and reported back to *Victory* that the enemy were thirty-three in number. During and after Trafalgar she was kept busy collecting survivors – one, a young French woman called Jeanette, an *Achille* crewman's wife

found clinging tenaciously to an oar, was taken aboard 'perfectly naked' after her ordeal. The *Pickle*'s crew were a typical – that is not to say a motley – cross-section of Nelson's navy: of the thirty-two men on board, there were seventeen English, including five from the West Country, two each from Kent and Sussex, and one from London; nine Irish (were they, one wonders, United-men?); two Americans, one Norwegian, one Scot, one Welsh, and one Channel Islander. The Master was George Almy from Rhode Island, and it is his log that provides a graphic detail of the voyage.

At noon on the 26th *Pickle* made sail for England, and so began a voyage of perhaps a thousand miles or more. Although there was still a chance of encountering the enemy, the greatest danger was the weather – a winter passage across the Bay of Biscay was never going to be easy. The Master's log methodically records the changing, but seldom favourable, winds and seas and the crew's reaction; an endless round of making and shortening sail, sending up and down topmasts and yards. Almost before clearing the area of battle they met with the *Nautilus*, Captain Sykes. The news was leaked and taken into Lisbon by Sykes, who then himself set off for London. It is not overtly stated but Lapenotière was probably under orders to communicate not a word en route, but human nature and wise precaution obviously dictated otherwise. (Sykes, by common account, met Lapenotière again at the Admiralty door). By 30 October *Pickle* was northwest of Lisbon, and the following day, as she rounded Cape Finisterre, a southwesterly gale threw a heavy sea across the ship; she was taking on water faster than her pumps could clear it. The crew worked through the night in a worsening gale, but to little avail. Friday, 1 November was perhaps the worst day; despite all efforts *Pickle* could not be kept on course. Lapenotière decided to cast overboard four of the ship's carronades to lighten her, and during the morning the ship sailed virtually under bare poles until, in the afternoon, the gale blew itself out. Sails were set again, and on the Saturday following, *Pickle* found the entrance to the Channel; the course was northeasterly and with a following wind the Lizard should only have been a day's sail away. But now the weather showed its other side; the wind died away completely and Lapenotière had to order the crew to man the sweeps to keep some steerage way on her until it returned. They were 60 miles from the Lizard when they encountered HMS *Superb* (74) whose Captain Keats was, ironically, hastening to join his patron Nelson before the expected battle. Shortly afterwards the burden of the news was again apparently communicated to some Cornish fishermen who hastened into Penzance to inform Mayor Giddy, interrupting his banquet at the Union Hotel. He in turn told it to the company gathered beneath the minstrel gallery before setting about the commissioning of a commemorative banner that would lead the procession up the hill toward the parish church.

Marryat conjured up a similar scene in Poor Jack (1853-4):

> '...we were abreast of the Ram Head when the men in a pilot boat...waved their hats and kept away to speak to us...
>
> "Have you heard the news?" cried one of the men.
>
> "No."
>
> "Lord Nelson has beat the French and the Spanish fleet."
>
> "Glad to hear it - Huzza!"
>
> "Lord Nelson's killed."
>
> "Lord Nelson's killed!" the intelligence was repeated from mouth to mouth, and then every mouth was hushed; the other boat hauled her wind without further communication.'

Pickle continued her voyage, now contending with the tidal stream of the Channel, until at last the Lizard Light was seen. The most well known landfall in England was only some 9 miles distant. Finally, the Master's log records, *Pickle* hove to in Falmouth Bay (at 9.45am) on 4 November, nine days after parting with the fleet, and Lieutenant Lapenotière was rowed ashore.

Midday saw him already aboard the post chaise to London on the last lap of his urgent and arduous journey. News must have continued to leak, for the coach displayed on a hastily rigged broomstick flagpole, the Union Flag flying above a tattered Tricolour. A stagecoach to London usually took a week, but by dint of changing horses a reputed nineteen times (the news passing to every ostler and innkeeper perhaps?), and thanks to the oddly unsea-sonable weather, the 266 miles to London was covered in something like thirty-eight hours by way of Truro, Tavistock, across Dartmoor, Exeter, Honiton, Yeovil, Salisbury, Andover and Basingstoke – the sense of urgency no doubt quickening with every milestone.

In the early hours of 6 November and in a thick London fog – 'too thick,' *The Times* said, 'for the King to go out riding yesterday,' – he arrived. The Secretary, Mr Marsden, was still at his desk at 1.00am when an otherwise unknown thirty-five year old naval officer, inevitably travel weary, but in what passed for his best uniform, was ushered in and dutifully delivered his Admiral's dispatches.

'Sir,' Lapenotière reported with due poise and precision, 'we have gained a great victory; but we have lost Lord Nelson.'

Marsden responded with professional equanimity. Immediately he set in motion a most surprisingly sophisticated communications network. Lord Barham, First Lord of the Admiralty, was located and awakened: 'What news Mr M?' he mumbled unsurprised, resurfacing from sleep to the alert. Dressed, the first task must have been to digest, summarise and duplicate the dispatch which gave chapter and verse to Lapenotière's graphic but terse precis.

Lapenotière makes haste along the Turnpike Road, clutching Collingwood's dispatch.

'Admiralty Office, Nov. 6 at One A.M. - Lieut Lapenotière, of the *Pickle* schooner, arrived last night with dispatches from Vice-Admiral Collingwood, announcing a glorious victory gained by His Majesty's fleet off Cadiz, under the command of Admiral Lord Nelson. - On the 19th of October the enemy's fleet, consisting of 33 ships of the line, four frigates, and two brigs came out of Cadiz, and on the 21st, at noon, were brought to action by the British fleet, consisting of 27 sail of the line (seven having being previously detached under Rear-Admiral Louis), four frigates and two smaller vessels. The engagement lasted four hours, and terminated by 19 of the Enemy's line striking their colours, and being taken possession of, exclusive of one that blew up in the action. Lord Nelson's ship being closely engaged with the *Santissima Trinidada*, and others of the enemy's ships, a musket shot fired from the top wounded his Lordship, and deprived him of his most valuable life. A gale of wind at the S.W. coming on the next day, and on the 24th and 25th increasing in violence, many of the prizes drove adrift, and being close to lee shore, it is supposed that many of them must have been wrecked, and the Vice- Admiral had make [sic] a signal for destroying all that could not be brought away. Two ships, from which the prisoners could not be removed, made their escape into Cadiz. The *Santissima Trinidada* was sunk, and two others of the line before the Lieutenant left the fleet. Admiral Villeneuve, who commanded in chief, and many others of rank, are amongst the prisoners. Besides the loss of Lord Nelson the country has to lament the loss of Capts. Duff and Cooke, and about 500 men killed. The *Belleisle* was totally dismasted, and the *Temeraire* and the *Royal Sovereign* also suffered very much; but not one of His Majesty's ships was lost in this most glorious conflict.'

With an economy of words – this is roughly a quarter of Collingwood's original dispatch – the event is cut and trimmed with the skill of a master butcher into news. Before dawn, messengers were sent (some with copies of the entire text) to Windsor, to Downing Street, to Lady Nelson, to Emma Hamilton, to the City via Lloyd's, and lastly, but vitally, to the office of *The London Gazette* in order that the intelligence might be officially broken and broadcast.

Pitt, Nelson's contemporary as well as his professional acquaintance, slept in close proximity to the Admiralty, and so was awakened to the news. Perhaps it woke him from his horrid nightmare – the one that always ended the same way, with the rolling up of the redundant map of Europe. Certainly, he confessed to Lord Malmesbury, it was the first time in his long and eventful career that he found himself unable to compose himself and go back to sleep again.

The Royal Family received the news at around 7.00am. King George, perhaps realising the truth of the rumour, mislaid his customary loquaciousness and was silent for a full five minutes. Then they read the dispatch out loud and wept en famille, and repaired to the chapel to give thanks to Almighty God for the success of His Majesty's Arms at Sea. Finally the guns in the Great Park fired a *feu-de-joie* to mark the occasion. Later, when news had sunk in, it is rumoured that King George met Lapenotière and, on the spur of the moment, grabbed the first thing that came to hand – a silver cruet – and presented it to him as a reward for his singular service.

Lady Nelson's immediate reaction to the official announcement of her husband's death appears to have gone largely unrecorded, despite the fact that to her alone, the First Lord wrote personally. Her biographers refer only to her stoicism and fortitude; her stiff upper lip. According to Lord Minto, it was the crown of thorns that marked the culmination of an afflicted relationship. There is, it might be noted, a certain bitter irony in the effect the news would have upon her; latterly denied his physical presence and emotional company, she would at least be well provided for now her husband was dead.

Not so Emma. ('Poor Emma! Brave Emma!') At this precise point she did not know of the codicil to Nelson's Will, made on 20 October in which he formally turned her over to the country, just as, years before, Sir William Hamilton's nephew had passed her on to him. One wonders though if she hadn't already a touch of the forlorn about her. She heard the Tower guns at Merton, but did not immediately understand their significance. Five minutes or so later Captain Whitby arrived with the news. She was bro-

Gillray's famous image of Emma, 'Dido in Despair', first published in 1801.

ken hearted, but did not (because she would not or could not) suffer in silence.

'Never mind your victory...', she screamed out loud, uncontrollably, before collapsing at the feet of the greatly embarrassed messenger, who was quite unprepared for such an hysterical reaction. Two images come to mind. Firstly Gillray's sardonic, and in a sense prophetic, 'Dido in Despair' of 6 February 1801, in which he caricatured the lamenting Emma, bereft at Nelson's departure for the Baltic. But this time it was underscored by finality. Secondly her destitution is described in the scribbled footnote she appended to his last, unfinished letter to her, dated 19-20 October 1805: 'O miserable wretched Emma, O glorious and happy Nelson.' Arguably, Nelson's death meant more to Emma than to anyone else. During his life she had basked in the reflected light of his authority and reputation; his death eclipsed all that. She was robbed not only of his love and companionship, but also of her association with him. It condemned her to the worst sort of fate, a life of tatty and rather sordid former glory without material support and eventually without comfort of any kind.

The Reverend Dr William Nelson, it is recorded, was tactfully told the news in the Cathedral Close by Mr Bristow, the Mayor of Canterbury, to prevent his getting it from the Public Reading Room where he was in the habit of retiring every day in order to keep abreast of the news.

The Times published the following paragraph on the inside of a special late edition on 6 November.

> 'We know not whether we should mourn or rejoice. The country has gained the most splendid and decisive Victory that has ever graced the naval annals of England; but it has been dearly purchased. The great and gallant NELSON is no more: he was killed by almost the last shot that was fired by the enemy. The action took place off Cadiz, on the 21st ult; the enemy were thirty-three sail of the line, Lord Nelson had only twenty seven.'

The first sentence unwittingly defined the manner in which the whole country would react to the news. That evening London was partially, almost apologetically illuminated with small mourning lamps in the windows, and shops and homes were decorated with branches of laurel and oak leaves. The people celebrated the victory but their hearts were not in it; as Lord Malmesbury recalled: 'I never saw so little public joy'. Reference was first and foremost to the loss of Nelson, rather than to the victory. It should have more than compensated for the disaster suffered by the Austrians at Ulm where on 20 October the hapless General Mack had surrendered the entire Austrian army (28,000 men) to the French. But had the price been too high? 'Britain's Darling Son' was dead.

At Covent Garden, after the evening's performance, an extempore tableau was presented; a portrait of 'The Hero of the Nile' descended from the flies before a backdrop of the British fleet at anchor, whereupon the orchestra played 'Rule Britannia', followed by the Dead March from Saul. The same was true in the streets of the capital: 'The illuminations began', said Lady Elizabeth Hervey, 'but were discontinued, the people being unable to rejoice.' As *The Times* reported:

'The victory created none of those enthusiastic emotions in the public mind which the successes of our naval arms have in every former instance produced. There was not a man who did not think that the life of the Hero of the Nile was too great a price for the capture and destruction of twenty sail of French and Spanish men-of-war. No ebullitions of popular transport, no demonstrations of public joy marked this great and important event. The honest and manly feeling of the people appeared as it should have done: they felt an inward satisfaction at the triumph of their favourite arms; they mourned with all the sincerity and poignancy of domestic grief their hero slain.'

In the City the Stock Exchange remained cautious but Government securities suffered as investors weighed the news of Trafalgar against the dispatch recently received from Ulm. The Lord Mayor though, put his faith in Pitt. At the annual banquet held on 9 November, he raised his glass to the Prime Minister whom he called 'the Saviour of Europe'. But Pitt, not long for this world, made the sober and prudent reply that, 'Europe is not to be saved by any single man. England has saved herself by her exertions, and will, as I trust, save Europe by her example'. An Address would be presented (on 21 November) by the Mayor and Corporation of London to the King. It was one of many that were presented to the

Throne from all parts of the Empire, all of which congratulated His Majesty on the recent most glorious and decisive victory off Trafalgar, expressed the highest admiration for Nelson, the deepest grief for his loss, and did not forget to note the obligations that were owed to the brave survivors.

Lloyds responded to the news in a practical and entirely commendable way, just as it had in the aftermath of the Battle of the Nile. Within a month the Committee for the Patriotic Fund sat for a special session. The resolutions passed fell into two categories: reward and relief, the one merging into the other; the list drawn up in the strict hierarchical declension of the period. Commemorative vases – valued at between an astonishing £300 and £500, and 'ornamented with emblematical devices and appropriate inscriptions, illustrative of the transcendent and heroic achievements of the late Lord Viscount Nelson' would be presented to his 'relict', Lady Viscountess Nelson, to the Earl Nelson of Trafalgar (William's advancement was announced in *The London Gazette* on 9 November), and to Admirals Collingwood, Northesk and Strachan. Likewise, there would be swords 'of the value of one hundred pounds each with appropriate inscriptions [for] the surviving Captains and Commanders...who shared in the dangers and glory of those memorable Actions'. Lapenotière received such a sword along with his command.

At this point in the list of resolutions the rewards turn into hard cash: 'Resolved, that the sum of £50 be presented to each of the officers of the third class...who was severely wounded; and the sum of £30 to each officer of the same rank who was slightly wounded.' Forty pounds would be awarded to a Seaman or Marine for the loss of a limb, £20 (in round figures, this was the annual wage of an able seaman) for the severely wounded, £10 per man slightly wounded. This relief extended also to the widows, orphans, parents and relatives depending for support on those 'who so gloriously fell in the cause of their Country'.

Upwards of £100,000 was collected in churches and chapels on 5 December, the day appointed by the King for a General Thanksgiving for the Victory. 'All the churches and chapels were crowded,' the Annual Register reported. 'All distinctions of sects were done away, and Christian and Jew, Catholic and Protestant, all united in the expression of one feeling of piety and gratitude to the Almighty.' All ranks from the highest to the lowest vied with each other in their patriotic gifts. At Mr Rowland Hill's Chapel in Blackfriars Road, a halfpenny was found on the collection plate, wrapped in a £100 note, and labelled 'a Widow's Mite'.

Was this true nationwide? Generally it was. Don't just take Southey's eloquent word for it either. Look up any provincial newspaper archive for mid November 1805; any record of Parliamentary proceedings; look at the pictures and verses published by the spring of 1806, and you will find it so, even to the extent described by that cynical double act, Edinger and Neep, writing in the 1930s:

> 'Innumerable odes, monodies, elegies, dirges, tributes and laments buried Nelson beneath a tumulus of platitude. The shop windows filled with weeping Britannia's clasping funeral urns, doleful lions gazing at tattered Union Jacks, and anaemic Nelsons exhorting rubicund mariners to do their duty.'

At Chester the bells rang out a peal of rejoicing alternating with a solemn tolling – dumb peals, as they were called. (The language of church bells has been largely forgotten, but at this period they still provided a rudimentary but effective broadcasting system which was presumably as eloquent as it was widely understood, and rapid and far-reaching in its transmission.) In the village of Maidwell in Northamptonshire the ringer was actually turned out of the belfry for being too enthusiastic – his conduct was considered improper: 'like a drunkard at a funeral'. Likewise, in Norwich, a city with a long tradition of free thought, we find evidence of a certain syncopation. The week-long Official Mourning ordained by the Town Corporation left William Firth, Steward of the City, dismayed and disappointed. Why, he complained in an open letter (privately printed) to Edward Rigby, the Mayor, had the magistrates refused a license? He had hoped that Norwich, capital of Nelson's own county, 'would have been the first to have testified her joy at the salvation of the country being accomplished by the hand of one of her sons, who bravely died in the great strife'. He had rather anticipated 'the merry sound of the pipe and tabor, or the mellow cadences of the distant horn,

the dance of many a gay fantastic round, the livening huzza of a multitude, the busy crackling of the flame, the abrupt splendour of the firework...Is it nothing to break up for ever the destructive conclaves of Bonaparte and the dark and capacious mischiefs of his midnight mind.' That, he (erroneously) asserted, was the form everywhere else other than in the 'Polar Regions' of Norfolk. Mayor Rigby was unmoved: celebration had to be counterbalanced by mourning. Such a spree was neither proper, as the Act allows, nor was it good taste.

Look, too, at the monuments that sprang up, not only in British towns and cities but as far afield as Canada and Barbados. The first of these was apparently at Cork, 'sketched and planned by Captain Joshua Rowley Watson RN, and built by him and 1200 of the Sea Fencibles, assisted by eight masons,...erected in only *five hours* on 10 November 1805'. Likewise, the prehistoric standing stone that was re-erected at Taynuilt by the workmen of the Lorn Furnace (manufacturers of cannonballs for the fleet). The manifestation of national gratitude, in the form of a 'Monument in the Metropolis', may have been, as Sir Nicholas Harris Nicolas sourly notes, tardy in its coming to fruition (Trafalgar Square was opened in 1843), due to 'the neglect of the Public to raise sufficient funds – the indifference of the Government – the necessity of accepting the donation of a Foreign Monarch – and the design...lamentable', but this appears to be very much not the case during the period when the news was hottest.

At Christ's Hospital, for instance they had fireworks and then a little glass of sherry wine was drunk in solemn silence. This memory was taken down, some eighty years after the event, still potent in the mind. Likewise someone who died towards the end of the nineteenth century remembered:

> 'The church bells had been peeling and dancing with glee, swinging high and low like a wedding chime. It was impossible to miss the infection of their merriment. Then, quite suddenly, they stopped. Stopped; and with a solemn boom came the muffled monotone, the dull clang of the passing bell. Toll! Toll! The presage of gloom and woe and misery. "Have you heard the BAD news?" asked the turnpike keeper. "We have taken twenty ships but – we have lost Lord Nelson."'

FALSEHOOD

TRUTH

JOHN BULL, Exchanging NEWS with the CONTINENT.

George Woodward's caricature entitled 'John Bull Exchanging News with the Continent'.

In the ports, garrisons and military stations of the country celebration was enforced and somewhat institutionalised. There were salutes, *feus-de-joie* fired, but full mourning was observed: the colours as well as band instruments were draped in crêpe ribbon. Likewise the sailors of Sir Richard Strachan's squadron, who had mopped up Dumanoir's fleeing ships, came ashore, it is reported, wearing a love knot of black crêpe above the left elbow. The same is true throughout the fleet. They were, we are told, for many days 'useless for duty'. In the words of a seaman on *Royal Sovereign*: 'All the men in our ship...are such soft toads, they have done nothing but blast their eyes and cry...God Bless you! chaps that fought like the devil, sit down and cry like a wench'.

In France the news was hushed up. No official report of the Battle of Trafalgar was ever published. This was relatively easily done; after all, it was easier to carry on boasting of the triumph at Ulm. Moreover, as Lanfrey wrote, 'an event did not officially exist until it had been duly stated and legalised by the *Moniteur*.' French newspapers often made reference to British journals, but only via the censor. Truth, that is the reporting of it, was something the British, with some justification, felt proud of. See, for instance, George Woodward's caricature (above) published on 11 December 1805, in which the well-fed figure of John Bull standing proudly on his home ground (TRUTH) and holding aloft the *Gazette Extraordinary*, trumpets the news of the 'Total Defeat

of the Combined Fleets of France and Spain' across the Channel where lurking behind the rocks (of FALSEHOOD) Boney and a lean minion churn out their fibs whose only purpose appears to be to obscure the actual event still clearly visible in the middle distance.

Sometimes news proper leaked through the underground (radical) press, but even then it tended to be vague and evasive. Thus on 7 November the Paris papers gave uncertain particulars of an engagement at sea, which took place off Cadiz, but it was little more than a gathering of rumour. They claimed it a draw and whistled loudly in the dark. By 30 November the *Journal* carried an extraordinarily disingenuous item: it reported the *London Gazette's* proclamation of the General Thanksgiving to be observed on 5 December, but omitting to mention that it was for the late signal and important victory obtained over the combined fleet of France and Spain.

In Spain the official announcement was made on 5 November by the *Gazet de Madrid*. Perhaps because by the beginning of November the news was already well known in Cadiz and Gibraltar, the Spanish papers made no bones about it: it was a disaster. But equally the English loss in this engagement had not to be underestimated – Lord Nelson having been killed. Ironically, a version of the truth made its way from Madrid to Paris. On 7 December the *Journal de Paris* spoke of the state of the British fleet after the battle of 19 October in a report remarkable for its economy with the truth. If, as was asserted, it was such a great victory, why had the French Government failed to celebrate? This wasn't news, but propaganda. Truth was already on the casualty list.

Of course the British made good use of the news as well. As quickly as it had arrived in London, the news was neatly packaged and dispatched abroad; 3000 copies of the *Gazette Extraordinary* were sent to the continent via Yarmouth. Thus by 15 November it was well known in Holland, and naturally well received. The essential message of a victory was clear; the detail of how, and at what cost it had been won, was indistinct. The British victory at sea was something to set against Napoleon's triumphal progress on land. In a comparatively very short time the news would become universally known having trickled along the trade routes. Thus, at Kingston, Jamaica, for instance, a funeral pyre 47 feet high and

47 feet wide was set alight at forty-seven points; forty-seven guns played an ovation while forty-seven muskets played in between. Forty-seven fireworks then exploded.

Napoleon himself first got news of Trafalgar, according to Marbot, on 18 November, he being at that time at Znaim en route for Austerlitz. He displayed no emotion, concealed the news, and simply wrote to Decres that 'he should wait for more particulars before forming a more definite opinion in the nature of this affair...cause all the troops that are on board [the Cadiz squadron] to come to me on land'. For Napoleon it was business as usual.

The Grande Armée inevitably found out at about the same time. The Austrians, still smarting from the capitulation at Ulm teased their victors with the news, as did prisoners of war in France, who made long bacon at their captors. At Verdun a subscription for supper and wine was immediately set on foot. The method the French had used to dispatch news of Ulm was mimicked, and an unmanned boat bearing the details was floated towards the coast of France.

Napoleon's only other direct reference to the event was on 2 March 1806 (at about which time news had reached Calcutta) when in an Imperial Address he referred to 'les tempetes nous on fait perdre a quelques vaisseaux apres un combat imprudemment engagé' [We have lost several vessels to storms after a battle imprudently engaged]. Yet only a month before, an Imperial Decree had been published, that these words be prominently painted up on every French man of war:

'La France compte que chacun fera son devoir.'

Lieutenant Lapenotière did his duty, and he was rewarded for it (even if his name was misspelt on his presentation sword). He was made commander, a promotion due to him anyway by seniority but was not made post for nearly another six years. Apparently he received no invitation to the funeral. His brief fame soon faded and the rest of his career was spent in the relative obscurity of the Baltic blockade, where he would suffer awful injury in an accidental explosion, and then be invalided home to a desk job in Plymouth and eventual retirement. He has no particular monument. He is however remembered, albeit with some tongue-twisting difficulty by more than a few for the part he took, which was the carrying and delivery intact of some of the most momentous news ever to reach our shores.

Perhaps it is not so surprising after all: the message is always inevitably more important than the messenger. There again, some material herein has been both anecdotal and apocryphal. Not altogether surprisingly, there is no real evidence, for instance, of *Pickle* passing information to fishermen, or of that news being transferred and told by Mayor Giddy in any of the usual sources. This does not however detract from the image of an eager lieutenant carefully carrying a guttering candle. On the other hand, if Collingwood's dispatch was only a sketch, it was an accurate and scrupulous one. Casualty figures and their consequences would follow as well as a myriad technical details that gradually completed the jigsaw. But nothing would contradict it.

Above all, the point is this: Collingwood trusted Lapenotière with this tremendously significant document, and because we can so readily trace its provenance and by cross reference, verify its content, we take it to be an authentic version of events. We are willing to accept it as the truth. Thus, we put our faith in it – which is how and why the banner found its way into a Cornish church.

Anthony Cross joined Warwick Leadlay Gallery as a History graduate in 1978. Despite his landlocked upbringing, he has always recognised the deep and significant role played by the sea in Great Britain's past. His interest in antique engravings has led him to become an acknowledged authority on the Nelsonian era, and he is particularly well versed in those images which illustrate the life and achievements of his Noble Lordship. His recent contribution *In Nelson's Footsteps*, a biopic narrated by Colin White was well received. Currently, he looks forward to the bicentennial decade with anticipation and relish – pen and spyglass in hand.

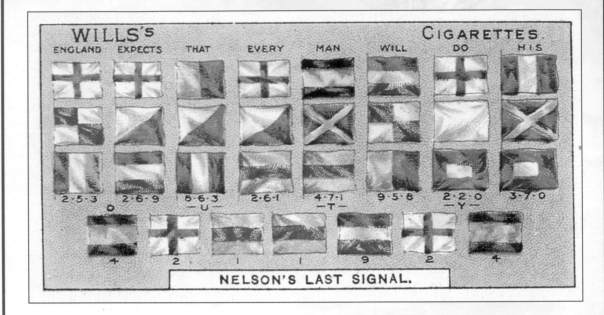

NELSON'S LAST SIGNAL.

TELEGRAPHIC SIGNALS, OR MARINE VOCABULARY

Captain Sir Home Popham's book published in 1800 revolutionised the transmission of signals between friendly ships. By means of a numerical code Popham transformed the restricted vocabulary of a few well known commands into the ability to send speech. This was achieved by designing ten numeral flags allocated singly or in pairs to letters of the alphabet, groups of two or three flags were allocated to a predetermined vocabulary of several hundred words, the advantage of which was to minimise the complex and time consuming task of hoisting them.

Observers of the famous hoist at Trafalgar should note that it contains both vocabulary and words spelled out. They should also note that Popham used No 9 for I and J and that in the eighteenth century V came before U in the alphabet.

ENGLAND EXPECTS

In 1663 the Marquis of Worcester proposed a plan of signals and a telegraph was suggested by Dr Hooke in 1684. M. Amontons also produced a telegraph at this time. The Duke of York (later James II) devised a set of naval signals which Kempenfelt modified in 1780. Popham produced his dictionary in 1800. Practical progress was achieved by M. Chappe who produced the first French telegraphs in 1792, and by the British in 1796, when two telegraph devices were erected over the Admiralty building in London. A semaphore replaced them in 1816.

MARIE ANTIONETTE
(1755-1793)

The fourth daughter of Maria Theresa of Austria, Marie was married to Louis XVI, then dauphin, when she was only fifteen. From the time she became queen in 1774, her favour towards Austria earned her the distrust of the people. Later, she further alienated Revolutionary France by openly showing enmity to Turgot and Necker and a dislike to monarchists such as Lafayette and Miraebau. The 'Austrian woman' was accused of extravagances, failed to understand the troublesome times in which she lived and attempted to flee from France. She was captured and incarcerated in the Conciergerie, a prison for common criminals, where she was convicted of treason. Her execution by guillotine followed on 16 October 1793.

1803 To His Excellency Hugh Elliot Esq. from Victory in Agincourt off Madalena Islands: 'Our crews...have now been upwards of five months at sea. But our health and humour are perfection, and we only want for the French fleet out'.

1800 Rear-Admiral Sir Home Riggs Popham's 'Telegraphic Signals and Marine Vocabulary' is first published. It was adopted by the Admiralty in 1803.

1803 To William Locker Esq. from St Omer, France: 'We set off at daylight for Boulogne....This place is full of English, I suppose because the wine is so very cheap'.

1755 Marie Antoinette is born. It was said 'The miseries of France became identified with her extravagance and prompted the poor vacillating King into a retrograde policy to his own undoing.'

1792 To HRH The Duke of Clarence: 'In what way it might be in the power of such an humble individual as myself to best serve my King, has been a matter of serious consideration; and no way appeared to me so proper as asking for a ship'.

1805 The 'Hibernian Journal' publishes a letter from Benjamin Franklin claiming the cause of the United States is that of Ireland.

1804 To Captain Gore, Medusa, from Victory: 'I wish you could get hold of a First Rate, loaded with money; not that you or I should get any of it...but a few millions would be useful to the state'.

1805 Lieutenant Lapenotière, Pickle, conveying Collingwood's dispatch regarding the victory at Trafalgar and the death of Nelson lands at Falmouth, and immediately sets off on the road for London.

1804 To Nathaniel Taylor, Naval Storekeeper at Malta: 'Our Master-Ropemaker is a child of thirteen years of age, and the best Rope-Maker in the Fleet'.

1800 'The Times' announces Dr Herschel's lecture to the Royal Society: 'A paper of singular curiosity: on the power of penetrating into space by telescopes.'

Flying the signal, 'I have urgent dispatches', HM Pickle arrives at Falmouth by Gordon Frickers, courtesy of Nicholas Varley Victary 2005 Ltd.

1800 To Evan Nepean, at the Admiralty, from Yarmouth: 'Sir, I beg you will acquaint their Lordships of my arrival here this day....I trust that my necessary journey by land from the Mediterranean will not be considered as a wish to be a moment out of active service'.

1789 John Carroll, of Irish descent, is appointed Bishop of Baltimore, the first Roman Catholic Bishop in the United States. The Dublin Society of United Irishmen is set up.

1st

2nd

3rd

4th

5th

6th

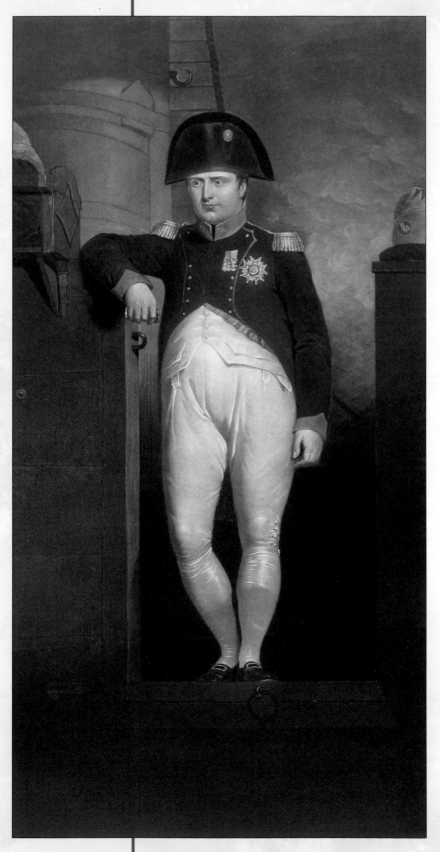

NAPOLEON BONAPARTE (1769-1821)

During Nelson's lifetime, and for much of the nineteenth century the man who had more influence on the course of European history than any other was, arguably, Napoleon Bonaparte. Born in Corsica, he became an artillery officer in the French Revolution, and his moment came at the siege of Toulon. From then on his political progress was rapid: he was appointed a Consul; then First Consul; then Consul for Life; and lastly from 1804, self-proclaimed Emperor of the French. His continuing military successes were almost uninterrupted until Nelson's victory at the Nile put paid to Napoleon's eastern ambitions. Likewise the Battle of Trafalgar, although not the only reason, turned his attention away from the invasion of Britain.

Napoleon was crowned Emperor of the French on 2 December 1804 in the cathedral of Nôtre Dame, Paris. The Pope was present to perform the ceremony but Napoleon seized the crown and put it on his head with his own hands. Later, in Milan on 28 May, 1805, Napoleon put the Iron Crown of Italy on his head saying, 'Dieu me l'a donnée; gare à qui y touchera.' (God has given it to me; woe to him who touches it.) On the same day he instituted The Order of the Iron Crown of Italy; this was temporarily abolished in 1814 but revived in 1816.

Napoleon had, by 1812, overreached himself – his armies were fighting in Russia and in Spain, and were finally defeated in both theatres. The subsequent decline seems inevitable: he was defeated by the Allies in 1814 and exiled to Elba, from where he escaped for the brief Waterloo campaign. The Emperor surrendered to the British on HMS *Bellerophon*, and he was sent to the remote Atlantic island of St Helena, where he died in 1821.

The Emperor Napoleon as he presented himself on the gangway of HMS Bellerophon *in Portsmouth harbour in August 1815.*

1805 'The Times' carries the news of Trafalgar.

1783 *The forger John Austen is executed in London; it was the last public hanging at Tyburn. Afterwards, and until 1868 executions were held at Newgate.*

7th

1800 Nelson arrives at Nerot's Hotel, St James Street. A letter to the Reverend Dixon Hoste states: 'His reception by Lady Nelson is said to have been extremely cold and mortifying to his feelings'.

1784 *The Treaty of Fontainbleau is signed between the Dutch and Emperor Joseph II, giving the Austrians access to the Scheldt.*

8th

1800 St Vincent remarks to Nepean: 'It is evident from Lord Nelson's letter to you on his landing, that he is doubtful of the propriety of his conduct. I have no doubt he is pledged to getting Lady Hamilton received at St James's and everywhere, and that he will get into much brouillerie about it'.

1799 *In the coup d'etat Brumaire Napoleon overthrows the Directory and becomes First Consul and unchallenged dictator of France.*

9th

1800 Lord Mayor Day in London. Nelson dines with the Lord Mayor, and receives the sword voted to him by the City of London: 'Sir, it is with the greatest pride and satisfaction that I receive from the Honourable Court this testimony of their approbation of my conduct, and, with this very sword, I hope soon to aid in reducing our implacable and inveterate Enemy to proper due limits; without which, this country can neither hope for, nor ever expect a solid, honourable, and permanent peace'.

1770 *Voltaire writes, 'If God did not exist it would be necessary to invent him.' On the same day in 1793 a 'Festival of Reason' was held in Nôtre Dame.*

10th

1796 The opening paragraph of a long letter to the Duke of Clarence: 'What may be thought of in England of our embarkation from Bastia I know not, but I conceive myself to have a fair right to be well spoken of, as the few facts which I shall state will evince. (I shall relate them to your Royal Highness, to give you an idea of the state of our Army and the Viceroy on my arrival.)'

1778 *Colonial settlers are massacred by British Loyalists (Tories) and their Indian allies in New York's Cherry Valley.*

11th

1794 To Fanny from St Fiorenzo: 'I have been sent to look after the French fleet, who had again given Admiral Hotham the slip. I found them in Toulon. The French say they will take Corsica again. There has been a most diabolical report here, of Agamemnon's being captured and carried into Toulon, owing to my running into the Harbour's mouth. I hope it has not reached England. Never believe what you may see in the Papers about us'.

1797 *Napoleon informs the directory that he has 'given all the necessary orders for moving our columns to the ocean.'*

12th

1798 Nelson signs his first letter using his new title of honour announced on 7 October. It is from his camp at St Germaines to Spencer and relates to the French Army: 'Thirty thousand of, as [General] Mack says, "la plus belle Armeé d'Europe", was drawn out for me to see, and as far as my judgement goes in those matters, I agree, that a finer Army cannot be'.

1797 *Napoleon sends Andréossy to Paris to prepare the artillery to the same calibre as English field pieces to accept their cannon balls.*

13th

ROBERT FULTON (1765-1815)

⌐—◆—⌐

Fulton was born on 14 November 1765 on a farm near Pennsylvania. He started work for a jeweller at the age of seventeen, saving hard to fund a small farm for his mother and sister. He was always keen on art and went to London to study under Benjamin West, but was encouraged by his English friends to turn his hand to engineering.

This was immediately successful; he invented a number of devices useful in the newly developing canal industry such as dredging machines, rope-making devices and canal-locking arrangements and quickly established an interest in steam propulsion for use on the rivers and waterways while others were concentrating on its application to pump out mines and transport goods or spoil by rail.

He investigated military applications of steam designing a steam-powered submarine capable of firing a torpedo. This rather comical looking design had sails to supplement its propulsion. It was known as 'Fulton's Folly' and confounded its critics on 17 August 1807 when the *Clermont*, as she was named, made a trial trip from New York to Albany, no less than 150 miles against the stream in roughly thirty hours. He went on to build the first steam-powered warship for the United States in 1815. Thereafter the demise of sail was rapid.

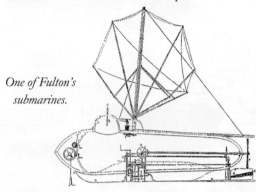

One of Fulton's submarines.

A Blanchard balloon.

FLIGHT

⌐—◆—⌐

Flight may have its genesis in Daedalus and Icarus but the first practical use of heavier than air apparatus was during Nelson's lifetime. The first important step took place near Annonay, France on 5 June 1783. A linen bag was made by the Montgolfier brothers. It was supported by a frame construction; under it straw was burnt filling the bag with hot air and causing it to rise to a great height. It was airborne for ten minutes and came to earth over a mile away. The brothers believed they had harnessed smoke, without realising that it was the expansion of air through heat that had caused the ascent.

On 27 August in the same year a French scientist J A C Charles, filled a varnished silk bag with hydrogen. It rose 3000 feet and travelled 15 miles. After it descended terrified peasants hacked it to pieces with pitchforks believing it to be the work of Satan.

On 19 September 1783 a sheep, a fowl and a duck rose to 1500 feet in a Montgolfier balloon but the first human to ascend was Jean Pilâtre de Rozier, a native of Metz, Lorraine. He went up near Paris on 15 October 1783 but his balloon was tethered by cable. Five weeks later, together with the Marquis d'Ârlandes, he made an un-tethered ascent, remaining airborne for twenty-five minutes and traversing about 5 miles. The following year on 15 September an Italian, Vincenzo Lunardi, rose from the Artillery Ground London in a hydrogen filled balloon thus becoming the first man to fly over England. The English Channel was conquered on 7 January 1785 by another Frenchman, J P Blanchard, and an American, Dr John Jeffries. The flight took two hours.

1804 To all vessels on the Mediterranean station: 'Whereas Hostilities have commenced between Great Britain and the Court of Spain; you are hereby required and directed on falling in with any Spanish Ship or Vessel of War, or Merchantman belonging to the Subjects of his Catholic Majesty, or which may have Spanish property on board, and on doing so, you will use your utmost endeavour to capture, burn, sink, or destroy them'.

1770 James Bruce, the 'Abyssinan traveller', discovers the source of the Blue Nile, Lake Tana, Ethiopia.

14th

1804 Memorandum: 'Whereas I judge it proper, under the present uncertain state of affairs between Great Britain and the Court of Spain, that all Spanish Ships and Vessels of War, as well as the Trade of his Catholic Majesty, shall be detained till further orders. You are hereby required and directed to detain all Spanish Ships of War and Merchantmen.'

1802 The English portrait painter George Romney dies at his home at Kendel aged 67.

15th

1803 To Nepean, at the Admiralty: 'You will be pleased to acquaint the Lords Commissioners of the Admiralty, that this morning the Squadron under my command captured Le Rénard, French National Schooner, mounting twelve four-pounders, with six swivels, and manned with eighty men; also Le Titus, transport, having on board ninety-six soldiers from Corsica bound for Toulon'.

1796 Napoleon is victorious at the Bridge of Arcola, Lombardy.

16th

1798 To His Excellency the Admiral commanding the Ottoman Fleet: 'The Grand Signior having condescended to notice my earnest endeavours to serve the cause of humanity against a set of impious men, I should feel sorry to miss an opportunity of expressing to you how anxious I am for the success of the Ottoman arms, and how happy your Excellency would make me by telling me how I can be most useful to you'.

1771 Sollom Moss near Longtown in Cumbria erupts, destroying many houses with mud and moss.

17th

1795 To HRH The Duke of Clarence from Foudroyant, Genoa Roads: 'Every day produces such changes in the prospect of our affairs that in relating events I hardly know where to begin. A superior force to the French must always be kept here; but, I own, I think the French will make a push from Toulon to drive us away'.

1851 Louis Jacques Mandé Daguerre (b.1789), the French photographic pioneer, dies. He perfected a 'daguerrotype' process involving copper plate coated with silver iodide and bromide.

18th

1795 To HRH the Duke of Clarence on assisting the Genoese: 'My situation is more awkward, as what has happened does not relate to the English Minister, the breach of Neutrality being an Austrian business...I think I shall be attacked very soon by a much superior force from Toulon'.

1792 French National Convention, by the edict of Fraternity, offers to help people of all nations to overthrow their kings.

19th

1798 Parliament votes Nelson £2000 per year for life. To his brother: 'As to myself, the probability is that I shall never take my Seat in the House of Peers. My health has declined very much, and nothing keeps me on service but the thought that I am doing good'. Two years later he takes his seat in the House of Lords and is introduced between Lords Grenville and Romney.

1780 War breaks out as Anglo-Dutch relations collapse on the news the Dutch have been supplying France and Spain arms to the American rebels via the Dutch Caribbean.

20th

1800 To Hercules Ross: 'San Joseph [captured by Nelson at St Vincent] is to be my next Flagship'. He hoists his Vice-Admiral of the Blue flag on 17 January 1801.

1783 The first successful ascent by hot air balloon carrying a human is made from Bois de Boulogne, Paris.

21st

Silhouette of Tom Allen, Nelson's good and faithful servant, who died on 23 November 1838.

The English fear of a French invasion is graphically illustrated in Gillray's caricature of February 1798 in which he depicts Napoleon's flat-bottomed boats carrying they cargo of revolutionary ideals. (See 29th November.)

🐚 **1799** 🐚 Nelson appears to have identified a soul mate in Admiral Suwarrow. To Lord William Bentinck: 'We are anxious to hear of the success of our friend Suwarrow. Although I never had the pleasure of seeing him, yet, as an individual of Europe, I love, honour, and respect him. Others may love the great hero – Nelson loves the man, for I hear he despises wealth, if it stands in the road to fame'.

🐚 *1774* 🐚 *Robert Clive, former governor of India, commits suicide. He is buried at Moreton Say near Market Drayton.*

🐚 **1803** 🐚 To Captain Cracraft, Anson: 'You will take every means in your power for the effectual protection of Trade in the Adriatic, and in the Mouth of the Archipelago, and give such convoys as may be wanted, not only from Malta, but also from Trieste, Venice, Fuime, Patras, Zante, &c. The French Fleet are ready for sea, but where they are bound I cannot tell you'.

🐚 *1795* 🐚 *The French begin a two-day battle to defeat the Austrians at Loano.*

🐚 **1803** 🐚 To Sir John Acton, off Toulon: 'The French fleet yesterday at 2 o'clock was in appearance in high feather, and as fine as paint could make them. Our weather-beaten ships...will make their sides like a plum-pudding'.

🐚 *1758* 🐚 *Americans and British regulars under General Forbes capture Fort Duqesne.*

🐚 **1803** 🐚 To Dr John Snipe, Physician to the Fleet: 'The Commissioners for taking care of the Sick and Hurt Seamen and Marines, having acquainted me that they had appointed Mr John Grey to be Surgeon of a Naval Hospital to be established in Malta, I am, therefore, to desire you will proceed immediately, in Narcissus for Malta, for the purpose of examining the situation and necessary accommodation of such Hospital'.

🐚 *1796* 🐚 *The entire crew of an East Indiaman returning to the Thames are press ganged for service in Britannia.*

🐚 **1804** 🐚 To Marsden: 'Having acquainted you that the Squadron under my command had detained the Spanish Schooner Ventura which appeared in every respect well calculated for the service of this Country, you will be pleased to acquaint their Lordships that as Vessels of her description are particularly wanted for the service of Malta, I have ordered her to be...placed under immediate direction of Sir Alexander Ball'.

🐚 *1836* 🐚 *John Loudon McAdam, inventor of the road surfacing system which won a £10,000 award in 1782, dies.*

🐚 **1795** 🐚 The Austrians defeated, Nelson writes to Drake: 'nothing has been wanting on my part to give every possible energy to the operations of the Austrians'.

🐚 *1801* 🐚 *George III's sons Augustus and Adolphus are created Dukes of Sussex and Cambridge.*

🐚 **1803** 🐚 To Hookham Frere, Madrid: 'I trust that we shall be received in the Spanish Ports in the same manner as the French. I am ready to make large allowances for the miserable situation Spain has placed herself in; but there is a certain line beyond which I cannot submit to be treated with disrespect'.

🐚 *1780* 🐚 *Maria Theresa of Austria, Hungary and Bohemia dies, aged 63.*

🐚 **1796** 🐚 To Suckling: 'My professional reputation is the only riches I am likely to acquire in this war...however it is satisfactory to myself'.

🐚 *1803* 🐚 *Napoleon writes to his Minister of Interior: 'I want you to get a song written, to go to the tune of the Chant du Depart, for the invasion of England.'*

🐚 **1798** 🐚 To William Wyndham: 'I have been thinking all night of the General and Duke of Sangaro's saying that the King of Naples had not declared war against the French. Now, I assert, that he has, and in a much stronger manner than the ablest Minister in Europe could write a Declaration of War. Has he not received, as a conquest made by him, the Republican Flag taken at Gozo?'

🐚 *1782* 🐚 *Preliminary Treaty of Paris, recognising the independence of the 13 United States. is drawn up.*

I Have One More Signal to Hoist

THE LEGACY OF ADMIRAL LORD NELSON

Robin Neillands

'Saluting the Admiral', a late Victorian print of the painting by Albert Holden, exemplifies the spirit in which the memory of Nelson remained very much alive nearly a century after his death.

'There is an extraordinary, almost incredible atmosphere of living reality about the influence which the glorious naval hero of a century and a quarter ago exercises to this day among the men of the Royal Navy. Nelson is not a ghost, nor even a great tradition among the British Ships. He is living, flaming spirit.'

Those words were written by Lorne Bartram the naval correspondent of the *London Evening Standard* in October 1939, six weeks after the outbreak of the Second World War. Bartram had just returned from a voyage on an unnamed British battleship during which the officers had dined to commemorate Trafalgar Day and, in the midst of that wartime cruise, had raised their glasses to the immortal memory of 'Lord Nelson, Vice-Admiral of the White'. Bartram, their guest in the wardroom that night, could only marvel at how the very name of Nelson encouraged – and comforted – the men of the modern navy at the outset of a new and bitter war, for Nelson, too, had fought against all odds, and what had been done once, could be done again.

Horatio Nelson was born in 1758, at the dawn of the Industrial Revolution. He grew up during a time when ideas and inventions were being produced in great numbers and at a bewildering speed, and his brief life was marked by constant change in almost every sphere of human endeavour. His world was also marked by conflict, a world in which one war was no sooner settled than another war broke out. It was a world where slavery was still practised, where liberty was frequently curtailed and justice often had to be paid for. It was a dangerous world, but an exciting one, a place were a young man with courage and initiative could make his mark.

It was also a dying world, one that would be killed off by the advance of technology and the spread of revolutionary thought. The great sailing ships, the 'Wooden Walls of England', and the gallantry and romance that goes with the period would soon be gone, and when Lord Nelson died in the cockpit of the *Victory* much of his world died with him. We will not see his like again, but his influence endures to this day, not least in the Royal Navy.

The Royal Navy is a service that values its traditions and many of those traditions had already been laid down by the time Nelson sailed on his first commission in 1771. The Seven Years' War between Britain and France had been ended by the Peace of Paris which endowed Great Britain with all of Canada, Cape Breton and Senegal. These territories came from the French, but there was also Florida, which Britain acquired from the Spanish. Many of these useful acquisitions had been obtained through the efforts of the Royal Navy and the Royal Navy was not slow to point this out. In spite of the press gang and the harsh conditions of the Service, by the time Nelson was born the Royal Navy had taken a place in the hearts of the nation that it has never since lost.

In 1759, when Nelson was a baby, the Royal Navy had ensured General Wolfe's victory at Quebec, by controlling the St Lawrence river and landing troops by night below the Heights of Abraham, where Wolfe won his famous if Phyrric victory over the great Montcalm and gave half a continent to the British people. It was the Royal Navy that took British troops to India to beat the French at Plassey. It was the Royal Navy that protected the ships of the East India Company and all the other great trading companies that were creating a new prosperity for the British people. For a boy to go to sea was a natural thing to do in the middle decades of the eighteenth century, because the Royal Navy protected the nation and the Royal Navy sailed to glory.

Nelson's life is the story of the Royal Navy, a tale well worth re-telling. Horatio Nelson first went to sea on the *Raisonnable* in 1771. Once afloat, he would have soon become aware that the Royal Navy was both the practical extension of his country's growing economic strength and the means of British overseas expansion. He also served some time in the merchant service and saw with his own eyes just how much of Britain's wealth and influence depended on those solid, handy, unglamorous ships. Nelson was a vain and impetuous man but he was no fool, and he never forgot the lessons he learned in those early days at sea.

Other influences, the background to his duties, may well have passed him by for a boy on his first commission at sea, especially in the age of sail, had

Wounds received by Lord Nelson
His Eye in Corsica
His Belly off Cape St Vincent
His arm at Tenereffe
His Head in Egypt

Tolerable for one War

a lot to learn and little time for reflection. Even so, ideas were afoot in Europe that were to change the nation that young Nelson wished to serve and affect the world in which he was to make such a significant mark. Nelson was ambitious and his chosen vehicle was the Royal Navy; that stern service offered a young man all he could wish for in the way of danger, glory and possible advancement.

He rose swiftly, becoming a post-captain in 1779, at the age of twenty-one. He served in all the great stations of the naval command, in the West Indies and in the Mediterranean, and made his mark in the great naval battles of the period, displaying competence and daring in equal measure. Off Cape St Vincent, in February 1797, he disobeyed the Fighting Instructions and took his ship, the *Captain,* out of the line of battle to fling it in the path of the Spanish fleet and create a victory. Had it all gone wrong he might have been shot; as it was he became a rear-admiral. At the Nile in 1798, he defeated the French fleet and marooned General Napoleon in Egypt. At Copenhagen, in April 1801, he disobeyed the order to break off the engagement until he was sure the enemy had been defeated. That was the Nelson Spirit; to do the right thing and win the battle, whatever the odds or the orders, whatever the risks to himself or his career.

Nelson spent years at sea, where he was often in action, and in due course he paid the price of duty. He lost an eye and an arm and the cost of his victories in personal, physical terms can be seen by comparing the painting of the young Lieutenant Nelson by Rigaud (see page 32), which was paint-

ed in stages between 1777 and 1788, and the one painted by Hoppner just before Trafalgar (see page 54). The first shows a slim, handsome, young officer; the second an old man, prematurely aged, his face lined and his hair white, a man worn down by wounds and worry and the weight of responsibility, yet still willing to take up his burden and put to sea again with his beloved ships.

When the combined fleet was beaten at Trafalgar in October 1805, the Napoleonic Wars still had another ten years to run. Many battles and hard campaigns lay across the path to eventual victory; only a few weeks after Trafalgar the Emperor Napoleon crushed the Austrians at Austerlitz and Prime Minister Pitt told his secretary to roll up the map of Europe, which would not be needed for another ten years. If Napoleon continued to flourish, what then was Nelson's real achievement, and how important was the victory at Trafalgar to the outcome of the Napoleonic Wars?

The second part of that question is the easier to answer. Trafalgar changed the entire course of the Napoleonic Wars and thwarted the Emperor's dream of a world-wide French empire. This is not to say that Napoleon's ambition was immediately stemmed by the outcome of Trafalgar. In the years immediately ahead he was to thrash the Austrians and the Prussians, come to an agreement with the Russians, occupy Portugal and place his brother on the Throne of Spain. For several years after Trafalgar his star was on the ascendant, but Nelson's victory put a limit to his ambitions and tied him to the land.

After Trafalgar, Napoleon turned away from the sea and concentrated his energies in the creation of a continental empire, a decision that took him to disaster on the hot sierras of Spain and the freezing wastes of Russia. It has been said that when the Emperor crossed the River Neiman into Russia in 1812 he was taking a path that led inexorably to St Helena. It would be equally true to say that he was directed down that road when Admiral Nelson's fleet sailed into action off Cape Trafalgar seven years before. That naval victory thrilled Europe, encouraged resistance to French domination and proved that one part of Europe would never fall to this new and revolutionary conqueror. Britain would fight on; if necessary for years; if necessary alone.

Moreover, although the death of Nelson seemed to outweigh any benefits obtained from his victory at the time, British seapower continued to curb the French and encouraged resistance to French domination throughout the remaining years of the Napoleonic Wars. When Napoleon invaded Portugal in 1807 it was the Royal Navy which spirited away the Royal Family of the House of Braganza. When the Spanish juntas rose against the French in 1808 it was the ships of the Royal Navy that supplied them with muskets and cannon, food and powder. The Royal Navy took General Wellesley's army to the Peninsula and when the Duke of Wellington set out from Portugal on his march to the Pyrenees in 1812 he was supplied and supported all the way by the ships of the British fleet. Without the Royal Navy, the Peninsula War could not have been won.

The answer to the first part of the question, on the real achievement of Lord Nelson, is also encapsulated in the Royal Navy. Lord Nelson devoted his life to the naval service, a service which repaid him with respect and affection, and which he endowed in return with an undying legacy, still best known as the Nelson Spirit.

The Nelsonian precepts – duty, discipline, professional seamanship and a willingness to engage the enemy closely – stood the Royal Navy in good stead for the next hundred years. Nelson inspired the Royal Navy, for his victories gave the navy such a reputation, and so much self-confidence that by his death the command of the seas seemed to be Britain's natural inheritance, and seamanship seemed to be an in-built ability of every Briton. The Nelson Spirit of 'engaging the enemy more closely', endowed Britain's sailors with the belief that they could always trounce the men and ships of other navies, whatever the odds.

That Belief, that Spirit, may not always have been true, or at least not entirely true – the big

A First World War recruitment poster which again evokes the Nelson Spirit.

1805   "ENGLAND EXPECTS"   1915

ARE YOU DOING YOUR DUTY TO-DAY?

American frigates encountered in the War of 1812 proved to be the most formidable opponents – but that belief, in their fighting prowess and ability to keep the sea has stood the Royal Navy and the British nation in good stead in some difficult times since that long-ago fight off Cape Trafalgar. That self-confidence is still present in the naval service, not just in Britain but in all those nations – Australia, New Zealand, India, even the United States and Chile, where the skills and traditions of the Royal Navy are valued as part of their own naval history. In the naval world, there is only one Nelson.

Yet Nelson was only a man, and a very human one. If Nelson had survived the battle at Trafalgar, what would have become of him in future years? Triumph and accolades in plenty in the immediate aftermath of victory of course, but what then? Could he have returned to the fleet and found more glory? Probably not. His eyesight was failing and it is more than probable that in a year or two he would have become completely blind. His general health was not good and he cannot have expected another command at sea when the current commission with the fleet was over.

Yet Nelson ashore is hard to imagine. He belongs at sea with his ships and his friends and his fighting. Would he have been able to divorce Fanny, marry his beloved Emma and settle down to honoured retirement at Merton? One rather doubts it. Victories offer a transitory form of glory. Had Nelson survived Trafalgar and spent the rest of his life ashore, it is hard to believe that it would have been a happy one. Nelson needed Society and the praise of his peers. His life with Emma Hamilton was already an open scandal and must have led eventually to some form of social ostracism had it continued – and all the evidence suggests that he could never have given her up. On balance, therefore, it is better for the Nelson legend and perhaps for the man himself that a French sharpshooter found his mark that day on the quarterdeck of HMS *Victory*. By his death Nelson became immortal and his spirit lives on.

That Nelson was the leading naval figure of his time is beyond question, but he was not alone in high command. The Royal Navy swarmed with talent in Nelson's time and had done for decades. Great Admirals, Rodney and Hood, Barham and Hawke, Jervis and Saumarez, had always been on hand to command the British fleets; the Royal Navy was a nursery of talent. Nelson himself never ceased to praise and admire the skills and professionalism of his peers and he revelled in the company of his captains, his 'Band of Brothers', Fremantle, Troubridge, Berry, Hardy, the doughty Collingwood, Blackwood and the rest. These were the men who brought their ships into battle at his back; famous, fighting seamen whose courage was without question, and on whose skills he could rely. 'See how that noble fellow Collingwood carries his ship into action', remarked Lord Nelson at Trafalgar, watching the *Royal Sovereign* sail down on the enemy fleet. And it was Collingwood, in great personal distress, who had to take command of the battered British fleet when the battle was over and his beloved Nelson was dead.

In the nineteenth century the Royal Navy was the living embodiment of the will and aspirations of the British people, a source of hope and a sign of faith, especially among that growing number of British people who lived and served overseas in Britain's expanding list of colonies and dominions. As long as a warship flying the white ensign appeared off shore from time to time they felt secure, knowing that their country had not forgotten them. The security of the Kingdom and the success of Britain's trade depended on the Royal Navy and whatever else was stinted, the fleet was kept in being and steadily expanded, as Nelson would have wanted.

There is, of course, another side to Lord Nelson. He became larger than life, almost an institution, but he belonged to that class of institution which, over and above all other gifts, has the power of inspiring affection. His men, though fiercely disciplined and never spared the lash, still loved him because they knew he would do his best for them and share their dangers. His captains loved him because he led them to glory and protected their interests.

Posterity loves him because he was a hero and could use the English language with telling effect. His penultimate signal at Trafalgar has never been forgotten; but he also spoke well at other times and his words reveal his kindness, his humanity and his courage. When wounded off Tenerife – his

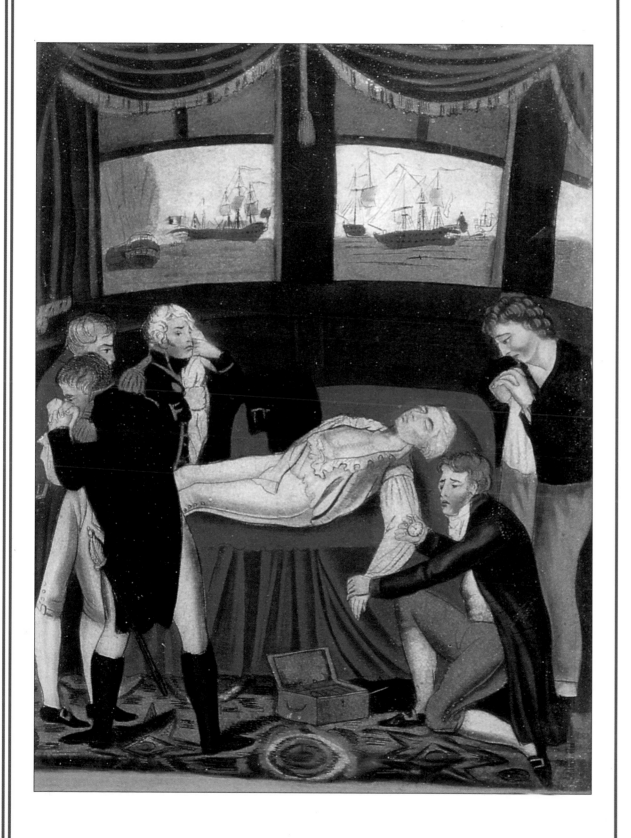

'They have done for me at last, Hardy.' In this simple but heartfelt rendition, produced no doubt for the popular market, the dying Nelson is attended to by Dr Beatty, while his officers and men already grieve the inevitable.

arm shattered – he refused to be taken on Captain Fremantle's ship because Mrs Fremantle was on board, 'and she must not see me in this condition when I can bring her no news of her husband'. And so, in great pain, he was taken to another ship, where his arm was taken off. Before Trafalgar he told his captains: 'In case any signals can neither be seen or perfectly understood, no Captain can do very wrong if he places his ship alongside that of an enemy'. His words, like his actions, were an inspiration to his men. 'He is so good and pleasant', said Captain Duff 'that we all wish to do what he likes without any kind of orders.'

The Royal Navy has never forgotten Lord Nelson; nor should it do so. Nelson and his captains thrashed the French and Spanish fleets at Trafalgar and gave Great Britain a naval supremacy over all other nations that was to last for more than a century, out of the age of sail and well into the age of steam. Thanks to Nelson the Royal Navy flourished throughout the century which followed and at the Fleet Review at Spithead in July 1914, just before the outbreak of the First World War, 42 miles of British warships, Dreadnoughts, battleships, cruisers, destroyers, frigates and submarines were drawn up for inspection by King George V, a display of seapower such as no two other nations could match. The British army might have been small, the Royal Air Force non-existent, but the British navy ruled the waves and carried the British Expeditionary Forces safely to that rendezvous with destiny in France.

The Royal Navy kept the seas and protected Britain's shores in that war, in spite of storms and submarines. There was a shock at Jutland in 1916 when the Germans sank more ships than the Royal Navy could manage to do, but in the end it was the High Seas fleet that broke off the action, surrendered in 1918 and scuppered itself at Scapa Flow. Thanks at least in part to Lord Nelson, the Royal Navy did not entertain the idea of defeat in that World War or in the one that followed. Great Admirals continued to command the fleet – Jellico and Beatty, Somerville and Vian – men who, like Lord Nelson, would hoist the three great battle

ensigns that the Royal Navy always flies in action and take their ships down on the enemy.

That was the Nelson way, the Nelson Touch, the way he had taught the Royal Navy to fight; to engage the enemy closely and drive him from the seas. 'You must be quick', Nelson said to his signal officer, Lieutenant Pasco at Trafalgar, ordering the hoisting of his famous signal (England expects that every man will do his duty), 'for I have one more signal to hoist, which is the one for Close Action'.

Nelson the man, a very frail and human man, much loved by all who knew him, lost his life on HMS *Victory* in 1805, but in a very real sense Admiral Lord Nelson is still alive. Every time the white ensign is hoisted, even on a 'stone frigate' far from the sea; every time one of the slim, grey ships of our greatly depleted navy slips out to sea, the thought of Nelson comes into the mind of the onlookers – and it is always Nelson, our only seaman.

Britain has been well served by her sailors, in peace and war, and it may seem strange that of all that great company Nelson is the only one that every Briton remembers. The Royal Navy, on the other hand, does not find that strange at all. Nelson was a seaman – the most famous sailor of all – and he deserves all the praise that posterity can bestow.

Robert Neillands is a journalist, a travel writer and one of Britain's busiest popular historians. He has written over thirty books on subjects as varied as the Hundred Years War, D-day 1944 and the lives and campaigns of Wellington and Napoleon. his most recent books are *A Fighting Retreat; The Military Campaigns in the British Empire, 1947-1997*, and *In the Combat Zone; The Story of Special Forces*. His next book, *The Great War Generals*, will be pubished in September, 1998. He served in the Royal Marines Commandos and when not travelling, he lives in Wiltshire.

Official feeling for Nelson is best illustrated by the number of monuments that were erected in memory of him, the most famous of which is Nelson's column in Trafalgar Square, London, pictured here c.1860.

William Pitt the Younger. (See 7 December.) Pitt's ministry lasted almost unbroken for twenty years, but all the good intentions of his early years were ruined by the necessities of war with France.

1798 Nelson writes of the Tuscan General Naselli: 'There is this difference between us – the General prudently, and certainly safely, waits the orders of his Court, taking no responsibility upon himself; I act, from the circumstance of the moment, as I feel may be most advantageous for the honour of the cause which I serve, taking all the responsibility on myself'.

1774 George Washington signs the Fairfax Resolutions barring the importation of slaves.

1st

1795 To Fanny on his fleet's failure to prevent the French attacking Austrian Posts near Borghetta in November, although his fleet is considerably outnumbered: 'Let the blame be where it may, I do not believe any party will seriously lay it at my door'.

1804 Napoleon, in Nôtre Dame, takes the crown from Pope Pius VII, and places it on his own head.

2nd

1796 To Jervis giving his account of events at Genoa, having been accused of breach of faith and being unworthy of his rank by the Marquis of Spinola: 'But I cannot allow the Marquis's Note to pass without severe reprobation. It is couched in Language which his rank as a Nobleman and representative of the Republic of Genoa, ought to have made it impossible for him to use'.

1800 The Austrians are defeated by the French and Bavarians at the Battle of Hokenlinden.

3rd

1804 Nelson hears that Vice-Admiral Sir John Orde is appointed to part of his old command, as commander-in-chief of a squadron off Cadiz. To Keats, Superb: 'I suppose, by the arrival of Sir John Orde in our vicinity that I may very soon be your troublesome guest [for passage home] therefore, that I may not hurry your Ship too much, I shall, with your leave, send some of my wine to the Superb this morning'.

1791 Britain's oldest Sunday paper, 'The Observer', is first published.

4th

1799 Writing to Sir Sidney Smith from Palermo: 'One of my greatest boasts is; that no man can ever say I have told a lie'.

1766 James Christie (the elder), auctioneer, holds his first sale in London.

5th

1798 Naples is at war with France, Malta has fallen to the French. To Commodore Ruckworth: 'I most heartily congratulate you on the conquest of Minorca - an acquisition invaluable to Great Britain, and completely in future prevents any movements from Toulon to the westward'.

1774 Austria becomes the first nation to introduce a state education system.

6th

1803 Off Toulon, to the Duke of Clarence: 'The French keep us waiting for them during a long severe winter's cruise; and such a place as all the Gulf of Lyons, so for gales of wind from the N.W. to N.E., I never saw; but by "always going away large", we generally lose much of their force and the heavy sea of the Gulf'.

1783 William Pitt the Younger becomes Britain's youngest prime minister at the age of 24.

7th

1797 Nelson, having regained his health, arranges a note to the clergymen of St George's, Hanover Square: 'An officer desires to return thanks to Almighty God for his perfect recovery from a severe wound, and also for the many mercies bestowed upon him.'

1757 Dr Bartholomew Mosse opens the Rotunda, a maternity hospital designed by Richard Castle.

8th

1799 Nelson begins another disputation over prize money for Ethalion, Alcmene and Niad, taken off Finisterre, when he contends his senior officers had quitted the station. He writes to Davison: 'I am cut short enough having no other emoluments. I, as the King gives me this, am determined no power shall take it from me'.

1783 The first executions at Newgate Prison in London take place.

9th

Joshua Reynolds (1723-1792)

Joshua Reynolds was arguably the finest portrait painter Britain has ever produced, ranking among the world's greatest. His portrait of Nelly O'Brien, now hanging in the Wallace Collection is considered by many to be one of his most accomplished works although he is better known for portraits of men, particularly those in his social clique such as Burke, David Garrick and Laurence Stern.

Reynolds was born at Plympton Earls in Devonshire on 16 July 1723, and was a student of painting from an early age. One of his patrons funded an expedition to Italy which was instrumental in raising him far above his contemporaries at home. He settled in London in the early 1750s and maintained a studio there until his death. He was principal founder of the Royal Academy in 1768 and as its first president received the honour of a knighthood. The aims of the Royal Academy were to give living artists the opportunity to exhibit and sell their work at the annual Summer Exhibition, and to train artists in drawing, painting, sculpture and architecture. The first students enrolled in 1769, at that time in Pall Mall. Today the academy is at its fourth premises – Bodington House in Piccadilly. It was at the Academy that Reynolds delivered his *Discourses* to the students.

The Boston Tea Party

On 5 March 1770, Parliament repealed the hated Townshend Duties, an Act similar in content to the former Stamp Act which had been the initiative of Chancellor of the Exchequer, Charles Townshend. On the same day five civilians were killed by a patrol of the 29th Regiment.

The Townshend measures were an elaborate attempt to transfer to the colonies the cost of keeping British troops in America by imposing tax on a variety of new commodities. Tax avoidance had been easy and rife; the rules were ineffectual, ignored and aroused no high feelings. What riled the colonials was a new determination to enforce the collection of dues and when the wealthy John Hancock's sloop *Liberty* was captured on alleged tax evasion charges, minds were concentrated spectacularly.

The repeal was not absolute; duty on tea remained for moneys needed to be raised to defray the cost of former wars and continue to protect the colonies. In marketing terms the passage from England to India with manufactured goods and tobacco from America to England were profitable but to take advantage of trade winds and complete a lucrative triangle a cargo had to be taken from India and sold in America. Tea was an obvious solution. Initially there was no reaction, duty was avoided by smuggling in Dutch tea but in 1773 Parliament granted the ailing East India Company a monopoly on the colonial tea trade. The Boston Patriots renounced such a monopoly and refused to land any goods from East India Company ships.

On 16 December 1773, a number of Bostonians dressed as Mohawk Indians boarded the tea ships, cut and split 340 tea chests and cast them into the harbour. The market value was about £9000. Sympathisers in New York burnt a consignment of tea and in Maryland an entire ship and its cargo were destroyed. South Caroliners confiscated tea which they subsequently sold on to help raise funds for the cause.

Parliament responded with the Coercive Acts (known in the colonies as the Intolerable Acts) compelling Boston to make full restitution for the ruined tea and to make the point it closed the harbour, stifling Boston's economy. This action had a catastrophic effect; a handful of Tories remained loyal to the Crown but most refused to comply. Neighbouring colonies supported Boston with food, livestock and money. General Gage was forced to request more troops for a show of strength and new regiments began to arrive in June of the following year. Meanwhile local militias began to drill two or three times a week. Fearful of armed conflict New York called for a new colonial conference whose objective was to convince Boston that it should repay the East India Company. But time had run out for the old order. On 5 September 1774, the first Continental Congress met at Carpenter's Hall, Philadelphia where Patrick Henry proclaimed: 'The distinctions between Virginians, Pennsylvanians, New Yorkers and New Englanders are no more. I am not a Virginian but an American.'

❦ 1798 ❦ On hearing that French privateers had been disarmed at Naples: 'The enemy will be distressed, and, thank God, I shall get no money. The world, I know, thinks that money is our God! And now they will be undeceived as far as relates to us'.

❦ 1768 ❦ The Royal Academy of Arts is founded by George III. Sir Joshua Reynolds is its first president.

❦ 1789 ❦ The Neapolitan general, St Philip, commanding 19,000 men, deserts to an enemy of 3000. His army fled: 'The Neapolitan officers have not lost much honour; for God knows they had but little to lose; but they lost all they had'.

❦ 1797 ❦ Mrs Phepoe, a celebrated murderess of the day, is awarded a sentence of execution at the Old Bailey.

❦ 1786 ❦ A note to Frances Nisbet: 'Our young Prince William is a gallant man: he is indeed volatile, but always with great good nature. There were two balls during his stay, and some of the older ladies were mortified that HRH would not dance with them; but he says, he is determined to enjoy the privilege of all other men, that of asking any lady he pleases'.

❦ 1792 ❦ The French fleet arrives at Naples and attempts to force Ferdinand IV to recognise the French Republic.

❦ 1797 ❦ 'We the undersigned, [Thompson, Waldergrave, Parker, & Nelson], serving in the Fleet, under the command of the Right Honourable the Earl St Vincent, conceiving, and having no doubt (except the table-money allowed to the Commander-in-Chief) that all emoluments – viz., Prize-money and Freight-money, belonging or appertaining to the Admiral or Flag-Officer in a fleet, where there is only one, must and does by right belong to the Flag-Officers jointly, where there are many.'

❦ 1784 ❦ The lexicographer Dr Samuel Johnson (b. 1709), best known for his dictionary which took eight years to complete, dies. He is buried in Westminster Abbey.

❦ 1803 ❦ To his brother: 'The main Battle is over, if I am victorious, I shall ask for my retreat – if, unfortunately to the contrary, I hope never to live to see it. In that case you will get an early Seat in the House of Lords'.

❦ 1799 ❦ George Washington (b. 1732), first US president, dies at his home on Mount Vernon. General Henry 'Light Horse Harry' Lee delivers his funeral oration. His last words were said to be 'tis well'.

❦ 1785 ❦ To his brother: 'I am in a fair way of changing my situation. The dear object you must like. Her sense, polite manners and to you I may say, beauty, you will much admire: and although at present we may not be a rich couple, yet I have not the least doubt but we shall be a happy pair: – the fault must be mine if we are not.'

❦ 1785 ❦ The Prince of Wales jeopardises his future and risks a constitutional crisis when he marries the Catholic Maria Fitzherbert.

❦ 1798 ❦ In consequence of the state of affairs at Naples, Nelson in Vanguard shifted her berth out of gun-shot of the forts. To Troubridge: 'Most Secret – Things are in such a critical state here, that I desire you will join me without one moments lost time. The King is returned here, and everything is as bad as possible. For God's sake make haste!'

❦ 1773 ❦ The Boston Tea Party. Three hundred and forty tea chests shipped to Boston by the firm of Davison, Newman and Co. are thrown into the harbour off Griffin's Wharf by men dressed as Mohawk Indians.

The Boston Tea Party.

10th

11th

12th

13th

14th

15th

16th

MUNGO PARK (1771-1806)

Mungo Park trained as a doctor, practised for a short time in Peebles, then became assistant surgeon on the *Worcester* bound for Sumatra, and in 1795 was accepted by the African Association. He spent much of his short life travelling in the Niger region of West Africa.

During his first expedition in 1795, sponsored by the African Association, he discovered about 300 miles of the course of the Niger. In 1796 he was captured by a Moorish chief but managed to escape. He related the story of his adventures in *Travels in the Interior of Africa* (1799). In the same year he married and resumed the life of a surgeon in Peebles, but it was a short practice. He was commissioned by the government in 1805 to make a second attempt to determine the 'termination of the Niger', writing prophetically in his journal, 'I shall set sail for Africa with the fixed resolution to discover the termination of the Niger...if I could not succeed in the object of the journey, I would at least die on the Niger.' His expedition began with a team of forty-five but by the time they reached the lower Niger only three were left. Then, near Bussa, their boat struck a rock. The party was attacked by natives and in an attempt to survive they took to the water but all drowned, save one friendly native who told the story.

Breadfruit (Genus artocarpus of the mulberry family) was intended to be used as cheap food for slaves working the plantations in the West Indies. (See 23 December.)

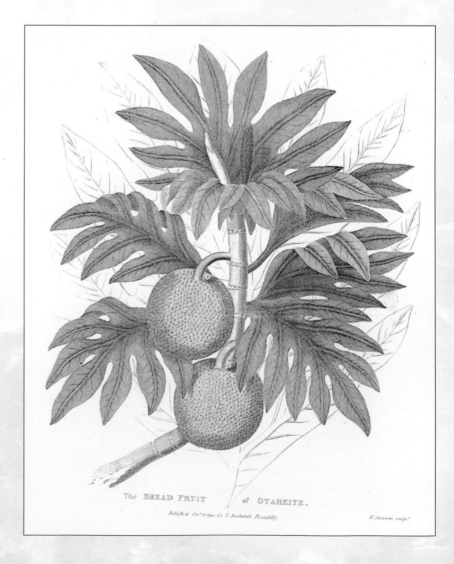

The BREAD FRUIT of OTAHEITE.

1798 Queen Maria Carolina commits 60,000 ducats in gold and her family diamonds to Nelson's war effort against Rome (which Nelson smuggled on board on the 19th). To Spencer: 'I have had the charge of the Two Sicily's intrusted to me, and things are come to that pitch, that I do not know that the whole Royal Family, with 3000 émigrés, will not be under the protection of the King's flag this night'.

1777 Louis XVI recognises the independence of the American colonies.

17th

1797 To Earl Spencer: 'I am just from Chatham. The Vanguard will be out of dock at half past one this day and ready to receive men whenever your Lordship is pleased to direct her being commissioned'.

1812 HMS Victory is paid off at Portsmouth. She was named by the Admiralty on 28 October 1760, and floated up on 7 May 1765.

18th

1804 To the queen of the Two Sicilies on Europe's attitude to Napoleon: 'Would to God these great Powers reflected that the boldest measures are the safest! They allow small states to fall, and serve the enormous power of France, without appearing to reflect that every kingdom which is annexed to France, makes their existence as independent states more precarious'.

1783 Pitt is appointed by George III as First Lord of the Treasury and Chancellor of the Exchequer.

19th

1798 Memorandum Respecting the Evacuation of Naples: 'Three barges, and the small cutter of the Alcmena armed with cutlasses only to be at the Victoria at half-past seven o'clock precisely. Only one barge to be at the wharf, the others to lay on their oars at the outside of the rocks'.

1798 Neapolitans mob outside the palace fearing they have been abandoned by Ferdinand and Maria Carolina.

20th

1798 To the Marquis de Niza: 'You are hereby required and directed to order Commodores Stone and Campbell to make preparations for burning the Guiscardo, St Joachim, and Tancredi, and you will be so particular on this service, that on no consideration you will sail until it is accomplished'.

1762 James Cook marries Elizabeth Batts at St Margaret's Church, Barking.

21st

1798 To Commodore Duckworth: 'I have only to tell you that their Sicilian Majesties with their august Family, arrived in safety on board the Vanguard last night at nine o'clock, feeling it a necessary measure in the present moment.'

1797 Mungo Park, the Selkirk explorer, returns to Scotland after two and a half years in Africa. He discovered the Niger River on 20 July 1796.

22nd

1799 To Evan Nepean from Palermo regarding Malta: 'Culloden, on going into the Bay of Marsa Sirocco, to land the cannon, ammunition, &c., taken on board that ship at Messina for the siege, struck a rock, and her commander [Troubridge] has informed me that the rudder and greatest part of the false keel are carried away....I have not as yet the least co-operation or assistance from Admiral Ouschakoff or the Russian fleet. They are, I believe, still in Naples Bay, and not any of their troops yet arrived at Malta'.

1787 Bounty leaves Portsmouth on its ill-fated voyage to collect breadfruit plants.

23rd

1796 Nelson had captured a Spanish ship but she was re-taken. He attempted a deal over captives with the Spanish captain general: 'The fortune of war put La Sabina into my possession after she had been most gallantly defended: the fickle dame returned her to you with some of my officers and men in her. I have endeavoured to make the captivity of Don Jacobo Stuart, her brave commander, as light as possible and I trust to the generosity of your nation for its being reciprocal for the British officers and men'.

1799 The French Directory is ended as a new constitution is approved; Napoleon is installed as Dictator.

24th

1804 Swiftsure joins the squadron at 8am. To Captain Mark Robinson: 'I would not trouble you to come out of Swiftsure with this swell, not being sure that you are not in Quarantine, and therefore I might be deprived of the pleasure of seeing you on board Victory; and also, hearing from Captain Cracraft that you have lately had the gout.'

1799 The Consulate is formed. It lasts until 20 May 1804. This was the period of Napoleon's influence and progress of French arms.

25th

1804 To Marsden on Swiftsure joining his squadron: 'I shall, agreeable to their Lordships' orders, take the said Ship under my command. The Fleet is in perfect good health, and good humour, unequalled by anything which has ever come within my knowledge, and equal to the most active service which the times may call for or the country may expect of them'.

1805 The Peace of Presburg. Venice is ceded to Italy. Napoleon consolidates his military gains in middle Europe, post Austerlitz.

26th

1798 To St Vincent on receipt of orders: 'I have just received your orders relative to the taking care of the Coasts of the Sicilys', also for the blockade of Malta and Toulon. I shall endeavour to comply with them all, by staying myself to take care of this Country, by writing to Commodore Duckworth to take care of Toulon, placing Captain Ball with a squadron at Malta and by sending Captain Troubridge to Egypt, to endeavour to destroy transports in Alexandria'.

1796 General Hoche's attempted invasion of Ireland with forty-three ships and 1400 men fails. His fleet scatters in storms before reaching Bantry Bay.

27th

1803 Nelson informs Mr Langstaff he has every species necessary except wine: 'I am therefore to desire you will immediately purchase such a quantity of wine at this place for supernumeraries at nine pence per gallon, and, very probably, considerably under'.

1756 The court martial of Admiral Byng commences. He is executed on 14 March 1757.

28th

1804 To Davison, lamenting Orde's appointment to a position to obtain prize money: 'I believe you could have hardly thought it possible that any man could have been sent to take the chance of a few pounds Prize-money from me, in return for all my service. At this moment, I am as poor as when I left you in Portsmouth...God knows, in my own person, I spend little money as any man; but you know I love to give it away'.

1766 Charles Macintosh (d. 1843), the Scottish manufacturing chemist who in 1823 patented and gave his name to Syme's method of waterproofing fabric, is born in Glasgow.

29th

1804 To Marsden on hearing he is to return to England to regain his health: 'I am much obliged by their Lordships' kind compliance with my request, which is absolutely necessary from the present state of my health, and I shall avail myself of their Lordships' permission, the moment another admiral, in the room of Admiral Campbell, joins the fleet unless the Enemy's Fleet should be at sea, when I should not think of quitting my Command until after the Battle'.

1777 Maximilian III, Elector of Bavaria dies without a successor.

30th

1798 Nelson learns that Sir Sidney Smith is trying to wrest some of his squadron. He writes to St Vincent: 'I do feel, for I am a man, that it is impossible for me to serve in these seas, with the Squadron under a junior Officer...Pray grant me your permission to retire, and I hope the Vanguard will be allowed to convey me and my friends, Sir William and Lady Hamilton, to England'.

1802 The Treaty of Basseino is signed by Wellesley and the Peshwa; the nominal head of the Mahrattas. The alliance led to war with Sindhia and Bhoslee and eventually to Wellesley's recall from India.

31st

SELECTED BIBLIOGRAPHY

AMERICA

Maclay, E S, *The History of the United States Navy, 1775-1894*, Bliss, Sands and Foster, London, 1894.

Mahan, A T, *The Influence of Sea Power and History, 1660-1783* [1890], The Major Operations of the Navies in the War of American Independence [1913].

BIOGRAPHIES

Thorne, J O, *Biographical Dictionary*, W&R Chambers Ltd, Edinburgh, 1961 edition (first edition 1897).

BRITAIN, THE COMMONWEALTH AND EUROPE

Carlyle, Thomas, *The French Revolution*, Chapman & Hall, London, 1894.

Chandler, David G, *Dictionary of the Napoleonic Wars*, Simon & Schuster, New York, 1993

Colley, Linda, *Britons: Forging the Nation 1707-1837*, Yale University Press, New Haven & London, 1992.

Cronin, Vincent, *Napoleon*, Collins, London, 1971.

Edwards, William, *Notes on British History* Parts III & IV, Rivingtons, London.

Farr, E, and E H Nolan, *The History of England*, Virtue & Co., London.

Harlow, V T, *The Founding of the Second British Empire*, 1952

Watson, J Steven, *The Reign of George III 1760-1815*, Oxford, 1960.

Williamson, James A, *The British Empire and Commonwealth*, Macmillan & Co. Ltd, 1935.

INDIA

Smith, V A, *The Cambridge History of India*, Cambridge, 1929.

NELSON

Clark & McArthur, *The Life of Admiral Lord Nelson, K.B.*, Cadell and Davis, London, 1809.

Hibbert, Christopher, *Nelson: A Personal History*, Viking, London, 1994.

Howarth, David and Stephen, *Nelson: The Immortal Memory*, (Conway Classics series), Conway Maritime Press, London, 1997.

Mahan, Alfred T, *The Influence of Sea Power upon the Life of Nelson, the Embodiment of the Sea Power of Great Britain* (2 vols), 1899 revised edition (first edition 1898).

National Maritime Museum, *Nelson: An Illustrated History*, Laurence King Publishing, 1995.

Nicolas, Sir Harris, *The Letters and Despatches of Vice-Admiral Lord Nelson* (7 vols), 1844-1846.

Oman, Carola, *Nelson*, Hodder & Stoughton, London, 1947.

Southey, Robert, *The Life of Lord Nelson*, Constable and Co., London, 1916 edition (first edition 1813).

Warner, Oliver, *A Portrait of Lord Nelson*, Chatto & Windus, London, 1958.

Warner, Oliver, *Trafalgar*, Batsford, London, 1959.

ROYAL NAVY

Callender, Geoffray, *The Naval Side of British History*, Christophers, London, 1924.

Clowes, Sir William Laird, *The Royal Navy: A History* (7 vols), Sampson Low, Marston & Company, London, 1897-1903.

WORLD AND GENERAL INTEREST

Family Encyclopedia of World History: The Events, Names and Dates That Shaped the World, Reader's Digest Association Ltd, London, 1996.

The World Almanac & Book of Facts, first published by the New York World, New York in 1868. Now Published annually by Newspaper Enterprise Association Inc., New York.

Vincent, Benjamin, *Haydn's Dictionary of Dates Relating to All Ages and Nations*, Ward, Lock & Co. Ltd, London, 25th edition (first edition 1841).

INDEX

Page numbers in *italics* refer to illustrations, and those in **bold** to the short articles that appear on the opposite pages to the diary entries. Relationships are to Nelson.

A

Abauzit, Firmin 47
Abercromby, General Sir Ralph 33, **48**, *48,* 49
Aboukir Bay 43, 47, *48,* 52, 110-11
  land battle of 107
  see also Nile, battle of the
Acheron, HMS 35
Achille, HMS **58**
Achille (Fr) 145, 156
Acton, Sir John 87
  letters from N 21, 171
Adam, Robert 43
Adams, John **18,** *18,* 19, 43, 99
Adams, Samuel **42**
Addington, Henry (Viscount Sidmouth) 45, 73, 76, 91, 96
  letters from N 35, 71, 73
Admiralty **34,** 57, **72, 106,** 121, 151, 156, 158, **164**
  corruption in 15
  letters from N 133
    see also Marsden, Nepean, Scott
Adolphus, Duke of Cambridge 171
Adventure, HMS **102**
Adventure (GB) **20**
Agamemnon, HMS 8, 31, 39, 45, 49, 63, **70,** 77, 85, **106,** 123, 133, 153, 167
Agincourt 165
Agincourt, HMS 13
Aix-la-Chapelle, Treaty of **86**
Ajaccio 119
Ajax, HMS 140
'A Journey through Europe' board game 133
Albemarle, HMS 19, 45, 67, 119, 149
Alcmene (Fr/HMS) 181, 185
Alexander, HMS 29, 71, 109, 126-7
Alexander I, Tsar 129
Alexandria 29, **34,** 47, 49, 110_11, 114, 123, 131
Algiers 107
Allen, Tom 80, *170*
Alliance, USS **136**
Almy, George 156
Amazon, HMS 29, 55, 123, 153
Ambuscade (Fr/HMS) 77, 123
America (US) **136**
Amherst, Field-Marshal Jeffrey 107
Amiens, Treaty of **44,** 45, *48,* 49, 61, 76, 129, 135, 139, 147
Amontons, M. **164**
Andersen, Hans Christian 55
André, Major John 147
Andrews, Miss 36
Angola **122**
Ankarström, Count 45
Ann (GB) 101
Anson, Admiral Lord George 99
Anson, HMS 171
Antarctic 17, **102**
Antigua 29, 36, 67, *68,* **70**
Archibald, James 133

B

Badger, HMS 83
Bahamas 149
Baird, Dr 135
Baird, General Sir David 135
Ball, Captain Alexander 35, 59, 126, *126,* 127, 129, 137, 171, 187
  letters from N 43, 73, 149, 153
Ball, Captain Edward 109
balloons 133, *168,* 169
Baltimore 165
'Band of Brothers' *10,* 15, 23, 111, 176
Bangalore 43
Bantry Bay 23, **58,** 93
Barbados 64, **72,** 83, 139, 149, 161
Barbary States 75, 131, 137
Barfleur, HMS 27
Barham, Admiral Lord 139, 157, 176
  letters from N 105, 123, 147
Bartram, Lorne 173
Basseina, Treaty of 187
Bastia **56,** 57, 59, 61, 75, **118,** 153, 167
Batavian Republic 31, **44**
Beatty, Dr 149, *177*
Beauharnais, Eugene de 75
Beaulieu, General 83, 89
Beethoven, L van 73
Belleisle, HMS 33, 144, 158
Bellerophon, HMS 103, 113, 154, 166, *166*
Benares 15
Bender 137
Bentinck, Lord William
  letter from N 171
Bering Straits **102**
Bermuda 156
Bernard, Governor Francis **42**
Berry, Captain Edward 9-10, 23, 25, 109, 111, *113,* 113-14, 123, *123,* 176
Beauharnais, Alexandre Vicomte de **44**
Bickerton, R/A 31
Bird, Major-General Sir David 15
Biscay, Bay of 117, 139, 156

Blackwood, Captain Henry 55, 139, 141-3, 156, 176
  letters from N 131
Blake, Admiral **20**
Blake, William **148**
Blanchard, J P 13, **168,** *168*
Bligh, Captain William **62,** *62,* 63, *84,* 85
Bohemia 108-9
Bolivia **102**
Bolton, Captain Sir William 49
Bolton, Lady 131
Bolton, Mrs (sister) 15
  letter from N 73
Bombay **86**
Bombay Castle, HMS 23
Bonaparte, General Napoleon 23, **44,** 45, 47, 50, **56,** 61, 76, 83, 85, **86,** 93, 95-7, 117, 140-2, 145, *150, 162,* 162-3, *166,* **166,** 169, 185, 187
  birth 119, **166**
  becomes First Consul 29, 117, **166,** 167
  crowned Emperor 75-6, 83, **166,** 181
  and Egyptian expedition 9, 19, 43, 49, 76, *104,* 107, 109-11, 114, 125, 149, 153, **166,** 174
  and invasion of Britain 31, **34,** 92, 109, 139, 171
  takes Malta 85, 124-5, 127, 129
  defeat of 103, 117, **166,** 174-5
Bonaparte, Joseph 49
Bonhomme Richard (USA) **136,** 137
Bonne Citoyenne, HMS 126-7
Boreas, HMS 7, 36, 47, 57, 64-5, 69, **70,** 83, 131
Borg, Vincenzo 127
Boston 85, 87, *87,* 119
Boston Massacre **42,** *42,* 43
Boston Tea Party 49, **90, 182,** 183, *183*
Botany Bay **16,** *17,* 33
Boulogne 94, 96, *97,* 119, 121, 137, 139, 165
Bounty, HMS **62,** 63, *84,* 123, 185
Boussole (Fr) 33
Boyce, William 31
Boydell, James and Josiah 27
Boyne, HMS 47, 156
Brame, Joseph
  letter from N 101
Brandlitz, battle of 19, 76, 163, 174, 187
Brandywine Creek, battle of 133
breadfruit *184,* 185
Brenton, Lt Jahleel 25, 27
Brereton, General 105
Brest **34,** 45, **58, 60,** 83, *83,* 94
  mutiny **58**
Bridport, Viscount *see* Hood, Admiral Lord
Briggs (pro-consul at Alexandria)
  letters from N 17, 29
Brilliant, HMS 19
Bristow, Mr (Mayor of Canterbury) 159
Britain 172-8
  blockading tactics 94-5
  colonies 31, 64-9, **86,** 89
    see also Canada, India, USA, West Indies
  and French invasion threat 11, 23, 31, **60,** 75-6, *92,* 92-7, 105, 107, 109, 119, 121, 139-40, 149, 153, **166,** *170*
    see also under Bonaparte, France
  mutinies 58, **58,** 59, **62,** 63, 73, 94, 103, 123
  peace with France *see* Amiens, Treaty of and possession of Malta 126-9, *128,* 139
  receives news of N's death 154-63
  taxation 15, 43, **76,** 93
    see also Hair Powder Tax, Stamp Acts, and under Boston
  trade and trade wars 7-8, 15, 35, 50, 64-9, 71, **82,** 93-5, 139, 173, 176
    see also Navigation Acts
  and USA *see* War of Independence under USA
  wars with France *see under* France
  withdraws from Mediterranean 23, 109
  see also Nelson, V/A Horatio Viscount
Britannia, HMS 45
British East India Company **88, 90,** 93
British Museum *16,* 17
Brown, Captain 147
Bruce, James 169
Brueys, Admiral F **60,** 110-13
Brummell, George ('Beau') 83
Brydges, R/A George **34**
Budd, Dr 38

Bunbury, Sir Charles 26
Bunker Hill, battle of 87, *87,* **90**
Burgoyne, General **86, 90-1,** 137
Burke, Edmund **100,** *100,* 101, **182**
Burnham Thorpe 8, 22, 26, **70, 106**
Burns, Robert **18,** 19, **148**
Bushnell, David 131
Bute, Earl of 59
Byng, Admiral John **44,** 45, 187
Byron, Lord George 40, **70**

C

Cadiz 9, 23_4, **60,** 99, 101, 103, 109-10, 131, 133, 137, 139-40, 142, 145, 147, 156, 158, 162-3, 181
Cadogan, Mary 15, 37-8, 41
Cadogan, William 37
Caen 83
Cagliari (Sardinia) 19
Ça Ira (Fr) 9, 45, 49
Cairo 105, 110
Calais 41
Calcutta **86, 88,** 163
Calder, Captain Sir Robert 24, 27, **60**
Calvi, siege of 85, **106,** 107-8, 117, **118,** 119
Camden, battle of 121
Campbell, Admiral 187
Campbell, Cdre 185
Camperdown, battle of **62,** 76
Campo, Formio, Treaty of 151
Canada 31, 76, 87, **90, 102,** 107, 133, 161, 173
Canning, George 57
Canning, Mr 133
Cape Breton 173
Cape St Vincent 33, 133, 137, 139
  battle of 8, 10, 22-7, *25,* 33, 55, 57, 92, 108-9, 174
Cape Town 15, **102,** 135
Capri 81
Captain, HMS 8, 22, 24-6, 33, 77, 85, 101, 153, 176
Captain Pacha
  letter from N 85
Caracciolo, Prince Francesco 81, 91, 103
Caroline, Queen of England 57, 77
Carroll, John 165
Cartagena 23, 77
Cartwright, Edmund 61
Casabianca, Count of 113
Casabianca, General **118**
Castiglione, battle of 117
Castle, Richard 181
Castlereagh, Viscount
  letter from N 147
Catherine II, Empress of Russia 35
Censeur (Fr) 9, 45
censuses 91
Centaur, HMS **58**
Chappe, Monsieur 103, **164**
Charles, J A C **168**
Charles Emmanuel, King of Sardinia 61, 71
Charles III, King of Sweden 33
Charles the Young Pretender 21
Charles V, Emperor 126
Charlotte, Queen of England **12,** 93, 133
Chatham, Earl of (William Pitt the Elder) 73, **90,** 119, **146,** *146,* 147
Chatham, 2nd Earl of (First Lord) 13
Chatham Dockyard 8, *30,* 103, 185
Chatterton, Thomas 123
Cherry, Mr 15
Cherry Valley 167
Chesma, battle of 101
Childers, HMS 49
Chile **90,** 176
China 35
Chollet, battle of 151
Christian, Fletcher **62,** 63
Christie, James 181
Cisalpine Republic 31
Cisneros, R/A 143
Civitavecchia 110
Clarence, Duke of *see* William Henry, Prince
Clarke, Captain 61
Clarke, General 135
Clermont (USA) **168**
Clinton, Sir Henry 147
Clive, Robert Lord **86, 88,** *88,* 89, 171
clocks and chronometers **72,** 73, **102,** 121
Coburg, Duke of 89
Cochrane, Admiral Lord 10
Cockburn, Captain 105
  letter from N 131
Code Napoleon **46,** 47

Coercive Acts **90, 182**
Coleridge, Samuel Taylor 47
Colles, Abraham 131
Collingwood, Admiral Cuthbert 8, 23-4, 55, **60**, 67, 109, 140-1, 143-5, 151, 154, *154*, 156, 158, 160, 163, 165, 176
   letters from N 10, 137
Collingwood, Captain Wilfred 8, 65, 67
Colossus, HMS 147
Columbia 83
Concord **90**
Congo 122
Congreave rockets 147
Constable, John **84**, 85
convict ships **16**, 17
Cook, Captain James **16**, 17, **62**, **72**, *74*, 75, **102**, *102*, 103, 147, 153, 185
Cooke, Captain 158
Copenhagen, battle of 10, 29, 43, 45, 50-3, *51-2*, 55, 57, 61, **62**, 71, 76, 89, 96, 133, 159, 174
Corday, Charlotte 103
Cordoba, Admiral 23-4
Corfu 111
Cork 161
Cork, Earl of 105
Cornwall, Marquis of 49
Cornwallis, Admiral Sir William **34**, *34*, 35, 96
Cornwallis, General Charles, 2nd Marquis 43, **91**, 121, 151
Correglia, Adelaide 79-80
Corsica 8, 10, 23, 25, 45, 49, 89, 94, 99, **118**, 123, 153, **166**, 167, 169
   see also Ajaccio, Bastia
cotton gins 15
Countess of Scarborough, HMS 136
Count Bernsdorff (Den) 69
Courageux, HMS 23
Cowper, William 61, **122**
Coyley, George 137
Cracraft, Captain 187
   letter from N 171
Crete 111
Cuba 31
Culloden, HMS 24, 26, 29, 105, 113, 127, 131, 185
Cumby, Lt W Pryce 154
Cyprus 111

D

Daguerre, L J 169
Danton, G J 55, **106**
Darby, Captain Henry 113
Darby, G, Admiral 57
Dartmouth, Lord 19
D'Aubant, Brigadier-General 59
Davison, Alexander 36, 40-1, **120**
   letters from N 19, 29, 45, 61, 77, 121, 149, 181, 187
Davison, Newman and Co 183
Davy, Sir Humphry 33, **84**
Dean, Silas 99
'Declaration of the Rights of Man' 123
Decres, Denis 13, 163
Defence, HMS 147
Defiance, HMS 133
Denmark 50-3, 57, 61, 71
   colonies 64_6, 69
   see also Copenhagen, battle of
Derby race 71
Desmoulins, Camille 105
Diadem, HMS 33
'Diamond' *70*, 71
Diamond, battle of 135
Discovery, HMS 103
'Dolly' (whore) 36
Dolphin, HMS 75, **106**
Dominica 67
Donnelly, Captain 15
Drake, Admiral Sir Francis 141
Drake (GB) **136**
Drake Francis (Minister at Turin) 171
Drinkwater, Colonel John 22-7
Duckworth, Admiral John 131, 187
   letters from N 131, 181, 185
Duff, Captain 140, 158, 178
   letter from N 147
Dumanoir, Admiral 162
Dumas, Alexandre 107
Dumouriez, General 123
Duncan, Admiral Lord **58**, **62**, 73, *148*, 149
Dundas, General **56**, 77
Dupleix, General JF **86, 88**

E

Eagle, HMS **102**, 131
East India Company **20**, **86**, **136**, 171, 173, **182**
Edinger and Neep 161
Egypt, French expedition to 9-11, 19, **34**, 43, 47, 49, **60**, 76, *104*, 105, 109-10, 123, 131, 133, 187
   see also Malta, Nile
El Arish, convention of 19
Elba 23, 99, 101, **166**
Elephant, HMS 52
Elizabeth, Tsarina 13
Elliot, Sir Gilbert
   letters from N 99, 119
Elliott, Hugh
   letters from N 89, 107, 147, 165
Elliott, Sir George 23
Elphinstone, Admiral Lord 96, 135
Emmet, Robert 105, *134*, 135
Emmet, Thomas Addis 49
Endeavour, HMS *74*, 75, 83, **102**, 147
Ericsson, John 107
Ethalion, HMS 181
Euryalus, HMS 133, 137, 140, 143, 151, 154, 156
Excellent, HMS 24, 33

F

Fairfax Resolution 181
Falkland Islands *18*, 19
Falmouth 157, 165, *165*
Fearney, William 26
Ferdinand IV, King of Naples and the Two Sicilies 38-9, 43, **56**, 78-81, 87, 103, 117, 126-7, 153, 171, 183
Ferrol **60**
Fetherstonehaugh, Sir Harry 38
Finisterre **60**, 181
Firth, William 161
Fischer, Captain Olfert 51, 53
Fishguard 31
Fittler, James 27
Flamborough Head, battle of **136**, 137
Fleurus, battle of 89
Flin, Edward 133
Florida 31, 173
Flushing 61, 96-7
flying machines 137, **168**
   see also balloons
Foley, Captain Thomas 23, 57, 112
Fontainebleau, treaty of 167
Foote, Captain 103
Forbes, General 171
Formidable, HMS **58**
   letter from N 165
Fort Bouron 47
Fort Duqesne 171
Fort Edward 107
Fortiguerra Mr 61
Fort Louisburg 107
Fox, Charles James 59, **76**
Fox, General 127
Frampton, Mary 93
France 13, 17, 28-9, 31, 33, 36, **44**, 45, 47, 49, 56_7, 61, *130*, 153-4, 156, 160, **168**, 171
   and battle of the Nile 9, 108-15
   and battle of Trafalgar **60**, 131, 139, 141-4, 162, 174-5, 178, 185
   in colonies 19, 31, 64, 66, **86**, **90**, 101, 173
   Egyptian expedition *see* Egypt
   fleet conditions 53, **58**, **60**, 92, 96, 112, 141-2
   and invasion of Britain 31, **34**, 92-7
      see also under Bonaparte, Britain
   in Italy 43, 77, 79_80, 83, 89, 93
      see also under Naples
   and Malta 124-9, *128*
   peace with Britain *see* Amiens, Treaty of
   Revolution 8, 16, *16*, 55, 71, 75, 77, 87, 89, 92, **100**, 103, 105-6, *118*, 119, 121, 123-4, 133, 135, 141, 147, 149, 151, 164, **164**, **166**, 167, 169, 185
   Royalists 78, 89, 93, 105, 151
   support for USA 64, 91, 101, **136**, 153
   trade and trade wars 64, **82**, **86**
   war with Britain (1777/8) 29, 101
   war with Britain (1793) 31, 76, 151
   war with Britain (1803) 10
   see also Bonaparte, General, Code Napoleon, Legion d'Honneur, and individual cities and ships
Francis I, Emperor 43
Franklin, Benjamin 28, *28*, 29, 59, 99, **136**, 165
Frederick, Crown Prince of Denmark 50, 53
Frederick, Prince of Wales **132**
Frederick II, King of Prussia 33
Fremantle, Captain Thomas 79, 176, 178
Frere, Hookham
   letter from N 171
Freya (Den) 50
Friendly Islands **102**
frigates *21*, 35, 94
   N's reliance on 55, 109-10, 123, 147
Froebel, FWA 59
Fry, Elizabeth 75
Fulton, Robert **168**
Furneaux, Captain Tobias **102**

G

Gage, General Thomas **42, 182**
Ganteaume, Admiral **34**
Garnerin, A J 151
Garrick, David **182**
Gaspee, HMS 85
Généreux (Fr) **60**
Genoa 19, 89, 101, 117, 135, 169, 181
   N's engagement off 45, 49, 83
Gentili, General **56**
George, Prince of Wales (George IV) 57, 77, **183**
George II, King of England **146**, 153
George III, King of England 29, 38, **44**, 45, 55, 63, 67, 71, **72**, 73, 76, **76**, 79, **86**, 87, 93, 99, **100**, 101, 119, 121, **132**, 133, **146**, 147, 153, 157-8, 160, 183, 185
George V, King of England 178
Germanstown, battle of 147
Germany 33, 178
Gibbon, Edward **148**, 149
Gibraltar 10, 13, **14**, 23, **44**, *56*, **56**, 57, 59, 77, 80, **91**, 109, 131, 139, 147, 149, 162
Gibraltar, HMS 23
Gibson, Mrs (Horatia's wetnurse) 19, 73, **152**
Giddy, Mayor 157, 163
Gillespie, L 11
Gladiator, HMS **58**
Glasgow, HMS 83
'Glorious First of June', battle of **20**, 76, **82**, *82*, 83, 89, 141
Golden Hill, battle of 17
Goldsmid, Abraham **152**
Goliath, HMS 112-13, 126
Gordon Riots 83
Gore, Captain
   letter from N 165
Gosling, Mr 123
Gould, Captain David 112
Goya y Lucientes, Francisco José de 49
Graham, Brigadier-General Sir Thomas 127, 129
Graham, George **72**
Graves, Admiral Thomas **20**
Gravina, Admiral 13, 87, 141, 144-5
Greathead, Henry **20**
Green, Captain John 35
Greenwich **14**, **72**
   Royal Naval College 13
   Royal Naval Hospital 151, *170*
Gregorian Calendar 35
Grenada 67, 69
Grenville, Richard (Earl Temple) **16**, **42**, **122**
Greville, Hon Charles 38
Grey, John 171
Grey, Sir Charles 47
Guerrier (Fr) 113
Guillaume Tell (Fr) **60**
guillotines **16**, 55, 123, 133, 149, 164
Gustavus III, King of Sweden 45

H

Hair Powder Tax 43
Halley, Edmund **72**
   comet 45
Hallowell, Captain Benjamin 23, *74*, 75, 77
Hamilton, Captain
   letter from N 119
Hamilton, Emma Lady 11, 15, 19, 29, 36-41, *37*, 43, 55, **70**, **78**, 79-81, *81*, 96-7, **106**, 127, 131, 139-40, **152**, 167, 176, 187
   letters from N 31, 45, 73, 75, 101, 135, 137, 141, 149, 151, **152**, 167
   and news of N's death 158-9, *159*
   death of 17
Hamilton, Sir William **12**, 36, 38-9, *39*, 41, **70**, 78-9, 81, 87, 91, 126-7, **152**, 158, 187
   letters from N 49, 87, 131
   death of 40, 55, **152**
Hancock, John 19, **182**
Handel, George Frederick 57
Hanover **44**
Hardy, Captain TM 143-5, *145*, 176
Hargreaves, James 73
Harrison, John **72**, 73, **102**, 121
Harrison, William **72**
Harvey, R/A Henry 33
Haslar 151
Hastings, Warren 76, **86**
Hatfield, James 73
Havana 23
Hawaii **102**
Hawke, Admiral Lord **122**, 141, 176
Hawkins, Sir John **122**
Haydn, Joseph 9, 115
Hazlewood, William 131
Hazlitt, William 57
Heights of Abraham *132*, 173
Henry, Patrick 77, **182**
Herbert, John Richardson 36, **70**
Herschel, Sir William **44**, *44*, 45, 165
Hervey, Lady Elizabeth 160
Hill, Rowland 161
Hoban, James 149
Hobart, Lord
   letter from N 71
Hoche, General 89, 93, 105
Hohenlinden, battle of 181
Hompesch, F von 124
Hood, Admiral Lord (Viscount Bridport) 7-8, 19, 39, **56**, **58**, 78, 85, **118**, 141, 176
   letters from N 107, **118**
Hood, Captain Samuel 112
Hooke, Dr **164**
Hoppner, John 55
Horse Guards 83
Hoste, Rev. Dixon
   letters from N 91, 167
Hotham, Admiral Sir William 9, 19, 45, 57, 107, 167
   letter from N 105
Howe, Admiral Lord 49, **58**, 76, **82**, *82*, 83, 117, 131, 141
   letter from N 15
Howe, General **90**, 133, 147, 153
Hubertusberg, Treaty of 33
Hughes, Admiral Sir Richard 8, 43, 47, 65, 67
Hughes, Lady 47
Humboldt, Alexander von 83
Hungary 108-9
Hyder Áli **86**, *86*, 87, 99

I

Incendiary, HMS 126
Indefatigable, HMS 15
India 10, **34**, 43, **76**, **86**, 87, **88**, 89, **90**, **91**, 93, 99, 109, 121, **132**, 163, 173, 176, **182**, 187
   see also Benares, Calcutta, Hyder Ali
Inglis, Dr Charles 119
Ireland 11, 13, 23, 31, 49, **58**, 66, 73, 75-6, 89, 93, 105, 109, 117, 135, 139, 149, 156, 161, 165
   Act of Union 13, 29
Italy 43, 77-81, 85, 91, 117, **166**, **182**
   see also Genoa, Milan, Naples

J

Jamaica 101, 162-3
James II, King of England 141, **164**
Janus, HMS 123
Java **100**
Jefferson, President Thomas 91, *91*, 99
Jeffries, Dr John 13, **168**, *168*
Jemappes, battle of **82**
Jenner, Edward **72**, 73
Jervis, Admiral Sir John *see* St Vincent, Admiral the Earl of
Johnson, Dr Samuel **148**, 183
Jolly, John 101
Jones, John Paul **91**, **136**, 137
Joseph, King of Spain 174
Joseph II, Emperor 33
Josephine, Empress of the French **44**, 45, 89
Jutland, battle of 178

K

Keats, Captain 157, 181
Keith, Admiral Lord 29, **34**, 45, 47, 49, 81, 96, 105, 127, *130*, 131
Kelly, Mrs 38
Kempenfeldt, Admiral Richard **122**, *122*, 141, **164**
Kendall, Larum **72**
Key, Francis Scott 117
Kidd, Mrs 37
Kilcullen, battle of 75
King, Joseph 123
Knight, Miss 103
Knights of St John of Jerusalem 85, 124_7, 129

L

Lafayette, General the Marquis de **91**, 101, 131, 147, **164**
Lake, General 89
Lamourette, Bishop 15
Landias, Captain **136**
Lapenotière, Lt John Richards *156-7,*

156-8, 158, 160, 163, 165
La Pérouse 33
La Scala 117
Latona, HMS 29
La Touche-Tréville, Admiral 29, 119, 121, 139
Laurence, Dr 19
Lauriston, General 142
La Vengeance (Sp) 135
Lavoisier, A L 123
League of Armed Neutrality 35, 50, 53, 71
Lechmere, Captain 147
letter from N 133
Lee, General Henry 183
Lee, Sgt Ezra 131
Leeward Islands 7, 47, 68
Leghorn 43, 47, 59, 77, 79, 99, 101, 105, 123, 137
Légion d'Honneur 47
Leopold II, Emperor 33, 43, 59
Lexington **42**, 59, **90**, 131
Leyman, Captain 43
Liberty (USA) **42**, 85, **182**
lifeboats **20**, 21
Ligurian Republic (Genoa) 83
Lindsey, Captain 45
Linley, Samuel 38
Linley, Thomas 37-8
Lion, HMS 127
Lively, HMS 22, 24-5
Livingston Philip 99
Livorno *see* Leghorn
Lloyd, Captain 83
Loano, battle of 171
Locke, John 99
Locker, Captain William (cousin) 26, *26, 32*, 141
letters from N 33, 47, 64, 69, 83, 133, 149, 165
Lorient **136**
Louis, Admiral 140-1, 147, 158
Louisbourg, battle of **102**
Louis XVI, King of France 39, 71, 73, 77, *88*, 89, 101, 103, **106**, 147, **164**, 165, 185
execution of *16*, 17
Louis XVIII, King of France 153
Lucas, Captain 144-5
Lukin, Lionel **20**, 21
Lunardi Vincenzo 133
Lunéville, Treaty of 31, 96
Lutine (GB) 149
Lyons 15
Gulf of 10, *17*, 139, 181

M

Macintosh, Charles 187
Mack, General *150*, 151, 160, 167
Madalena Islands 165
Madeira 139
Madras **86**, 87, **88**
Madrid 142
Treaty of 137
Magic Flute **136**, 137
Magon, Admiral 142
Maidstone, HMS **89**
Maitland, Captain Frederick 103
Majestic, HMS **58**
Majorca 10, 45
Malmesbury, Lord 158-60
Malta 10,11, 13, 33, 35, **44**, 45, 49, 75, 85, 87, 89, 91, 110-11, 124-9, *125, 128*, 137, 139, 153, 165, 171, 181, 185, 187
'Promotion Hook' 126-7
Malthus, Thomas 33
Man, Admiral 59
Marat, Jean Paul 103, *103*
Marengo, battle of 85, 93
Maria Carolina, Queen of Naples 38-9, 79-81, 87, 103, 127, 185
Maria Theresa 123
Maria Theresa, Empress of Austria **136**, 149, **164**, 171
Marie Antoinette, Queen of France 38-9, 73, 89, 147, 149, **164**, 165
Marie Thérèse (Fr) 73
Marquesas Islands **102**
Mars, HMS 140, 147
Marsden, William 154, 157
letters from N 31, 35, 45, 59, 77, 83, 107, 119, 123, 181, 187
Marseilles 123, 153
Martello Towers 94, *94*
Martin, R/A Pierre 45
Martinique 47, 73, 89
Maskelyne, Dr Nevil 13
Masséna, General 137
Maximilian III, Elector of Bavaria 187
McAdam, JL 171
McDougall, Alexander 17
medals **20**, *116*, 117, **120**

Medusa, HMS 165
Meles, Baron von 85
Menou, General 123
Merton Place 41, *41*, 123, 139, *150, 151*, **152**, 153, 176
Methodism 48
Micheroux, Chevalier 147
Milan **166**
Miller, Captain Ralph 23-5, 33, 87, 112
Minerva (Sicily) 91
Minorca 10, 13, **44**, 45, 81, 87, 105, 127, 151, 181
Minorca, HMS 127
Minotaur, HMS 126
Minto, Lord 103, 158
letters from N 17, 35
Mirabeau, HGR, Comte de **164**
Mitchell, Admiral **58**
Monarch, HMS **44**, 45
Monmouth, HMS **34**
Monserrat 65, 67
Montagne (Fr) **82**
Montcalm, Marquis de 101, *101*, 133, 173
Montgolfier brothers **168**
Moore, Colonel Sir John **56**, **118**
Morse, Samuel F B 61
Mosse, Dr Bartholomew 181
Mouat, Captain 59
Moutray, Commissioner 29, 36
Mozart, W A 73, **136**, 137
Murat, Joachim 107
Murdoch, William 87
Murray, Captain Sir George 23
mutinies 58, 103
see also Nore, Spithead, and under Britain
Myers, Sir William 83

N

Naiad, HMS 181
Naples, Kingdom of 10-11, 13, 38-9, 49, 61, 73, 78-81, 87, 89, 101, **106**, 109, 123, 125-7, 183
allied with Britain 8, 181
rebellion and French attack 31, 39, 55, 79-81, 87, 91, 103, 117, 185
Narcissus, HMS 171
Naselli, General 181
Nautical Almanac 13
Nautilus, HMS 156
Naval Chronicle 94
Naval General Service Medal **20**
Navigation Acts 8, 43, 64-9, **90**, 139
Necker, J 33, 87, **164**
Neep 161
Nelson, Rev. Edmund (father) 13, 33, **70**, *79*
Nelson, Emma (daughter) **152**
Nelson, Frances Lady (wife) 8-9, 15, 27, 33, 36-7, 39-40, *40*, 41, 43, 61, 68, **70**, 79-80, 96, **106**, 133, 149, 160, 167, 176
letters from N 13, 19, 35, 39, 43, 45, 57, 63, 71, 83, 85, 87, 117, **118**, 121, 181, 183
receives news of N's death 158
death of 71
Nelson, Horatia (daughter) 19, 41, 43, 73, 151, **152**, 153
enters Navy 7, *12*, **12**, 13, 173
at battle of Cape St Vincent 22-7, 24, *27*, 33, 93
at battle of Copenhagen 45, 50-3, 55, 57, 61, 76, *174*
pursuit of Bonaparte to Egypt 9, 17, 21, 59, 109-10, 126
at battle of the Nile 9-11, 19, **34**, 55, *78*, 107, 109-14, 141, 174
pursuit of Villeneuve 11, 19, 33, **34**, **60**, 73, 87, 139
at battle of Trafalgar 17, 133, 139-45, *140, 143*, 151, **152**
boarding technique 24-7, 108, 144
care for crews 10-11, 13, 15, 22, 45, 47, 49, 53, 59, 69, 71, 81, 87, 89, 95, 99, 101, 112-13, 121, 123, 133, 165, 176, 185
character 7-10, 19, 33, 39, 43, 45, 47, 49, 55, 71, 77,80-1, 85, 87, 89, 91, 96-7, 99, 105, 107-8, 110, 117, 127, 138, 151, 153, 176, 178, 181, 183
in Downs command 19, 96-7
honours 8, *9, 16*, 17, 19, 27, 35, 43, **46**, *46*, 47, 55, **56**, 89, 108, 115, *115*, 167, 169
letters *see under* recipients
loss of arm 9, **70**, 80, *106*, 107-9, 121,

149, 153, 174, *174*, 178, 181
loss of eye 8, 52, *53*, 85, 94, 108, *108*, **118**, *174*, *174*
and Malta 126-7, 129
marriage 40, 68-9, **70**, 80, **106**, 135
in Naples 78-81, 126
private life 17, 31, 36-41, 43, 45, 61, **70**, 71, 78-80, 96, 101, **106**, 121, 123, 127, 131, 133, 135, 137, **152**, 167, 176
and prizes 61, 67, 83, 89, 145, 165, 171, 181, 183, 187
see also Davison, Alexander
promotions 7, 9, 33, 57, 108, 174
reputation and legend 11, 22, 26-7, 39, 41, 43, 89, 97, 109, 113-14, 117, 159-62, 173-6
tactics and 'Nelson Spirit' 9-11, 17, 19, 24, 27, 33, 36, 52-3, 71, **82**, 87, 105, 111-12, 113, 119, 140-1, 147, 174-6, 178
in West Indies 64-9
death of 27, 97, 139, 144-5, *145*, 151, *154, 155*, 158,162, 173, 17-56, *177*, 178
news of death *162*, 165, *165*
coffin *11*, **14**, *14*, *74*, 75
will 43, 131, **152**, 158
funeral 11, **14**, *14*, 22, 163
memorials 154, *154*, 160-1, 163, *172, 175, 179*, 185
reputation and legend 78-9, 96, 145, 147, 154-7, 176, 178
see also Burnham Thorpe, Merton Place, and under frigates, Genoa
Nelson, Mr
letter from N 101
Nelson, Catherine (mother) 36
letter from N 49
Nelson, Tom (nephew) 73
Nelson, Rev. William (brother) (Earl Nelson) 13, 40, 57, **70**, *159*, 160
letters from N 17, 21, 31, 49, 59, 87, 119, 151, 153, 183
Nepean, Sir Evan 151, 167
letters from N 15, 75, 117, 165, 169, 185
Nepomuceno 142
Netherlands **48**, 49, 66, **86**, 87, 89, 91, 93, 96, 108-9, 119, 162, 169, **182**
Nevis island 7, *8*, 36, 40, 65, 67, 69, **70**
New Brunswick 87
New Caledonia **102**
Newcomen, Thomas **84**
Newfoundland **102**
New Guinea **102**
Newton, Sir Isaac **72**
New York 17, **42**, 73, **91**, 99, 101, 131, 153, **168**, **182**
New Zealand **102**, 147, 176
Nibbs, George 64
Nicolas, Sir Nicholas Harris 161
Niger, HMS 133
Nile, battle of the 9-11, 15, 19, 23, **34**, 41, 55, **60**, 75, *78*, 79-81, **82**, 92, **106**, 107-15, *112*, 117, **120**, 139, 141, 160, **166**, 174
Nisbet, Frances (Viscountess Nelson) *see* Nelson, Frances Lady
Nisbet, Frances (wife of Josiah) **106**
Nisbet, Dr Josiah 36, **70**, 106
Nisbet, Josiah (stepson) 36, 39-40, 43, **70**, 80, *106*, **106**, 107
Niza, Admiral the Marquis de
letters from N 15, 185
Nore **14**, 149
mutiny 58, *58*, 73, 87, 91, *91*, 94
Norfolk Island **102**
North, Lord 19, **76**, **86**, **91**, **132**, 153
Northesk, Admiral 160
Northumberland, HMS 127, 131
Norway 50
Norwich 27, 161
'Nostra Signora di Belvidere' 105

O

Observer 181
O'Connell, Daniel 117
'Olive Branch Petition' 121
Oliver, Andrew **42**
Orange lodges 135
Orde, V/A Sir John 110, 181, 187
Orient (Fr) 75, 110, 113-14, *114-115*, 125
Original (GB) **20**
Orion, HMS 71, 109, 112-13
Orlov, Admiral 101
Otis, James 75
Ottoman Empire *see* Turkey
Otway, Commissioner 13

P

Paine, Thomas 99, 135, *135*
Palermo 10, 29, 31, 34, 43, 47, 55, **70**, 79-81, 103, 117, 127, 153, 181, 185
Pallas (Fr) **136**
Pandora, HMS **62**, 123, 153
Paoli, Pasquale **56**
parachutes 151
Paris, Treaties of
(1763) 31, **86**, **130**, 137
(1783) **91**, **130**, 131, 171
(1814) 129
Park, Mungo **184**, 185
Parker, Admiral Sir Hyde 23, 43, 45, 47, 50, *50*, 51-3, 55, 57, 76
Parker, Captain Edward 55, 97, 135, 137, 183
letters from N 123
Parker, Richard **58**, 91, *91*
Parker, Sir Peter
letter from N 123
Pasco, Lt 142, 178
Paul, Tsar 35, 47, 50, 53, 71, 124
Payne, Captain John Willet 38
Pearson, Captain Richard **136**
Pearson, Lt 25
Peel, Sir Robert *28*, 29
Pégase (Fr) **34**
Pegasus, HMS 67, 69, **70**
Pelham, Henry **146**
Pellew, Captain Sir Edward 15, 96
Pembroke 93
Pembroke, HMS **102**
Penelope, HMS 55, 127
Peninsula War 175
Peru 83, **90**
Peter III, Tsar 13
Phepoe, Mrs 183
Phillip, Captain Arthur **16**, 17, 19
Phoebe, HMS 139
photography 169
Pickle, HMS 156-8, 163, 165, *165*
Pines, Island of **102**
Pitcairn Island **62**, 63
Pitt, William, the Elder *see* Chatham, Earl of
Pitt, William, the Younger 9, 15, 19, 21, 29, *29*, 45, **76**, *76, 77*, 93, 119, **122**, 123, 147, 158, 160, 174, *180*, 181, 185
Pius VII, Pope **166**, 181
Plassey, battle of **86**, **88**, 89, 173
Plymouth 19, **34**, 40, 103
Poland 71, 153
Pollard, John
letter from N 59
Pope, Alexander 37, **148**
Pope, William 133
Popham, Admiral Sir Home Riggs 15, 135, 141, **164**, 165
Portsmouth *7*, 9, 45, 57, 133, 139-40, 185, 187
Portugal 23, **86**, **122**, 126, 137, 156, 174-5
Pressburg, Peace of 187
press gangs 13, *30*, 59, 171, 173
Preston, Captain Thomas **42**
Priestley, Joseph **120**, 121
Princeton, battle of **90**
Principe de Asturias (Sp) 144-5
privateers 64, 83, **136**, 137, 183
prizes and prize money 19, **20**, 23-4, 29, 45, **66**, 67, 123, 129
see also under Nelson, V/A Viscount Horatio
Prussia 33, 50, 108-9, 119, 153, 174
Pyramids, battle of *104*, 105

Q

Quartering Act 17, **42**
Quebec 36, **46**, 49, **102**, **120**, 133, **146**, 173
see also Plains of Abraham
Queen Charlotte, HMS 47, 59, **82**, *82*, 83
Queensbury, Duke of 41
Quiberon Bay
battle of (1759) **122**
landing at 89, 93, 105

R

Raffles, Sir Thomas Stamford *100*, 101
railways 35, **84**, 107
Raisonnable, HMS 7, 13, 73, 173
Ranger (US) **136**
Ransijit, Bosredon de 124
Rattler, HMS 65
Raven, HMS 31, 43, 45
Raynal, Abbé **122**
Redoubtable (Fr) 144-5
Regency Bill 76

Regulation Act **86**
Renard (Fr) 169
Rennes **60**
Resolution, HMS 17, **62**, 103, 153
Resource, HMS 83
Revere, Paul 59
Reynolds, Sir Joshua 35, **182**, 183
Rhodes 126
Richard, Ebenezer **42**
Richery, Admiral 59
Rigaud, JF *32*, 33
Rigby, Edward 161
Riou, Captain 52
Royal Sovereign, HMS 162
Robespierre, Maximilien de 55, 71, **106**, *106*, 107
Robinson, Captain Mark
    letter from N 187
Rochefort **60**
Rodney, Admiral 141, 176
Roman Catholic Relief Act 83
Rome 21, 79-80, 121, 185
Romney, George 38, 169
Romney, HMS **42**
Rose, George
    letters from N 73, 147
Rose, Mr 133
Rosetta 110, 114
    Rosetta Stone 105
Rosily, Admiral **60**, 140, 142
Ross, Hercules 85
    letters from N 119, 169
Rotherham, Captain 151
Roundwood 39
Rousseau, J J **106**
Rowe, John 133
Royal George, HMS **122**, 123
Royal Sovereign, HMS 133, 141, 143-4, 158, 176
Rozier, Jean Pilâtre de **168**
Ruffo, Cardinal 80
Russell, Lord John 121
Russell, Thomas 49
Russia 35, 50, 75-6, 101, 117, 119, 131, 133, **136**, 137, 141, 153, **166**, 174, 185
    and Malta 124, 129

S

Sabina (Sp) 185
Saint George, HMS 23
Samuel and Jane (Br) 131
Sandwich, HMS **58**, *58*, 91
Sangaro, Duke of 171
San Josef (Sp/HMS) 24, 26, 63, 169
San Nicolas (Sp) 24-6
Sannova, Don Juan de
    letter from N 135
Sans Culotte (Fr) 45
Santa Anna (Sp) 143
Santa Cruz 9, 103, 105, **106**, 107, 121
    see also Tenerife
Santissima Trinidad (Sp) 23-4, 55, 143-4, 158
Saratoga, battle of 87, **91**
Sardine, HMS 99
Sardinia 8, 10-11, 17, 19, 45, 61, 71, 77, 89, 108-9, 109-10, 137
Saumarez, Captain Sir James 109, 111-12, 176
Saunders, V/A Charles **146**
Saxony 33
Schiller, C F von 73
Scott, Sir William 143
    letter from N 71
Seahorse, HMS 17, 121
Sekker, Sgt 144
Selkirk, Earl of **136**
Senegal 31, 173
Serapis, HMS **136**, 137
Seven Years' War 31, **90**, **146**, 147, 173
Sheridan, Richard Brinsley 101
Sherman, Roger 99
Shirley, Sir Thomas 7, 64-7, 69
Sicily 8, 10-11, 17, **34**, 43, 47, 73, 78-81, 87, 89, 109, 111, 185, 187
    see also Naples, Palermo
Sidmouth, Viscount *see* Addington, Henry
Sierra Leone 121
signals and telegraph 10, 17, 33, 57, *57*, 83, 103, 112, 135, 137, 140-3, 145, 158, **164**, *164*, 165, 178
Simcoe, General John 107
Simpson, James 75
Simpson, Mary 36
Singapore *100*, 101
Sirius, HMS **16**, 55
Sistoua, Peace of 117
Slater, Samuel 15
slavery and slave trade 15, 64, **76**, 89, 99, **122**, *130*, 131, 181, *184*

Sloane, Sir Hans 17
Smith, Adam 105
Smith, Alderman 41
Smith, Captain Sir William Sidney 43, *46*, 47, 187
    letter from N 181
Smith, John Spencer 153
    letter from N 153
Snider, Christopher **42**
Snipe, Dr John 49
    letter from N 171
Soberano (Sp) 55
Solano, Marquis of 43
Solebay, HMS **102**
Sollom Moss 169
Somerset, James 89
Sotherton, Captain
    letter from N 55
Southey, Robert 71, 119, 161
Spain 10, 19, 43, 45, 49, 83, 101, 103, 124-5, **130**, 141, 149, 156, **166**, 171, 185
    allied with Britain 21, **44**, 78, 108-9
    allied with France 13, 23, 35, 57, 77, 87, 91, **91**, 107, 109, 121, 135, 137, 147, 169
    at Cape St Vincent 8-9, 22-3, 33, 55, 57, 108, 174
    colonies 31, 64, **90-1**, 173
    at Trafalgar **60**, 131, 139, 141, 154, 160, 162, 178
    see also Cadiz, Madrid
Spencer, Earl (First Lord) 9, 22, 24, 81, 109-10, 115, 127, 158, 167
    letters from N 43, 137, 185
Spinola, Marquis of 181
Spithead 11, **14**, **62**, 63, 71, **122**, 123, 145, **152**, 178
    mutiny *57*, **58**, 59, 94
Stamp Acts **28**, **42**, 47, 77, 153, **182**
Stanislaus II, King of Poland 71, 153
St Croix island 66
Stephens, Philip 131
    letters from N 123, 147
Stephenson, George Louis **84**, 85
St George, HMS 43
St Helena 103, 117, 166, 174-5
St John island 64-5
St Joseph, 17
St Kitts 65, 67
St Lawrence river **102**, 107, 173
St Leger 137
St Lucia 105
Stone, Cdre 185
St Paul's Cathedral **14**
St Philip, General 183
Strachan, Admiral Sir Richard 160, 162
Straits, battle of the 141
Stromboli, HMS 127
St Thomas Island 69
Stuart, Captain Don Jacobo 185
Stuart, General **118**, 119
St Vincent, Admiral the Earl of 9, 19, 22-3, *23*, 24, **34**, 39, 47, 55, 61, 73, 76, 94, 96, 99, 103, 109, 156, 167, 176, 183
    at Cape St Vincent 26-7, *27*
    letters from N 15, 17, 29, 31, 33, 59, 61, 75, 77, 79, 83, 85, 89, 97, 99, 101, 103, 105, 107, 110-11, 113, 121, 126, 135, 181, 187
    submarines *168*, *168*, 178
Success, HMS 127
Suckling, Captain Maurice *quoted* 12, 7, *7*, 13, 36
    letters from N 118, 171
Suckling, Sir William 153
Suffren, Admiral **86**
Superb, HMS 121, 157, 181
Sutton, Captain 75
    letters from N 13, 29, 63, 73, 153
Suwarrow, Admiral 137, 171
Swaine, Captain Spelman 31
Sweden 45, 50-1, 53, 71, 107, **122**, 137
Swiftsure, HMS 187
Switzerland 137
swords **20**, *20*
Sydney, Viscount **16**, 19, 65
Sydney (Australia) **16**, 19
Sykes, Captain 156
Syria 133

T

Tahiti **62**, 75
Talleyrand, C-M de 124
Tangier 156
Tate, General William 31, 93
Taylor, Nathaniel
    letter from N 165
Taylor, Simon
    letter from N 85
Taynuilt 161

Temeraire, HMS **58**, 144, 158
Temple, Earl, *see* Grenville, Richard
Tendra, battle of 133
Tenerife 9, **70**, 80, 103, 105, **106**, 107-9, 121, 178
    see also Santa Cruz
Termagant, HMS 55
Terpsichore, HMS 126
Texel **20**, **136**
Thalia, HMS 40, 43, **106**
Theseus, HMS 77, 87, 103, 105, 107, 112-13, 121
Thetis, HMS 113
Thomas, Honoratus Leigh 37
Thompson, Horatia Nelson *see* Nelson, Horatia
Thomson, Captain 183
Thomson, Horatia *see* Nelson, Horatia
Thunderer, HMS 133, 137, 140
Thurn, Count 91
Ticonderoga, battle of 101
Tigre, HMS 43, 47
Timor **62**, *84*, 85
Titus (Fr) 169
Tobago 83
Tone, Theodore Wolfe 149
Tonga **62**
Toronto 107
Tortola 64, 66, 69
Toulon 8-11, 15, 35, 45, 47, **56**, **58**, 59, **60**, 75, 77-8, 81, 83, 85, **86**, 94, **106**, 109-10, 123, 137, 139, 151, **166**, 167, 169, 171, 181, 187
Townshend, Charles **182**
Trafalgar, campaign and battle of 10-11, 19, 23, 27, 41, **60**, 76, 81, **82**, 94, 97, 112, 114, 133, *138*, 138-45, *144*, 154, 156, 158, **164**, **166**, 174-6, 178
    news of 154-63, 167
    Trafalgar swords' **20**
Trafalgar Square 161, *179*
Trekroner (Den) 53
Trevithick, Richard 35
Trevor, John
    letter from N 35
Trevor, Mr 77
Trincomalee, HMS **34**
Trinidad 33, 83
Tripoli 126
Troubridge, Captain Sir Thomas 13, 23-4, 26, 29, 47, 49, *49*, 55, 77, 96, 113, 117, 176, 185, 187
    letters from N 33, 75, 183
Tunis 137
Turgot, A R J **164**
Turkey 15, 35, 47, 49, 85, 101, 107, 109, 111, 117, 126, 133, 169
Turtle, USS 131
Tyrit, David 119

U

Ulm, battle of *150*, 151, 160, 162-3
USA **46**, 75, 93, **100**, 101, 117, **120**, 137, **146**, 156, 165, **168**, 176
    Declaration of Independence 91, *98*, 99, **99**
    trade and trade wars 8, 35, 64, 66-7, 73
    War of Independence 7-8, 17, **18**, 19, 21, 28-9, 31, **34**, 35, **42**, 43, 59, 64-6, 75, **76**, 87, **90-1**, 91, 107, 119, 121, **130**, 131, **132**, 135, 137, 139, **146**, 147, 151, 153, 165, 167, 169, **182**, 185
    see also Paris, Treaty of (1783)
    see also under France
Ushakov, Admiral 133, 141, 185
Ushant 15, **34**, 139
    see also 'Glorious First of June'

V

vaccination **152**
Valetta 49, 125, 127, 129
Valley Forge **91**
Valmy, battle of **82**
Vanguard, HMS 9-10, **44**, 43, 71, 77, 109-13, *115*, 153, 183, 185, 187
Vanneau, HMS 99
Vansittart, Sir Nicholas 51
Varennes 89, **164**
Vattel, Emerich de 99
Vaubois, General 126-7
Vendée rebellion 45, 151
Venezuela 83
Venice 35, 137, 171
Ventura (Sp) 171
Verdi, Giuseppe 45
Victory, HMS *14*, 45, 63, 71, 73, 75, 77, 83, 105, *120*, 121, 123, 133, 165, 185, 187
    at Cape St Vincent 23-4

at Trafalgar 11, 27, 140, *140*, 143-4, *145*, 149, 154, 156, 173, 176, 178
Vigo Bay 139
Villaret-Joyeuse, Admiral **34**, **82**, 83
Ville Franche 45
Villeneuve, Admiral 11, 19, 33, **34**, 35, **60**, *60*, 73, 87, 94, 126
    at battle of Trafalgar 139-43, 158
    death of **60**, 61
Villettes, General **56**, 75
    letter from N 135
Vincejo, (Sp/HMS/Fr) 127
Vinegar Hill, battle of 89
Virgin Islands 64-7, 69
    Coral Bay 64-5
Voltaire 167

W

Waldegrave, Captain 183
Wales 93, 156
Walker, John **102**
Walpole, Sir Robert 21, **90**, **146**
War of 1812 176
War of Jenkins' Ear **90**
War of the Austrian Succession **90**
Washington, President George **18**, 63, *63*, **90-91**, 99, 133, 147, 149, 153, 181
    dies 183
Waterloo, battle of 166
Watson, Captain Joshua Rowley 161
Watt, James **84**
Wedgwood, Josiah 12, **12**, 13
Wellesley, General Arthur (Duke of Wellington) 93, 175
Wellesley, Marquess of **86**, 187
Wells, Captain 47
Wesley, Charles **48**, 49
Wesley, John **48**
West, Benjamin **168**
West Indies 7-8, 11, **34**, 59, **60**, **62**, 64-9, *65*, **70**, 71, **72**, 73, **86**, 93, 119, **122**, *130*, 135, **136**, 139, 174, *184*
    see also individual islands
West Point 147
Weymouth 93
Wheatley, Phillis 131
Whieldon, Thomas **12**
Whitby, Captain John 158
    letter from N 33
White, Pte Hugh **42**
White House 149
White Plains, battle of 153
Whitney, Elias 15
Whitworth, Lord 50
Wieland, CM **136**
Wilberforce, William **76**, **122**, 123
Wilkes, John 61, *61*, 147
William Henry, Prince, Duke of Clarence (William IV) 26, 40, 67-9, **70**, 79, 108, *153*, 183
    letters from N 43, 61, 63, 83, 153, 165, 167, 169, 181
Williamson, Captain 13
Winthuysen, Admiral 27
Wolfe, General James 49, 107, *132*, 133, **146**, 173
Woolward, William 36, **70**
Woolwich Dockyard *148*, 149
Worcester, HMS **184**
Worcester, Marquis of **164**
Wordsworth, William 55
Wouldhave, William **20**
Wyndham, William
    letter from N 171

Y

Yarmouth 43, 50-1, **70**, 162, 165
York, Duke of **48**, 55
Yorktown **91**, **132**, 151
Young, Captain 75

Z

Zealous, HMS 23, 105, 112-13
Zurich, battle of 137